JURISPRUDENCE IN INDIA

JURISPRUDENCE IN INDIA

Through the Ages

D.D. Aggarwal

KALPAZ

Published by

Kalpaz Publications
C-30, Satyawati Nagar,
Delhi – 110052
Ph.: 011-47034999, 9811692060
www.kalpazpublications.com
E-mail: kalpaz@hotmail.com

Distribution Network
gyanbooks.com
India, USA, Canada, UK, Australia, France

ISBN: 978-81-7835-108-7 (HB)

Reprint in India, 2024
First Published, 2002

Printed at: Gyan Press, Delhi.

Jurisprudence in India: Through the Ages
Author: D.D. Aggarwal

Contents

Preface

I have been trying to focus the concepts of modern institutions existing in our ancient times through my books. In the books titled *Protocol in Ramcharitmanas, Protocol in Srimad Bhagwat, Protocol in Mahabharata,* I have projected the modern concept of protocol (political, religious, administrative, social and spiritual) and then the concept of independence in our ancient times. In the book *India Ever Independent—Why Only Fifty Years,* I have brought out these concepts existing since Vedic period and these had been eclipsed during Mohammedan period because they destroyed our literature and usages during the course of their six hundred years of rule over India.

Jurisprudence is another subject where English boast that there was no legal system or codes in India and they only gave a procedure and legal system in India. I started working on the proposition as to how in such an advanced country like ours' we had no legal system in our ancient times, and found that starting from Vedas, we have had a comprehensive legal system propounded in our Smritis and Shastras. The Raja with his Samiti and Sabha and the cabinet of ministers had been discharging the duties of governance of the state. The Samiti and Sabha were responsible for making of laws; The Raja's men enforced the same and the courts investigated the crimes and punished the criminals. With Indra, being the Raja of the state as he is Raja of Swarag too, he had Varun, Agni, Soma, etc. as his ministers in-charge of various Departments. Soma was the Minister-in-charge of judiciary and also the Chief Justice. He had to be a learned person, confident and well-versed in all vocations so that he was able to analyse any situation and understand the same before taking decision on any matter. The judicial department was responsible for eradicating violence from the kingdom by punishing the violent people, who harassed others. Such punishment was based on breach of Dharma as every person was supposed to act as per his Dharma and breach thereof was considered a crime. So Soma was also the protector of Dharma. For punishing the criminals, he had to be well-versed with the laws, usages, practices, customs, ordinances, statute, etc. This is what is required of law enforcing authorities in modern times too. Soma being protector of truth, had to go deep into the matter and find out the correct position based on evidence, etc.

Like the present day, there were courts at various levels. First the village Panchayat, which decided local disputes; then there was a court for ten villages, hundred villages, thousand villages, towns and then the final court of the Raja. The Raja was considered as the fountain of justice. The appeals lay from the Panchayat's decision to the courts of ten village, hundred villages and so oin culminating with the highest court of the Raja and the Raa's decision was considered to be correct and non-biased.

In Vedas, eight kinds of criminals have been mentioned viz. *rakshashas;* man eaters; those who always speak ill of others and harm others in one way or the other; those who indulge in doing illegal jobs like stealing, beating others etc; those who develop enmity with others; back biters; those who tell lies, etc. The crimes committed by them were decided in courts only after finding out the true and untrue aspects in the matter. The judges acquitted true persons and punished those found guilty. The criminals were put to pecuniary punishment; their limbs were amputated; they were sent to jail or hanged. The persons were thus punished after the charge had been proved in the court of law. The punishment differed from person to person and *varna* to *varna*. Lighter punishment was given on first crime and heavier on repeated crimes.

Like the present day, every suit had four parts—first a plaint was filed indicating the charge against defendant, the guilty person, supported by evidence, etc; the second part was calling the defendant, examining him and the evidence produced by him. The examination was given a limited time of two weeks within which he had to be present with his supporting evidence and if he failed, a short extension of time could be given and if he still failed, then the case was decided on the basis of the facts available. The third part was examination of the evidence, etc., produced by both the sides and the fourth was the judgement.

English people say that there were no detailed codes narrating thue procedure to be followed by the courts and punishments to be awarded in each case. The English had said so having thus seen the working of the courts during Muslim period. During six hundred years of Muslim rule in India, the courts decided cases as per the Shariat, wherein detailed procedure and limited punishments have been indicated. But in Hindu jurisprudence, the detailed procedure to be followed by various courts and punishment to be awarded in all sorts of cases—which could be enviased—have been given in our Smritis namely: Vishnu Smriti, Manu Smriti, Indra Smriti, Narada Smriti, Brihaspati Smriti, Yajnavalkya Smriti,

Parasara Smriti, commentaries and digests; and Dharmashastras. All, that is contained in the present day codes—Indian Penal Code, Criminal Procedure Code, Civil Procedure Code, Indian Evidence Act., is given in our Smritis and Shastras rather, it is with more details than in present day codes as our codes also recognised moral sins and religious sins too as punishable crimes which are not recognised as such by modern jurisprudence. So our ancient law was more comprehensive.

After having narrated the position of legal system in our ancient times, I have given the details of Mohammedan Law and the legal procedure in present day as given by the English and continuing even today. In this way this book is a comprehensive study of laws existing in our ancient period, during the Muslim rule and during the British period, which exists even today. The study shall also dismantle the British claim that there was no elaborate legal system available in India when they took over the governance of this country and a study of I.P.C., Cr.P.C., C.P.C., Evidence Act, etc. together with our ancient Smritis and Shastras would give a feeling that the present day codes have been more or less copied from our Smritis and Shastras.

In the end, I desire to express my gratitude to the writers of works available but for whose help I would not have been able to bring out this book. I am also thankful for the inspiration and assistance provided by my wife and other members of my family and friends in bringing out this book.

D. D. Aggarwal

PART—I

VEDIC PERIOD

1

SYSTEM OF GOVERNANCE IN VEDIC PERIOD

The history of India, from the earliest period to the present day, may be mapped out into five eras of pre-historic or Vedic period; the Hindu period; the Mohammedan period; the British period ; and the Post-independence period. The Vedic period commences from the advent of mankind from when Vedas are said to have come; the Hindu period commences from the dawn of history or advent of Buddha; The Mohammedan period commences with the invasion of the followers of the Prophet under Mahmud of Kabul in the middle of eleventh century A.D. ; the British period commences with the conquests of Robert Clive in about the middle of eighteenth century and the Post-independence period starts from the attainment of independence from the British in 1947.

Unlike the present system of governance in which the three ingredients of governance namely Legislative, Executive and Judiciary are independent organs with some checks and balances, the Vedic system, while speaking of these three organs, gave the king the overall power over all the three. Also unlike the present duration of legislative and executive for a period of 4-5 years, the Vedas speak of life-long duration of the king and the members of his Sabha and Samiti.

In Vedas, the Government consists of Indra as the King and Varun, Agni, Savita, Pusa, Soma, etc., as his ministers, although they too have been mentioned as the kings at many places. We take the duties, etc., of the king and his ministers from several places indicated in the form of advices and narration of these qualities and requests to them by the people. The collection of these only constitute the duties of the king and his ministers. Of course, the king (Indra) and his ministers (Varun etc.) are not the gods of Hindu mythology but they are the human beings and through these only the polity; science, art, etc., have been narrated. Since we are discussing the history of jurisprudence in India, and it is a part of the governance of the country in Vedic period, we have to first of all see the overall system of governance presented in the Vedas.

Evolution of Ancient Text

Vedas are considered to be the voice of Brahma and these came into being simultaneously with the advent of mankind and God had thought that the provisions in Vedas shall be necessary for the human beings to enable them to lead their lives since, as per Vedas, only God had created all creatures, trees, plants and all other necessities of life. Vedas provided for the four Varnas in human beings, besides the creation of trees, earth, sky, oceans, land, mountains and other things of past, present and future. Besides Vedas, there were Upvedas, Angas, and Upangas created by Aryan rishis, narrating the progress made by Aryans in the fields of spiritualism, philosophy, science and literature. These Shastras also deal with science of life (medicines, surgery, hygiene, chemistry, philosophy and anatomy); science of mechanics and handicraft; science of music and songs, dramas and dancing; science of war and weapons; science of phonetics and orthoepy; principles of law; Vedic ceremonies, rules of domestic ceremonies; principles of geometry; grammar; philosophy; prosody; astronomy; justice; yoga; logic; metaphysics; psychology; ethics and physics.

Ever since the creation of Vedas through the voice of Brahma, these were not brought out in black and white as these were considered so sacred and these could not be written by human beings and were learnt by heart by the gurus and then their disciples, and so on. These were written only in Guptas' reign, and in view of there having been no documentation about the existence of Vedas, these are considered to be only about 1500 years old, when these were first written. We do not want to be put in this dispute as this is not the subject matter of this book. We have to see the contents of Vedas, as they are. Even the original Vedas, as first written, had mostly been destroyed by Muslims, when they occupied India. It is said that such a vast treasury of books was available in Taxila, Vaisali, Varanasi, etc., universities that they kept burning for years and whatever was left was taken away by the Europeans and unfortunately Indians had to go to Europe to attain the knowledge of Vedas and other shastras which had been interpreted by Europeans in their own way.

Evolution of the Raja

A kingdom is the basis of any governance and it does not become as such overnight. It is the result of the constant evolution for centuries. At first, with the advent of mankind, Manu and Satrupa had come. Then a family and then a community and then a country came into being. At first, there was no government as the people were few and they were free. Then came the families, which were run by their heads and then as the population grew, the quarrels in various families started. This led to the creation of a community and to control the community, a Panchayat or a Mukhiya came into being. They made rules for compliance by the people in their charge. Then many strong persons became available, who, for a better governance, chose one man to head the region or a *Rajya*. He was called the 'Raja'. He was either an elected man or a strong man, who, by dint of his strength, became the governor of the people of the region. This evolution ended with the Rajas choosing one person (emperor) to govern the entire universe, comprising of many *Rajyas*. But since the Rajas or emperors could not solely govern their respective countries, the Samitis and Sabhas had been provided for their assistance along with teams of advisors.

Election of Raja : The Raja was an elected person as per Vedas :

त्वामग्ने वृणते ब्राह्मणा इमे शिवो अग्ने संवरणे भवान्

(ऋग. 3.10.1)

Meaning that the Raja was elected by Brahmins (members of the Samiti/Sabha). Further :

आ त्वाऽहार्षमन्तरभूर्ध्रुवस्तिष्ठाविचाचलिः
विशस्त्वा सर्वावाञ्छन्तु मा त्वद्राष्ट्रमधिभ्रशत।

(यजु. 12-11)

Meaning that the Raja has been called to live amidst the people, occupy the throne, and govern the kingdom keeping the well-being of the people in view.

Generally, the son of the Raja was elected to succeed him. Out of the sons too, the eldest had a right to be considered first and if he was not capable then only the next could be considered. At the time of finding a Yuvraja for Ayodhya, Raja Dasratha had chosen the eldest son Rama for this assignment. He first got approval of the Rajguru Vasistha for this purpose. Vasistha gave clearance but asked him to obtain the approval of the Samiti too. Since Samiti members had been elected by the people, the election by the Samiti was considered to be the choice of the people at large. So, after obtaining the approval of the Samiti only Rama was notified to become Yuvraja. But as is well known, the Queen Kaikayee desired her son Bharata to be the Raja. At that time Raja Dasratha had told her that he could choose Bharata too for this purpose but Rama being capable and Bharata being very obedient to him, he had wished to hand over the Rajya to Rama. Still if she desired he could make Bharata, the Raja but fearing that Rama may in course of time banish Bharata, she insisted Bharata to become Raja and Rama to go to forests for 14 years. The main tasks of the Raja at that time were to provide food to his people; their protection from enemies and criminals and to think of their well-being and for fulfilling these purposes, the Raja was chosen by the people.

In the Vedas, Indra has been specified as the Raja or emperor. He is not considered as God of gods but a human being in the capacity of a Raja. He is said to be :

1. पृथिवयाश्च सम्राट (ऋग. 1-100-1)
2. राजा यजाते वर आपृथिव्याः (ऋग. 3-53-11)
3. पटिर्वभूषा समोजनानाम (ऋग. 6-36-4)

Meaning that

1. Indra is the emperor of the universe.
2. That emperor works for the well-being of his people.
3. He is a unique ruler of the people.

Qualities of a Raja

Vedas have even prescribed the qualities to be seen while electing a person as the Raja. These are :

1. He should be learned knowing all Vedas and Shastras.
2. He should be speaking truth and sweet words.
3. He should be well-versed in driving chariot.
4. He should be above 25 years of age, i.e., should have completed Brahmcharya Ashrama and be strong.
5. He should be with deep thoughts.
6. He should be capable of undertaking all kinds of jobs.
7. He should be strong and earn appreciation from all.
8. He should be very intelligent, should be able to understand all situations.

9. He should be able to inflate the exchequer.
10. He should be able to discover/invent new things.
11. He should be married with children and be a good house-holder.
12. He should be having all qualities of the human beings.
13. He should be resourceful and be able to imbibe in his people the pleasures, Dharma, praise, intelligence, knowledge, and *vairagya.*
14. He should be a man of good character.
15. He should have all leadership qualities.
16. He should be able to know the qualities in other persons.
17. He should be able to meet all requirements of his people viz. of food, clothing, education, housing, etc.
18. He should neither be cruel towards his people nor do any harm to them.
19. He should be pious, God fearing and knowing his Dharma well.
20. He should be very handsome and wear impressive clothes and ornaments.
21. He should not be old.
22. He should be able to save himself from all vices.
23. He should be able to bear all kinds of difficulties, should lead simple life and should be prepared to help all his people in all kinds of difficulties.

Duration of Reign. According to Vedas, once a person is elected as a Raja based on his capability, he continues to rule for his entire life. But then he has to follow the canons of Dharma, according to which he has to pass his first twenty-five years in education as *brahmachari*, then enter *grihasta ashrama* and it is during this period only that he continues to rule as after *grihasta ashrama*, he has to follow *banprastha* at the age of around 55-60 years and then to pass his last years of life as a Sanyasi. It can be concluded from this provision in Shastras that a person could rule only for about 25-30 years and this in fact is the meaning of entire life for him.

Passing on the Reign : Reasons

There are instances of Raja Dasratha opting to go for *banprastha*, Raja Dhritrashtra too had gone to forests in his last years of life and died there only, and so on. This appears to have been prescribed in view of the fact that :

1. The Raja loses his strength, thinking power, etc., with the passage of time and he would not be able to protect the kingdom from enemies in old age.

2. The sons would become young during this period and they would aspire to become Raja. It is, therefore, better that the Raja passes on the kingdom to his sons himself rather than allowing the sons to ask for it, which can be in bad taste.
3. As per Dharma too, the Raja has to follow the ashramas and after having passed his youth period in *grihasta*, he is supposed to proceed for *banprastha*.
4. In Hindus, attainment of salvation is also to be cared for by everyone. Therefore, the Raja too has to proceed in that direction of bhakti during the last years of his life.

Election of Raja

Normally the sequence of election of a Raja is firstly out of the sons of the Raja, preference being given to the eldest son, if he is otherwise capable of becoming a Raja. If the Raja had no sons, then another person in royal family is elected to become the Raja. It is only in a situation in which a capable person is not available in the royal family that a person is brought from another *rajya*. But in that case such a person shall have to detach himself from his previous *rajya* and should consider himself as one amongst his people in the new *rajya*.

अर्वांचमिन्द्रममुतो ह्वामहे। (अथ. 5-3-11)

Meaning that we bring the emperor from another kingdom. Such an emperor shall think of

अस्माकमस्तु केवल

the kingdom where he is brought only.

Electorate. Question arises whether the election should be by all the people or some specially qualified persons only shall elect such a person or it should be election by the Samiti/Sabha alone. Vedas provide :

1. विशस्त्वा सर्वा वाछन्तु (यजु. 12–11)
2. त्वां ही इन्द्रावसे विवाचोह्वन्ते चर्षणयः (ऋग. 6-33-2)

According to these *shlokas*, the entire public chooses the Raja. But as already indicated at the time of choosing Rama as *yuvraja*, Muni Vashistha had asked Raja Dashratha to obtain the approval of the Samiti too. This shows that there was indirect election that is election by the elected representatives in the Samiti. There is also mention of Brahmins' concurrence being obtained in the election of the Raja. Raja Dashratha had obtained the approval of Guru Vashishtha. This provision might be to include the Brahmins in the electorate because Brahmins were considered to be impartial, they were learned and could find out the best man to hold the post and they had no consideration, being absolved of all wishes. To fulfil this provision, Brahmins would have been included in the electorate with some additional voting rights.

Ballot Paper. There is mention of the Parna Mani (पर्णमणि) for holding election. Parna Mani is like the present day ballot paper on which vote is cast.

Election Manifesto. There is mention of the candidates, for election as Raja, notifying an election manifesto as is being done by various parties these days. Since in ancient period there were no parties and the election was held on individual basis only, the election manifesto was issued by the individuals only. It indicated the merits / qualities of the candidate and his intentions—what he proposed to do, if elected. Unlike the modern times, when election manifesto is not acted upon and is for the purpose of fighting election only, the person elected as Raja had to act on his promises made in the manifesto. Further, it appears that the election of the Raja in those days was not out of many candidates but for or against one person proposed by the outgoing Raja. If that person was not approved then the next person was put for similar voting and a person, who was thus elected, became the Raja. Such an election was by majority of votes attained. Since the Raja was elected by the people based on his capability and promises made, he could be dethroned by the people if he did not act for the well-being of the people, including caring to provide for their food, clothing, house and their protection from enemy. In such a case, the Raja could be dethroned or killed. Raja Bains was such a Raja, who had been elected by the Samiti as there was no other son available and on his having been cruel to the people, he had been killed by the members of the Samiti and another person 'Prithu' had been made Raja in his place although he was still in Brahmacharya Ashrama. This only indicates that democracy was in best play at that time in India.

As per Vedas, although the Raja was respected and in fact, worshipped by his people as he provided them with all their necessities and protection from enemies, the things one expects to be bestowed by the God only, yet he was not considered a God or a representative of God as had been the case with some kings of England and some Muslim rulers of India.

Federal System of Kingdom

In Vedas, there is mention of Raja and emperor (Chakravarty Raja). This would indicate that there were Rajas, who ruled small states and these Rajas had chosen their emperor, so these small states governed by Rajas were similar to the present day federating units. Such Rajas were autonomous in their kingdoms. They had *samitis/sabhas* to assist them. They, however, paid certain amount to meet the expenditure of the emperor. There was the system of holding Aswamedha *yagyas*, in which the Rajas of all federating units used to come and offer rich presents/contributions to the emperor holding the Aswamedha *yagya*. Also the people of the emperor used to go about in his empire and collect money from the Rajas of the federating states. Arjuna in *Mahabharata* had been going for such a collection. For such collections, only a brave person, the son or brother, of the emperor was sent so that he was able to subdue in case any Raja refused to pay contribution to the exchequer of the emperor. Karna had also gone and collected huge amounts for Raja Dhritrashtra/Duryodhana. In lieu of getting contributions from his federating Rajas, the emperor was responsible for the protection of such Rajas in case of attack from another Raja or by one Raja of his empire on another Raja of the same empire.

Further, in case an emperor wanted to extend his kingdom, he would attack the Raja of the non-federating units and in case he was victorious, he would either hand over the kingdom to the defeated Raja if not killed in the battle or to his brother/son. But such a Raja or brother or son had to accept the suzerainty of the victorious emperor and paid annual contributions, etc., to his exchequer like the other federating units. Of course, such a Raja was autonomous to rule his kingdom within the purview of the suzerain ruler. Such examples are there in *Ramayana* and *Mahabharata*. Rama had handed over the Kiskindhya Rajya to Sugreeva, the brother of Bali after he was killed. Similarly, the Rajya of Lanka was handed over to Vibheeshana on the death of Ravana.

Welfare State

In Vedas, the Raja is said to be caring for the five persons (Panchjanya) (पंचजन्य). These Panchjanya are none other than the people of four Varnas and Dasyus, who were not included in any of the varnas. As per Vedas, there were four Varnas and four *ashramas*. After Brahmacharya Ashrama, i.e., after completing education, one was allowed to choose one of the four varnas as his Dharma. Varna means to choose and, therefore, the varna was choosen and did not come by birth.

After completing education, if one continued further studies and then resorted to teaching the same, such persons were Brahmins. Those, who did not study and had interest in fighting, such persons became Kshatriyas. The *rajkumars* generally came in this category. They were then taught further the tactics of warfare and rules of governance, i.e., Rajdharma. Those, who were not able to continue studies further and were not fit for fighting too, became Vaishyas. Their job was agriculture, trade, industry, etc. Still, the people, who could not be included in the above three Varnas, became Shudras. Their job was to serve the people of the other three Varnas, who ensured to provide them with the necessities of life. Once having chosen a Varna, the persons of all the Varnas had to follow the canons of their respective *varna-dharma* and since that *varna-dharma* was because of their choice only, they did not have any grudge against the people of other Varnas. There were still some persons, who could not be fitted in any of the above Varnas or who did not want to follow the canons of Dharma as per Shastras, they were called 'Dasyus'. They were allowed to live in the kingdom so far as they did not interfere in the compliance of the Dharma by the people of other Varnas and followed the rule of law. In case of default such persons were treated as 'Rakshasas' and killed. The annihilation of the Rakshasas (Ravana, Kansa etc.) was because they did not follow the Vedic Dharma and did not allow the people of the other varnas to follow the requirements of their respective Dharmas viz. holding *yagyas* by Brahmins/rishis; governance by Kshatriyas; trade by Vaishyas and their service by the Shudras. The killing of such persons is not prescribed as a sin in Shastras. On the contrary, if such Dasyus lived in cooperation with the people of other Varnas, they were allowed to live in the kingdom and they enjoyed all rights as enjoined by the people of the four Varnas.

The Brahmins were given special facility of expressing themselves freely as they only spoke for the welfare of the kingdom although the people of other Varnas too had the right to express themselves as a washerman in Ramrajya could speak on the conduct of Rama in having accepted Sita as his wife even after she had stayed in Lanka for about one year.

According to the Vedas, the women were entitled to hold any profession. They could even be elected as the ruler of the country; representative of the Sabha/Samiti; adopt any profession/vocation. They, however, had to adopt the *varna-dharma* of their husbands only after marriage. In ancient times, ladies had been poets, rulers, members of the Sabha/Samiti, and in other professions such as in trade, agriculture, etc.

Sabha and Samiti

Sabha was like the lower house of the present day and Samiti was upper house or Council of Ministers. The members in both were elected by the people. The Raja had to consult the Sabha and Samiti in all important matters and their advice was generally accepted. Although the Raja could over-rule their advice but in that case he had to give reasons for the same. Raja Dashratha had to consult the Sabha at the time of making Rama as his *yuvraja*. Even Rama, during the period he was in forests and had proceeded to fight with Ravana, had formed a Samiti of his advisers and had been consulting it in all important matters, like how to cross the sea, whether to accept Vibheeshana or not when he came to Rama for refuge after having been expelled by Ravana. At that time Sugreeva and others had advised not to accept Vibheeshana, as he was enemy's brother but Rama befriended him and gave convincing reasons for it. Atharva Veda says that :

1. The Raja requests the Sabha and Samiti to help him. They are like his daughters. The members should advise him whenever he consulted anyone in respect of his specialisation. This shows that the members had specialisation in their respective subjects and, therefore, their advice was considered as experts' advice.
2. The Raja used to address the Sabha and the Samiti individually and jointly and used to tell his planning in governance.
3. The advice of the members was without any bias.
4. The members were elected and their term of office was about 25-30 years, i.e., upto the limit of the *grihastha ashrama*.
5. The decision arrived at in the Sabha / Samiti was generally unanimous.
6. The Sabhas and Samitis were there at the level of the emperor as also with the Raja.
7. The Samitis/Sabhas exercised control over the Raja in the governance of the Rajya so that the Raja could not become an autocrat and act against the well-being of the people of the *rajya*. In that case, the Sabha / Samiti could dethrone the Raja. This would indicate that there was something like the procedure of impeachment of Raja in those days.

स विशोऽनु व्यचलत्।
तं सभा चसमितिश्च सेना च सुरा चानुव्यचलन।
सभायाश्च वै स समितेश्च सेना याश्च सुशयांश्च
प्रियं धम भवति य एवं वेद। (अथ. 15-9-1–3)

Meaning that when the Raja acted as per wishes of the people, his Sabha/Samiti/force/exchequer followed the Raja. Acting as per wishes of the people means acting for the well-being of the people. In this *shloka*, there is unanimity in the course of action of the Sabha/Samiti and the Raja.

8. The Samiti used to hold meeting in a special conference room.
9. The Sabha/Samiti used to frame laws, which were approved and executed by the Raja.
10. Even the Sabha/Samiti only could decide, who should become Brahmin, Kshatriya, Vaishya and Shudra in the *rajya*. In this way, the system of Varnas has been there not by birth but by adoption by individual and approval of the Sabha/Samiti.
11. In case of war also, the Sabha/Samiti gave approval for undertaking any war/battle. Of course, where the *rajya* had been attacked then there was no case for approval but the way of defence was organised by the Sabha/Samiti.
12. The Sabha/Samiti controlled the exchequer and suggested ways and means for raising more money.
13. Qualifications had been laid down for the person to be elected as member of the Sabha/Samiti. He had to be intelligent, learned, pious, unbiased, specialist in his field and had no vested interest. If one acted otherwise, he could be ousted from the membership of the Sabha / Samiti.
14. Out of the Sabha and Samiti, the indication is that the Sabha was the lower house and the Samiti was upper house. The members of the Samiti were more qualified than those of the Sabha. Unlike present day when lower house is more powerful, the Vedic upper house was more important. May be it was the Council of Ministers. The members of either Sabha or Samiti were chosen by people. Whereas the members of the Sabha could be ordinary persons, the members of the Samiti were specially qualified in their respective fields. Also there was the chairman of the Sabha and the Samiti appointed by the Raja out of the members.

Emperor of the World

There is mention in the Vedas of the '**Indrendra**' (इन्द्रेन्द्र) i.e., Indra of the Indras or the emperor of the emperors. Since as already indicated, the emperor was at the head of many Rajas and acted as their suzerain, the emperor of emperors would have been the emperor of the entire universe. This would indicate that the phrase '**वसुधैव कुटुम्बकम**', i.e., entire universe is one family was correct and there would have been an emperor of the entire world. He was more powerful than the present UNO as the present UNO is generally recommendatory whereas the emperor of the emperors had all the executive powers over other emperors. He had his own Sabha and Samiti and own force. He received contributions from the emperors to run his establishment. Such emperor of emperors was not elected by the people of the entire universe but was elected by the emperors *per se*. The emperor of emperors was :

1. Accessible to all the people.
2. All should obey the direction of the emperor of emperors.
3. He should see that the requirements of all the people and their emperors were met.
4. The emperor of emperors decided all cases of dispute between the emperors and their people.
5. This organisation was so well-established that the people of the entire universe could live in peace.
6. The emperor of emperors could be from any kingdom.
7. The institution of emperor of emperors would indicate that all inter-kingdom disputes could be peacefully solved by such institution. This would result in no inter-national disputes or wars and the entire universe could live in peace. If such an institution could be established today then there would be no race for the arms, army, etc., and the huge expenditure incurred on these — the major portion of the revenues of each country—could be used for the development and benefit of the people. Also there would be no killing, no international enmity and all round cordiality. In this way Vedas are in favour of establishing a universal Government based on the principle of federal Government.

Cabinet

The Raja could not perform all the duties of the Government. He was, therefore, assisted by his council of ministers, like the cabinet of present time. Indra had Agni, Aswani, Varuna, Soma, etc., as his Ministers. They were all called emperors too as they acted for their respective departments on behalf of the emperor only. Might be it is like the present system in which officers of a particular level are authorised to take decisions and issue orders "for and on behalf of the President" and "President is pleased" although such papers are not seen nor any orders issued by the President himself. Accordingly, the ministers of the Indra were also called emperors as they acted 'for and on behalf of the emperor' in their respective fields and their over-all emperor is Indra only. The following **shloka** further confirms such thinking :

अतश्चिदिन्द्रादभयन्त देवः (ऋग. 5-30-5)

(All ministers were afraid of Indra the emperor. All these ministers assisted the emperor). The emperor could seek their advice and entrust the job of their fields to them. Generally there was not much interference in the actions of the ministers by the emperor as they always had fear of the emperor and they acted without any partiality or vested interest. The jobs of some of the ministers of the emperor are indicated below. This is only symbolic and the number of ministers could be increased or decreased by the emperors according to their respective needs.

Agni. In Vedas, Agni is a god but in the context of the formation of the Government, Agni and other gods are only ministers. Agni accordingly is the Minister for External Affairs.

1. अग्ने यासि दूत्यम (ऋग. 1-12-4)
2. दूत्यानि विद्वान (ऋग. 4-7-8)

1. Agni works as an Ambassador.
2. Agni is well-versed with the job of an ambassador.

As Agni in the *yagya* gives the smell throughout the area so does the Agni as minister take the emperor's orders throughout the universe. Agni has been called Ambassador. In fact in those days, Agni being the incharge of Ambassadors and acting as an Ambassador too, could correctly be called the Minister for External Affairs as he collected the information received from all ambassadors under him, posted in various countries, considered it and put up for the information of the emperor and sought the emperor's guidance in cases where it was required. The duties of the ambassadors have also been indicated. He used to convey the message of his emperor to the other emperor, collected his reaction on the same and conveyed the same to his emperor. He also looked into the interest of his country in other countries. His people also acted as spies in other countries and conveyed the information collected by them to their emperor for suitable/timely action. The ambassadors were appointed out of the persons with specific qualifications.

1. सं दूतो अद्यौदुषसो विरोक (ऋग. 3.5.2)
2. उभयां अन्तरग्ने दूत ईयसे (ऋग. 4.2.2)
3. विभूपम्मग्न उभयां अनुव्रता दूतो देवानाम रजसी समीयसे,
   यत् ते धीतिं मुमतिमावृणीमहेऽध स्मा नस्तिवरूथः शिवो भव।
   (ऋग. 6.15.9)

1. The ambassador gets up early in the morning and starts his work i.e. he is always alert.
2. The ambassador works with all kinds of people — men and women — people of any varna or profession, etc.
3. The ambassador is the confidant of his emperor. He goes to the other Raja and his people and he is required to be available everywhere through his persons.

Apart from the above examples, the ambassador is to be handsome, strong, alert, very intelligent, able to change his form; should be affectionate to all; he is to be a young man meaning that old people should not be appointed as ambassadors.; he should have quality of befriending others; he should be a *grihastha* so that he may not get involved in the women of other countries and leak out all secrecies of his country; he should be able to protect himself in case of difficulty, etc. The ambassadors were immune from any action being taken against them in the matter of conveying the message of his emperor to the other emperor even if such a message was not of his liking. This is like the present day system of immunity to ambassadors. In *Ramayana* too when Ravana wanted to kill Hanumana on his having killed his son and having killed many other people and having deserted the garden, Vibheeshaṇa told him not to kill the representative of other king against law.

'नीति विरोध न मारिये दूता'।

. ***Aswani.*** Aswani is a god as also emperor Indra's minister. This is from the word Aswa (अश्व) i.e. horse or a means of transport. So he is the Minister for Transport. There is mention that he was incharge of all means of transport of the emperor such as chariots. He was a good chariot-driver as also maintained chariots, which were used in all kinds of battles and in tours of the kingdom by the emperor and his people. He also arranged chariots for transporting public from one place to another. He was responsible for transport of foodgrains, honey, ghee, milk, gold and silver, chemicals, arms and ammunition and other items required during the battles like animals, army troops, etc. His chariots could go anywhere in the country. The chariots could be driven during night also without any fear. Aswani also was responsible for construction of roads in plain and in hilly areas. He had means of transport to be used in seas (means there were ships and submarines); in air (means there were aeroplanes); vehicles without the use of animals to drive the same (means there were locomotives, engines, etc., too). The vehicles of Aswani could run with high speed and even there were vehicles which could operate as per desire (means there were electronically operated vehicles). The chariot used by Krishna for Arjuna in *Mahabharata* was such a vehicle and it vanished after the Mahabharata was over.

Aswani is also the docfor their assistance,tor of gods. So, in the universe, he acts as the minister for health too. The medicinal treatment at that time was both by medicines and surgery. There are instances of surgical expertise in the days of *Ramayana* and *Mahabharata*. The warriors could be treated with medicines and surgery over night and they were able to return to the battle-fields the next day.

Varuna. Varuna is Minister for Police Department although mythologicially he is the god of water. Varuna is said to be with handcuff (पाश). So he is the minister for police, who used to arrest the culprits. His job was to locate the sinners and culprits through his persons, who were spread in the entire area, arrest them and present them before the ruler for awarding punishment, etc. He had the handcuffs of three kinds — one to arrest the hardened criminals; second to arrest the criminals of medium level and third to arrest the criminals, who were involved in very light crimes. Varuna's people were intelligent enough to arrest only the sinners and culprits and not the others. He was brave as he had to face the criminals and had to get involved in encounters with them. Varuna also had his spies, who could mix up with the people and locate the culprits. These spies checked whether the Raja's land had been encroached upon by anyone; whether the specified part of the product was given to the exchequer or not, etc.

Varuna is also incharge of the prisons. As he arrests culprits and produces them before the judge for awarding punishment, he also had to arrange for the punished persons to be kept in prison for the decided period. He, therefore, provides and manages prisoners also. Varuna and his persons have to locate the culprits for the kingdom. They, therefore, have to be very alert and act very cautiously. He should be able to distinguish between the culprits and others as ultimately it is he, who proves his guilt before the judge. He is also in that case the protector of the gentlemen and in that capacity he is their protector and friend. Also Varuna could exceed his jurisdiction at times. For this purpose the emperor's people kept a watch on Varuna and his people so that they were not able to unnecessarily harass anyone.

Spash **(स्पश)**. He is minister of spies. There are spies with Agni, the minister for external affairs; spies with Varuna, the minister for Police and also spies with other departments like Finance, Agriculture, etc, to keep a watch that there was no misappropriation of funds and the specified part of the produce was handed over to the royal exchequer, etc. The spies were with the following qualities :

1. They should not have any fear from anyone and should act quickly.
2. They should keep a watch on the sinners and culprits and Dasyus so that they did not harass the people.
3. They should be handsome and attractive so that they could befriend anyone and mix up with the people at large to extract the correct thing out of them and locate the sinners etc.
4. They should be strong enough to face the culprits when caught by them.
5. They should be able to go from one place to another with speed.
6. They should be men of good character.
7. They should be alert and be able to smell the ill-doings of the people.

Mitra. He is Minister for States as also of External Affairs to keep liaison with other emperors as also the Rajas under his emperor. Therefore, his is field within the country and also outside country. He, in the discharge of his duties, has to be very alert, cautious, intelligent and good in manoeuverability. He is responsible for making friends in other countries and to keep a watch on the Rajas under his emperor so that they did not rise against the emperor. He should be able to even bring the culprits to right path; to keep the image of his emperor high in other countries and in the Rajas under him.

Soma. Soma is a god and here he is Minister-in-charge of Judiciary and is also the Chief Justice. Soma has to be a learned person, confidant, well-versed in all vocations so that he is able to analyse any situation and understand the same. Soma has been said to be :

विचर्षणि (ऋग. 9.40.1)	seeing carefully
विश्वचर्षणि (ऋग. 9.66.1)	seeing others carefully.

1. He has to be very alert always as he has to listen to others very carefully; read between the lines in what is stated by others and going deep into the spirit and meaning of the same because unless he listens carefully, he cannot take a decision in the cases presented before him as a judge.
2. The judicial department is responsible for eradicating violence from the kingdom. This is possible by punishing the violent people, who harass others.
3. Soma is the protector of Dharma. This is possible by punishing the sinners and criminals. He himself follows the canons of Dharma because unless he follows Dharma, he cannot expect others to follow the same.
4. For the purpose of punishing the sinners and criminals. he has to be well-versed with the law, usage, practice, customs, ordinance, statute, etc. These very aspects have to be taken into consideration in present times too. This would indicate how comprehensive our legal procedure had been in ancient times for which western people boast of having introduced the same in the universe.
5. Soma is the protector of truth. His duty as a judge is to save the true person and punish the untrue. For this purpose, he has to go deep into the matter, see the evidence available and statements of petitioner and the defendent. In this way only he can impart justice.
6. Soma favours gentlemen.
7. Soma becomes friendly with all persons.

Rudra. Rudra is the Defence minister and Senapati. We note that the Minister for judicial affairs is Chief Justice too and here the Defence Minister is Senapati as well. In the present system, the Defence Minister is a political person, whereas the Senapati is from armed force. The political leaders cannot properly visualise the requirements of the Defence personnel and armaments. It is, therefore, better if Defence Minister is Senapati as well as given in Vedas. Indra had Rudra as his

Defence Minister. Rudra means one who makes others cry. Since the job of Senapati is to kill the enemy, he is rightly under the charge of Rudra. He works for the organisation and strengthening of the force during peace time and to resort to fighting in battles. Then there is Marut (मरुत) too as an incharge of troops. Marut means one, who may have to die. Since the warriors during battle, either kill or get killed, they are Maruts.

Twastha. He is the Minister for Handicrafts and Industries. Twasta (त्वष्टा) is one who shines. Since he produces handicrafts which shine, he is incharge of this Department as also of industry. He is responsible for spreading the handicraft centres in the country and arranging their marketing and training the people in this vocation. He also establishes new industries in the country to meet the requirements of the people.

Brihaspati. He is the Raj Purohit. The god Indra had Brihaspati as his Guru. So in the universe too Indra as emperor keeps Brihaspati as the Raj Purohit. The emperor performs all his duties in consultation with the Raj Purohit. Vashistha was the Raj Purohit of Raja Dashratha. His duty was to teach the Rajkumars as also to advise the Raja on matters of Dharma and to help him in the pursuance of law of dharma in the governance. The Raj Purohit was one who was very learned and gave non biased advice. He was always a Brahmin, who did not have any involvement in the worldly attractions. Such a person only could give non-biased advice to the Raja. The Raja acts on the advice of the Raj Purohit in dealing with the Rajas of other countries; in battles; in raising *rajya* revenues and in all other matters including ensuring the following of their respective *varnadharma* by the people of the *rajya*. In this way, the Raj Purohit was virtually a super Raja to whom even the Raja had to bow. The Raj Purohit was also responsible for performance of the *yagyas* by the Raja, teaching the *rajkumars* and others; holding of the functions like christenings, *upnayan*, marriages, etc. He was responsible for character building of the Raja and his people. He used to check the Raja, whenever and wherever he acted against the canons of Vedic laws. He was the head of all Purohits in the *rajya*. He was not appointed, as such, on the basis of birth in the house of a Raj Purohit but according to his personal capability.

Pusa. He is a god and Minister of Indra (emperor) for Finance. Pusa is responsible for :

1. Finding ways and means to raise the revenues of the exchequer.
2. Execution of the existing system of raising the revenues by

obtaining the specified portion of agricultural products and cess on trade, industry, etc.

3. He has his people under him who evaluate the products and ensure that the Raj Bhag is correctly paid out of it.
4. There are spies also under the Finance Minister to oversee that there is no misappropriation or embezzlement of Government revenues. His people donot connive with the producers in under-evaluation of the products, etc.
5. He is responsible for preparation of budget of the Raja indicating the items of revenue and expenditure and balancing the same by finding new ways and means where the expenditure happens to be more than the revenues.
6. The Finance Minister also controls the expenditure incurred by the Raja on himself and in his palace.
7. He is responsible to see that everyone gets foodgrains to meet his requirement besides clothes and houses.
8. All expenditure on donations, *yagyas,* etc., is incurred with the concurrence of Pusa. The Raja could incur expenditure on *yagyas,* etc., out of the booty obtained after defeating another Raja and not out of the Raj Bhag obtained from out of the agricultural products, etc., Once Yudhisthra wanted to hold Aswamedha *yagya* but he was told that it could not be performed as there was no money out of the booty and the other money out of products could not be spent on Yagyas and on personal expenditure of the Raja. Then some money had to be found out from other Rajas and then only the Yagya could be performed.
9. Pusa has to ensure that the treasure is never empty and he is the controller of all finances of the kingdom.
10. The main source of income was the Raj Bhag from the agricultural products but there were other means too to raise the royal revenues like the income from mines, income from animals, income from textile industry and other industries, income from cess on traders, income from handicrafts, etc. Pusha, therefore, has to be very alert to see that the taxes to the extent due are collected and are not misappropriated. He is also responsible to make the people aware of the correct amount of tax leviable so that his men donot unnecessarily extract money from the people.
11. Pusa also listens to the complaints of the tax papers regarding any extraction, over-evaluation of the products, etc.

12. Pusa has to ensure that the amount of tax levied is not excessive and is within the paying capacity of the tax-payer.

Savita : Like Varuna, etc, Savita is a god as also a Minister of Indra emperor for Law. As already indicated, laws made by the Sabha/ Samiti are executed by ministers. 'Sav' and 'Prasav' indicate the Rajdharma, i.e., Law. Therefore, Savita is correctly assigned the Department of Laws —

देवः सविता धर्म साविषत् (यजु. 9.5)

i.e. the god Savita arouses Dharma in people or make people act according to Dharma. As already indicated, the following of laws was considered as the Dharma, the obediency of laws made by Raja and ***varna-dharma*** is the following of laws pertaining to one's Varna, codified in ***Manu** Smriti*. The laws made by Raja and assured to be complied with by the people through Savita cannot be breached by anyone and if anyone does so, he is taken as a culprit and caught by the Raja's men and produced before a judge to give the punishment according to the crime. These laws cannot be breached even by ministers or chief officials of the Government. The importance of other ministers too lies in getting the compliance of laws by Savita. Therefore, Savita's job is very important as the working of the entire Government depends upon the extent of compliance of laws managed by Savita.

Sun. Sun is another god of Indra and Minister of Indra emperor for Education. As education enlightens a person so does Sun light the universe.

उद् सूर्यो ज्योतिषा देव रुति (ऋग. 4.13.1)

Here Sun is said to be the god of enlightenment. This enlightenment can be the light we apparently see as also the internal light of human being, as sun is said to be having exhauastive knowledge. (ज्ञान) :

विश्वस्य मनस्पते विश्वस्य वचसस्पते सर्वस्य वचसस्पते। (यजु. 0.37.18)

Here Sun is said to be controller of mind and speech. Sun has the treasure of knowledge within himself, which he spreads in the universe through his rays; which are responsible for agricultural production; which feed the people and keep them alive. One attains knowledge on inspiration from Sun, who, without any fear, does his job of rising and reaching climax in noon and then setting. So do human beings attain knowledge, reach their climax and then see their end to rise again in the next life.

Vishnu. Vishnu is the God of even god Indra in mythological terms but here he is shown as acting as the Prime Minister of Indra emperor. So here Vishnu has been symbolised as the present day Prime Minister, who, like mythological Vishnu, has all powers and the emperor is only symbolical head of the state. He is at the head of all other ministers. He even supervises the working of the Sabha/Samiti; produces all legislative proposals for enactment and then gets them complied with by his ministers and other Government employees. He keeps the emperor informed of the state of affairs in the kingdom and the king issues instructions through him to other ministers for compliance from time to time. He is, therefore, a link between the emperor and other ministers. Mythologically, Vishnu is said to have had 'Vamanavtara' in which he measured the two *lokas* by his two steps and the third had to be placed on Raja Bali. So, in this universe, Vishnu, as Vamanavtara is the defacto ruler of the entire universe. Vishnu has been referred to as Health Minister, Controller of Exchequer, Incharge of Policing, Protector of Dharma, etc. This would indicate that in those days Prime Minister was the defacto ruler like the present day Prime Minister with President as symbolic head only.

Aryama (अर्यमा). He is a god with Indra emperor as the Minister for Judiciary and Chief Justice (Civil). This indicates the perfectness of judicial system in those days as has been attained in present day after a prolonged struggle by the West. In Vedas, Aryama has been shown as both Chief Justice as also the Judiciary Minister. Since Aryama is the master of wealth, he is considered to have been the Chief Justice (Civil). Aryama decides the cases on the basis of truth. He does not have any fear from anyone and cares for the wealth of all people. He does not decide in haste and goes deep in the cases to find out the truth. He favoured the true party and punished the wrong. Aryama registeres all births and deaths and marriages. For these cases, judges had been appointed at various places under the Chief Justice and Minister of Laws. In Vedas, Aryama has been the incharge of wealth and dealt with all cases pertaining to disputes on wealth, marriages, etc.

Bhaga (भग). He is a god and Minister incharge of Welfare and Agriculture. He is incharge of distribution of wealth and to evaluate the agricultural products and to see that the Raj Bhag is given to the royal exchequer. He earns money, is very strong and virtually the owner of the entire country so far as its wealth is concerned. He planned in a way that the people became resourceful and wealthy. The poverty was eradicated and all people used to live comfortably. But he also used to see that no one collected more wealth than specified. To this extent, the principle of socialism was at work. Bhaga also dealt with the earnings from mines; the booty received from other defeated Rajas, etc. Bhaga provided all kinds of comforts to the people of all races. This does not, however mean that Bhaga had been distributing wealth from the exchequer as it was not possible since it would lead to the exchequer getting emptied. What he did, therefore, was to find out ways for the people to earn money, through industry, trade, increased agricultural production, etc.

Saraswati. As her name implies, she is Godess of knowledge in mythology. For Indra as emperor too, she is the Minister for Education. She is the treasure of all knowledge, education and imbibes the same in the people. Accordingly she looks into the arrangements for imparting education to the people. In those days, the education was arranged by gurus in 'Pathshalas'. So all these *pathshalas* were arranged by the education minister.A part of the revenues of exchequer was set apart for education and from this money only the pathshalas were run. She was also responsible for the character building of the people as true education is to produce men of character. This was the theme in all pathshalas too where the students were taught not to involve themselves in worldly enjoyments. They were treated on equal footing whether they were *rajkumars* or a vaish boy. The schools of high level were also started for imparting higher knowledge to the deserving persons and as such, there were universities for this purpose. Taxila, Vaishali, etc., are known universities. Saraswati herself is quite learned and is the treasure of all knowledge. She only, therefore, spread the same amongst the people. Saraswati is also incharge of music. She bestows best brains amongst the people. In fact, this would mean that she arranged for high class education to the people as also best of teacher-pupil relation.

Parvat. Like Varun, Surya, etc., Parvat was also a god and was Minister-in-charge of all products in hills, forests, etc. The Parvat provides to the people :

1. Foodgrains and eatables.
2. Wealth in the form of diamonds, rubies, etc.
3. Wealth from forests.

4. He protects such wealth.
5. All herbal commodities and medicines made therefrom.

He is responsible for the protection of forests, hills, etc. Wherever forests were cut, new trees and plants were grown. Parvat had under him other people, who looked into the local developments in his Department.

Vayu. Vayu (Air) is the god and incharge of pollution control department under emperor Indra. This would indicate that the importance of pollution control, which is relevant in present times, was already known to our people in ancient times and there was one full important department under a minister for this purpose. As Air is responsible for cleansing all pollution, he has correctly been assigned this department. Air is responsible for the cleansing of body by providing good and healthy air to the people in breathing. Air also cleans the pollution in atmosphere. Air acts in two ways in pollution control—one cleansing the houses, cities, etc., from pollution by strong waves of air and another by providing fresh air in breathing. Air also provides strength to people. Air also works as a panacea for many diseases.

तन्नो वातो भयोमु वातु भेषजम (ऋग. 1.89.4)

Means that air brings the medicinal effects which affords pleasures to people. In fact, air is one of the three ingredients (कफ, वायु, पित्त) which run the human body. Also air is synonymous with Atma. When it goes out of the body, one is considered to have died. Air is also an essential ingredient in the formation of human body out of water, air, fire, space and earth.

Kutsa (कुत्स) He is a god and Minister for vigilance in Emperor Indra's Government. The word 'Kutsa', means finding faults. As vigilance looks into the faults of the Government employees in the discharge of their duties, it comes rightly under the minister for Vigilance Department. Kutsa acts secretly through his people and keeps a watch on the Government employees of all Departments. He has to see that employees in Finance Department do not misappropriate Government funds; the Agriculture Department employees properly evaluate the harvests and do not connive with the agriculturists ; and the traders pay their cess correctly and it is assessed correctly. Since in the discharge of these duties he has to earn the anger of all employees, he is in constant fear of any revenge being taken by them. Therefore, Indra provides proper protection to these people so that they could act fearlessly. Also they are supposed to catch the actual culprits only and are taken up if they falsely implicate any person. Therefore, some intelligence is put behind them with a view to see that they donot connive with anyone. The people in Vigilance Department are selected specially out of people of good conduct, resourceful, intelligent, alert and devoted to their duty. Kutsa specially keeps a watch on the Dasyu people as they are of low character. They are liable to act in misappropriations; acting against the Raja; creating obstacles in the employees discharging of their duties; harassing the people of four Varnas, etc. Kutsa also monitors that each person does his best in the interest of the *rajya*, that is, an agriculturist produces maximum; the industrialist produces maximum; trader accordingly does his maximum and in case the output is shown less, then Kutsa investigates into the matter lest it is wrong projection to avoid taxation. Similarly, Kutsa's people keep a watch on the other Government servants to see that they discharge their duties well; there is no lethargy or slackness on their part or connivance with the producers, etc. Wherever such slackness is found, such employees are caught and produced before the Raja for due punishment. In this way, Kutsa was responsible for :

1. Ensuring that each person worked hard to have full production and give the Raj Bhag to Government exchequer, which was ultimately spent on the welfare of the public at large and less production would deny that well-being of the public.
2. Ensuring that there was no corruption in Government servants in misappropriation of royal funds as also in connivance with the producers.

In the above analysis, it has been narrated that emperor Indra had twenty-one gods, who worked as his ministers in charge of various jobs. They were all tiny emperors and generally worked autonomously without interference from the emperor, so much so that they were considered as emperors themselves. Here Indra is the suzerain emperor having many Rajas under him. He, therefore, had to keep a watch on all the Rajas under him as also the other Rajas,emperors with a view to protect his kingdom from any attack. For this purpose, the role of the vigilance and police departments was very important and whichever emperor had given importance to these Departments, he had been a successful ruler and those who left these departments unattended, had to face disintegration of the kingdom.

Rajya and Judiciary

Raja as Dharmadhikari. One of the jobs of the Raja is to punish the people who harass the public. This implies the setting up of courts to deal with such people as it is in the courts only that the culprits and non-culprits could be judged as every culprit on prosecution pleads non-guilty. Now whether he is culprit or not has to be ascertained by the court only and on his having been found guilty, he is to be punished adequately. Dharma was generally taken as the code of conduct in Vedas and commitment of any crime was considered as the breach of the canons of Dharma. The duties of each person had been defined in the *varna-dharma* of each person and he is supposed to be following the same. Then, there are the Raj Dharma, Spiritual Dharma, etc, also. In Raj Dharma, one had to contribute the specified portion of his products to the exchequer and be prepared to present himself for the protection of the *rajya* whenever called upon to do so. In Spiritual Dharma, one had to follow the ashramas and, if followed correctly, the spiritual requirement shall be met. In *Ramayana*, Rama considered it as his duty to coach people about the attainment of salvation through *bhakti* although it was not strictly within the preview of the Raj Dharma. Therefore, Rama too, after coaching the Dharma, left it to the people to follow it or not as per their volition. Therefore, Spiritual Dharma, though necessary, could not be enforced by the Raja. Then there are Samajik Dharma, Parivar Dharma, etc., indicating what are the duties of an individual in Samaj. For instance, giving alms to beggers is a social Dharma but one cannot be forced to do it. Similarly, in Parivar Dharma, one is obliged to bring up the family, arrange for their proper food, clothing, education, living etc. Though there are no set standards for it but one has to fulfil this obligation as per one's position. Since the judges of the court see the compliance or breach of the laws made by the Government, and the compliance of these laws is stated to be one's Dharma, they are also called Dharmadhikari or Dharmadhakshya, and the courts are named as 'Dharmadhikaran'. Therefore, it is essential for the Raja to :

1. Establish the courts to interpret law and punish the criminals found to have involved breach of laws.
2. There should be laws made out by the Raja. These laws are based on truth, Dharma, etc., as defined in various Shastras.
3. There should be a code of punishments to be awarded for each crime like the present day penal code.

4. There should be a procedure to detect the criminal; produce him before the court; levelling charges against him; giving him a chance of defending himself by documentary and oral evidence and then deciding the case and imposition of punishment, if found guilty.
5. There should be a machinery to watch compliance of the judgement of the court that is there should be a jail to keep the criminal to undergo punishment of conviction and arranging execution in case of death sentence.

The Cabinet as per the Vedas

Here, Indra has been stated to be the emperor and Varuna, Soma, etc., as his ministers for different portfolios. Varuna, as the minister for Police Department, is responsible for the maintenance of law and order in the kingdom and to detect, prosecute and present the culprit before the court for enabling the court to award punishment for the crime in which he is involved. For this purpose Varuna has to frame the chargesheet and present proof of the apprehended person having committed the crime. Spash is the minister for spies. The spies too wander about in the kingdom and detect the criminals secretly and on such detection arrest and present the criminals before the court for punishment. The police and spies act independently and jointly for this purpose. Soma is the minister for the Judicial Department as also the Chief Justice. We see that in Vedas the same person is Minister incharge as also the head of the Department. He also monitors the working of all other courts in the kingdom. Rudra is the minister for defence and commander-in-chief of the army. During battles/wars too the prisoners of war are arrested and they are also punished by the court. Also the booty obtained from the defeated Raja is properly appropriated by the civil court. Pusa is Finance Minister. His department also detects the people, who misappropriate Government funds and also hide their products and do not pay the Raj Bhag properly. Such people are presented by the employees of this Department before the court (civil) for adequate punishment. Savita is the Law Minister. His job is to get the laws framed by the Sabha/Samiti and then application of the same through the courts on the criminals having been apprehended. He is responsible for establishment of all courts, manning the same and application of laws in punishing the detected criminals. Bhaga is the Agriculture Minister. He overseas that all producers give the specified portion of Raj Bhag to Government exchequer and to apprehend the criminals, who did hide the products and getting them punished by the courts of law. Bhaga is also responsible for proper distribution of the money from the Government exchequer and to see that the same is used for the purpose for which it is allotted and not misappropriated. Parvat ensures the adequate production in forests, mountains, seas, etc., and to see that these are not exploited or misappropriated by unauthorised persons. Brihaspati is Dharma minister. He looks into the fact that each person had been following the *varna-dharma*, Raj Dharma and Spiritual Dharma and getting the criminals punished where the crime is punishable as per law or getting such persons morally degraded, where not punishable under state laws. Kutsa is the minister for Vigilance Department. His job is to keep a watch on the Goverment servants, ministers, etc. to see that they do not misappropriate government funds, do not connvive with the producers in hiding the produce and not giving the Raj Bhag of the produce to the Government exchequer. On having detected the persons involved in such acts of breach of laws, they are presented before the court with charges levelled against them and getting them punished. And overall, the Prime Minister Vishnu is there to oversee that each Minister and his Department had been acting as per laid down laws and bringing the untoward incidents to the notice of the emperor Indra.

As already indicated, the emperor in Vedas is not only a tutorial head like the present Emperor of England or President of India but he had all powers of governance bestowed on himself and is answerable to the Sabha/Samiti, public at large and the God for not discharging his duties properly as laid down as Raj Dharma in *Manu Smriti*. The emperor attends the proceedings of the Sabha/Samiti and issues directions from time to time as may be considered necessary for the consideration of the Sabha/Samiti. He has to act on the advice of the Sabha/Samiti and in case of non-agreement, he can undo the same but has to give reasons for the same acceptable to the Sabha/Samiti. He is the controller of all ministers and their departments and their working as head of the executive. He is responsible for the execution of all laws framed by the legislature and to earn revenues to run the Government, protect the kingdom from foreign invasions and for this purpose raising adequate army with armaments required by the army. He executes all jobs for the welfare of the public such as construction of roads; provision of transport; provision of *sarais* in cities and on highways; keeping the kingdom free from any fear of thieves/robbers/dacoits; arranging food, clothing, housing and education for all the people in the kingdom. On judiciary side, he is considered as the fountain of justice and the overall justice of the country. Final appeal in judicial cases lie to him only and his decision is final.

Criminals : Types of in Vedas

In Vedas, eight kinds of criminals have been mentioned as rakshasas ; man-eaters ; one who always speak ill of others and so harms others in one way or the other ; those who are always busy in doing illegal jobs ; those who steal ; those, who develop enmity with others ; those who beat others; those who are back-biters ; and those who tell lies. The crimes committed by them are decided in courts after finding out the truth and untrue aspects in the matter. The judge acquits the true persons and punishes those found guilty. The criminals are either put in jails on conviction or are entrusted to be hanged. In this way, a person is not punished simply on having been charged with any crime but only after the charge has been proved in the court of law. Vedas amply make it clear that there were courts established in those days.

Code of Punishment as per the Vedas

There was also the code for punishments. Some of the criminals mentioned are those mentioned above. Some of the other criminals mentioned are enemies of : Brahmins or education, yagyas, gentlemen, country, Raja and wanderers during night with bad intentions, thieves, robbers, womanisers, etc. The punishment for these crimes has also been mentioned. It indicates that there was a code of crimes and punishments like the present day penal code and this code is more exhaustive. The punishments prescribed are pecuniary (monetary), conviction for specified period of imprisonment, death sentence, etc. At first, efforts are made on the first crime committed by a person to warn him not to repeat the crime ; on second crime, some physical punishment (amputation of parts of body) is given and death sentence is given on repeated crimes. The harshness or otherwise of the punishment differed from one Raja to another. Although some punishments for crimes have been illustrated in the Shastras, there was sufficient scope for reducing or enhancing the same by the judge depending on the situation of each case. Vedas speak of reforming the criminals first and if they are not reformed then only they are punished. During their punishment of imprisonment too, efforts are made to reform them. It may, however, be remembered that according to Shastras, the system of punishing the criminals is with a view to save others against whom crime has been done and not simply to punish the criminals. So by punishing the criminals, the Raja is doing his job of protection of his people from criminals within and without the kingdom.

Soma is stated to be the judge in Shastras. The judge should be :

1. Truth speaker;
2. Pious;
3. Strong enough to protect himself if attacked by criminals in isolation;
4. Should be able to go deep into the matter to find the truth and false in the case;
5. Should not have any vested interest in the criminals;
6. Should be without any fear or favour;
7. Should be leading a simple life and not luxurious life as one who indulges in luxury is liable to do wrong jobs himself. Soma only awards the punishment commensurate to the crime committed as proved and it is then for the men of the Raja to punish him accordingly. In this action of granting punishments, Soma develops enemity with the criminals and they could harm Soma. Therefore, the Raja had to grant him proper protection. Also Soma is granted complete freedom in dealing with the criminals and there is no pressure or interference from other departments. This ensured independence of judiciary, which is even now granted as any decision to punish the criminal under pressure cannot be a correct decision and can lead to either punishing a wrong person or acquitting the real culprits. Soma, for this purpose, even tries the Kshatriyas against crimes committed by them. There is special mention of punishing the Kshatriyas with a view to see that Soma does not, out of fear acquit them or grant a milder punishment as Kshatriyas are brave people and could harm Soma for the punishment awarded to them. That is why Soma is said to be a fearless and non-biased person since his job is to grant punishment to all. Also there is speical reference to the trial of Brahmins as Brahmins are basically non-biased, non-greedy, God fearing people and do not generally commit crimes. They should be specially dealt with during their trial and if found guilty, should be given milder punishments and given a chance to reform themselves. Sometimes it may be sufficient to warn and acquit them if they undertake not to repeat the crime again. But such leniency is not exercised for all brahmins but for those, who are away from material wants ; quite learned and selfless but due to some unfortunate circumstances, fell to commit crime.

2

HINDU LAW AND DHARMA

The above is the origin of a concept of life or a way of life or the law governing the life as per Vedas. The Hindu Law of today, therefore, is not exactly what it originally had been many centuries ago. The fate of law is a change—a constant change with the change in society. Hindu Law is undoubtedly one of the most ancient systems of law and can be compared only with the oldest systems of law known to the world namely the Babylonian Law, the Egyptian Law and the Roman Law. In its height of perfection, richness of details and wealth of juristic and philosophical speculation. Hindu Law can be compared favourably and advantageously with any of the other systems of law. As indicated in Vedas, Hindu Law was originally assigned the true 'Dharma'. What was 'Dharma' was law too and vice versa. The true Dharma passed through several transitions of meaning and ultimately its prominent significance can be confirmed to, "The privileges, duties and obligations of man, his standard of conduct as a member of the Aryan community, as a member of the one of the castes of a person in particular stage of life".

Hindu Law is generally believed to have been derived mainly from Vedas, as already explained, followed by Dharmashastras, which are supposed to have been preceded by and elaborated from the Dharmasutra. But still Dharma could not mean positive law, civil law, private law, or public law in the modern sense of the term. Dharma was in fact a much wider term including religion, social, moral, domestic and other regulations including legal rules as well. This term was used in the most comprehensive sense to cover and regulate the conduct of one Aryan or a Hindu from all points of view. The ancient Hindu jurists generally distinguished between the rules relating to religious and moral observances (आचार और प्रायश्चित) on the one hand, and those relating to positive law (*vyavahar* व्यवहार) on the other.

Eras of Hindu Law

The Vedas or the shrutis (As heard from God), were in theory the root and original source of 'Dharma'. These have been further interpreted and elaborated in Smritis, which means 'recollection'. The Shrutis were accepted as the original utterings of the Great power and Smritis were couched in the words of the rishis or sages since antiquity, who saw or received the revelations. Hindu law thus falls in three eras :

1. The Vedic era.
2. The era of Dharmashastras:
   (a) The Sutra period;
   (b) the Smriti period.
3. The post Smriti era.

The contents of Vedas as the source of jurisprudence have already been narrated. The subsequent periods are discernible successive strata of legal thought, progressive evolution and expansion and growth of a system of traditional law claiming its foundation in the law of revelation and having Smritis as its ancient framework. The era of Dharmashastras was the golden age of Hindu Law, although the more critical period was the post-Smriti period, where the system became more refined and simpler and was the most productive period of Hindu Law.

The Smritis

The Hindu jurisprudence regards the Smritis, which are often designated as Dharmashastras, as constituting the foundation of an important source of Law. The Smritis or Dharmashastras are the earliest extant treatises from which our knowledge of the line of development, which Hindu Law has pursued during the second epoch of its history, is derived. Composite in their character, the principle Smritis blend religious, moral, social and legal duties. The Smritis or the Dharmashastras announcing rules and percepts of Dharma are expressions understood in a broad and comprehensive sense and a clear perception of Hindu Law is not possible unless it is properly appreciated that the blending of religion and ethics with law by these jurists-theologians was in a large measure the natural result of a philosophy of life, which had emphasis on the supremacy of inward life over things external.

The extant Smritis were compiled at different times and in different parts of the country but they all purported to record one traditional law. Smriti was not automatic law which is the result of a true form of legislation or is promulgated by state in its own person. The rishis, who compiled the Smritis did not exercise temporal power nor did they owe their authority to any sovereign power. The authority or imperative character of their legal injunctions was partly derived from the reverence in which they were held and the accepted principle that what they laid down was agreeable to good conscience. There are a number of texts in the Smritis on the subject of ownership, which show that the jurisprudential concepts reflected through them remarkably accord with the views of the most modern writers on jurisprudence. Further, there are a number of texts in the Smritis on the treatment of the law of prescription. These law-makers evinced practical insight and legal acumen of high order. In law of succession, they announced the identity of husband and wife and on that assumption rested the rule that, in case of a person, who died sonless, his widow could succeed in preference to all other heirs recognised by law. A maxim that found favour was that reason and justice are more to be regarded than mere texts and some of the ancient rules of law propounded by the law-makers surprise us by their strikingly modern character and remarkable insight into jurisprudential concepts for insight which does not depend on modernity.

The Smritis of Dharmashastras are divisible into two classes. The first of these are the 'Sutras'. Complete Sutras' work contain aphorisms on sacrifice, aphorisms on ceremonies requiring domestic fire and aphorisms on law and customs, treatment of temporal duties of men in their various relations. The principal extant Dharmashastras are those of Gautama, Baudhyama, Apastamba, Harita, Vashistha and Vishnu. The Smritis were more specifically so called namely the institute of Manu, of Yajnavalkya and of Narada and the Smritis of Parashara, Brihaspati, Katyana, and others belong to the second category of Dharmashashtras. Of the Smritis, the first and foremost in rank of authority is Manu Smriti of the Institute of Manu. There is a striking resemblance and agreement among the Smritis on many questions and they purport to embody one traditional law and all the Smritis in course of time came to be regarded as of universal application.

After the Vedic period and before the advent of Smritis, the advent of Buddhism is the first standpoint in the annals of India. It forms in fact, the only true commencement of Indian history. Its founder Gautama Buddhha is said to have been born in 623 B.C. and to have died in 543 B.C. at the age of eighty. The history prior to Buddha is not supported by any documents and is hence called the Vedic period or Mythological period and is not accounted for in the factual history of India.

The first important feature of the Hindu Era is the broad distinction, which originally existed between the Vedic and Brahmanic elements in the early history. The Vedic Aryans, who colonised North Western India, in a remote antiquity, were worshippers of spirits or elements of the universe as gods and godesses and invoked those deities in old Sanskrit verses known as Vedic hymns. Subsequently the Brahmins effected changes in Vedic ideas and usages which are found invested with a deep significance. The Vedic Aryas had neither temples or idols nor rigid caste distinctions. They worshipped their deities as living existences and they apparently offered their own sacrifices and invocations and performed their own domestic rites without the aid of any caste or priest whatsoever. It was in subsequent Brahmanical Era that the Brahmins appear to have encouraged the construction of temples and to have set up images or idols, which were worshipped individually and collectively, or representatives of one supreme being. Brahmins also seem to have distributed the people into castes or at any rate to have recognised and sanctioned such castes' distinctions and they arrogated to themselves the position of an exclusive and hereditary priesthood through whom alone the people could arrange sacrifices. The Kshatriyas, who governed the kingdom, were responsible to protect the people from outside aggressions and inward crime. The Vaishyas were engaged in trade, agriculture and industry and the Shudras were there to assist and help the people of other three castes perform their functions. It was in this era that every legend and tradition had systematically Brahmanised for the purpose of bringing all the religions, laws and usages of the differant races of India into conformity with Brahmanical ideas. It is when they were stripped of those Brahmanical grafts and overgrowth that the legends and traditions are found to have been finished in large illustration of Hindu civilisation.

The Buddha Era

In Vedas, the gods have been invested with the governance of universe. Indra as a deity, appears as a sovereign ruler of the gods and the king of the universe, as has already been explained. This was followed by Buddha Era, which spread in India in about fifth century B.C. This brought The Brahmanical philosophy of caste, religion, idolatory, etc., to a naught and instead the Buddhist concepts of faith in Divine, non-harming to any creature, being pious and sympathetic to all, etc.

flourished. In such an environ, there was practically no crime but whenever there was crime it was strenuously dealt with. It was at this time that Alexander invaded India. At that time, Chandrgupta Maurya had been coming up in Magadha. Alexander could not stay for long in India and died on his way back. His lieutenants too had been eliminated in his absence. This gave a chance to Chandra Gupta Maurya to bring entire India under his control under the able guidance of Chanakya (Kautilya).

Maurya Period

The civilisation that prevailed in the great Gangetic empire of Chandra Gupta Maurya was essentially different from that of the Panjab Kingdom under Porus. The people were strictly divided into castes and hereditary professions. Further, the army was not composed of contribution from feudatory princes but was a vast standing camp,maintained solely at the charge of the king. The Government too was not administred by feudal or vassal chieftains, under a Suzerain or Lord Paramount but by a network of officials, which were spread over the entire empire. The Raja was an all powerful despot. He was not merely the Sovereign of his dominions but the actual proprietor of the land in the European sense of the word; and the *ryots* cultivated the land as labourers and received a share of the produce as wages. Thus, a large proportion of the produce of the empire was stored up every year in the royal granaries and partly sold to the trading and manufacturing classes and partly devoted to the maintenance of the army and civil administration. The internal administration of the Gangetic kingdom was conducted by a separate class of civil servants, inspectors and magistrates. Some of them were appointed to the city, some to the camp and some to the districts and provinces. The duty of the magistrates combined the ordinary routine of the executive with other measures of supervision and surveillance which are of essentially oriental character. They also worked for espionge. Even women were engaged in such jobs and they are said to be working more efficiently compared to men.

City Magistrates : Divisions. The Magistrates of the city were formed into six Divisions, each of which consisted of five officials. One division maintained a close supervision over the working of all arts and manufactures. A second division presided over the sale of all such articles to prevent old goods from being sold as new ones. A third division presided over all sales and exchanges in produce. This division apparently comprised royal brokers, who received the produce from the royal granaries, after the payment of the share to the cultivators and then supplied it to the retailers in the *bazaars*, and maintained a supervision over the trade. The fourth division collected the tax for the king which amounted to one tenth of the price of the article sold and any attempt at fraud in the payment of this tax was punished by death. The fifth division registered all births and deaths, with every particular of time and place for the two-fold object of levying tax and punishing concealment. The sixth division entertained all strangers or foreigners, who came as envoys or might possibly be spies. In addition to these special duties pertaining to each division, the city magistrates perfomed other duties in their collective capacity. They took charge of the markets, harbours and temples; they repaired all public works and they fixed the price of all articles and commodities that were sold in the shops and *bazaars*.

Inspectors. The duties of the inspectors as magistrates in the Districts are same but slightly touched upon. Some of the District officers had charge of the rivers and measured the land. They observed the effect of yearly inundations during the rainy season. Others inspected the great tanks or reservoirs from which water was distributed by canals so that all might have an equal share in the irrigation. Others again superintended the shepherds and hunters and rewarded those who kept the fields clear of birds and vermins, whilst punishing those who neglected their duties. They collected the taxes and superintended all the various work-people, who were engaged in connection with the land, such as wood-cutters, carpenters, workers in brass and mines generally. They all superintended the public roads and placed pillars at intervals of every ten stadia to indicate the by-ways and distances.

The seventh class, including officers of state, must be dismissed with a bare notice. It consisted of counsellors and assessors of the king and that to these persons belonged the offices of state, the tribunals of justice and the whole administration of affairs. The people were happy because of the simplicity of their manners and their frugal mode of life. They had but one extravagance and that was a love of ornaments which to this day is a characteristic of all classes of the community. They never drank wine, excepting at sacrifices. Their laws were so simple that they had few law suits and none whatever in the case of pledges and deposits. They required neither witnesses nor seals but made their deposits and confided in one another. Even their houses and property were unguarded. They had no written laws and were even ignorant of writing and regulated every thing by memory. The Brahmins possessed a sacred literature.

Gupta Period

Fahien, who visited India in about fourth century A.D. during the reign of Guptas, has indicated that the people were prosperous and happy for there was no registration of families for the purpose of taxation. No one paid any portion of the produce as rent excepting those who farmed the royal demesnes and they were allowed to give up the land whenever they pleased. Offenders were not subjected to corporal punishment, but only fined. Rebels, however, convicted of repeated rebellions, were deprived of their right hands. No one except the *chandals*, killed any living being or drank anything intoxicating or even dealt in living animals. There were no shambles or wine shops.

Harsha's Period

Of course later during Harsha's time, when Hiuen Tsang came to India in seventh century A.D., he has stated that the administration of justice amongst the Hindus was exceedingly mild. They had no capital punishments. Even rebels were not put to death but only imprisoned for life. They were neither beaten nor whipped but simply left to live or die. But those, who violated justice or failed in their fidelity or neglected their duties towards their parents, were condemned to lose their ears, noses or hands and feet. Sometimes they were expelled to barbarous regions beyond the frontiers. Other offences were punished with fines. The administration of justice was concealed as much as possible from the public gaze. Neither staff nor whip was employed to induce offenders to confess their crimes. If the accused frankly acknowledged his fault, he was awarded suitable punishment. If he obstinately denied it or sought to palliate it, he was tried by the four ordeals of water, fire, weight or poison, and by these means his innocence or guilt was established without further question. The whole system of Government was based upon the benovolent spirit of Buddhism. All governors, magistrates and officials received lands for their maintenance. India was divided into 124 kingdoms. Each of these kingdoms was independent and self contained like a Hindu village. The villages were a permanent institution and they had their own self governance.

We were considering the sources of law in ancient India. After vedas, we have Dharmasutras. In Dharmasutras, those of Gautama can be mentioned. These contain sources of law, initiative, rules of purification, duties of four ashramas, rules and forms of marriages, castes, lawful occupations and livelihood, duties of a king, civil and criminal law, witnesses, impurities, funeral, oblations, study of Vedas, eatable and forbidden foods, women, penance and inheritance.

Under civil law, the treatment of Gautama includes taxation, sources of ownership, treasure-trove, guardianship of minors' wealth, rules of money-lending, payment of debts, deposits, rules about witnesses, partition, *stridhan*, twelve kinds of sons, inheritance, etc.

Under criminal law, Gautama deals with punishment for libel, abuse, adultery and rape, thefts, privileges bestowed on Brahmins as regards punishments. Disputes between cultivators and landowners, disputes between cowherds and masters, qualifications of judges too have been dealt. In crimnial law, the punishments vary according to the Varna of the man and woman. The Shudra is to be punished for abuse or claiming equality. However, for homicide or theft, the Brahmin is to be made blind (by tying cloth) and kept in secret confinement until amendment and if he does not amend, he is banished.

Vashistha Dharmasutras

Vashistha borrows many Sutras from Gautama. He quotes many verses of extant Manu. The contents of Vashistha Dharmasutras are sources of law, the Aryavrata, sinful persons, five *mahapatakas, upapatakas*, rules for acquiring wife from lower varnas, six forms of marriages; Brahmins as law-givers and their privileges; tax on wealth; the four Varnas; the *upanayana* and its importance; the lawful occupations of the four Varnas, condemnation of usury for Brahmins and Kshatriyas; different rates of interest; rules of treasure-trove; constitution of a Parishad; rules of purification; dependence of women and father on husband and sons; the rules of day-to-day conduct; legal procedure; inheritance; mixed castes; duties of the king; penances; gifts; administration of justice; three-fold proofs—documentary, witnesses and possession—quaifications of witnesses; perjury; inheritance; partition between brothers; sixth part of wealth as tax; rates of interest, etc. The discussion of criminal law is not found in Vashistha Dharmasutras.

Vishnu Dharmasutras

Brief contents of Vishnu's Dharmasutras are: The great Boar myth; duties of Varnas; kingship; coins and measures; crimes and punishments; rules of debt; rates of interest; sureties; documents; witnesses; ordeals; twelve kinds of sons; rules of inheritance; mixed castes; *shradhas*; rules and forms of marriages; Various kinds of sins, diseases due to sins; penances; householder; duties of kings; stridhana; three kinds of documents. The discussion on criminal law includes treatment of crimes and punishments.

3

THE CONTENTS OF ANCIENT LITERATURE : SMRITIS AND ARTHASHASTRA

The Smritis are the works that laid the foundation of Hinduism. Smritis, as they themselves claim, were written to show the right path to the people. After Buddhism, it was necessary for revival of Brahmanical values to compose new codes of law based on old ones. Smritis were the answers to this challenge.

Manu Smriti. This is the oldest amongst Smritis and is considered to be the most authoritative word of law. Hindus all over India hold its dicta in high esteem. Manu recounts the story of the origin of the institutions of law as well as the universe. The present text had many changes. Narada, Markandeya and Sumati condensed the text of Manu successively. Manu enumerates four and Yajnavalkya fourteen different sources of Dharma. In these sources, Dharma has been used in the 'Varnadharma, sense of Varnadharma and not in the sense of 'Vyavahara' or positive law. Therefore, in reality, the different aspects of Vyavahara, which have been enumerated as Dharma, Vyavahara, or Charitra. Hence the word Dharma has been used in the sense of truth or principles as embodied in the Dharmashastras used in the most comprehensive sense to include the whole of scriptural literature which constitutes the literary source of Hindu Law. The term Dharma has been used in the sense of Dharma literature, including the Dharmasutras and the Dharmashastras, the Shrutis having practically very little of secular or positive law. In ancient India, there was no arrangement of law reports and hence no decision could be preserved. The expression literary sources, as used in connection with Hindu Law, comprised the Shrutis, the Smritis and the commentaries of which the first played a very significant part as a source of secular law or "Lawyers' Law" and the last could not be forseen by the authors of the Smritis as they were produced much later. The present text of *Manu Smriti* has twelve chapters :

1. Introductory myth;
2. Sources of law, various sanskaras, studentship;
3. Marriage and duties of householder;
4. Rules for a Sanataka; study of Vedas;
5. Permissible and forbidden foods; impurity and rules of purification; duties of wife and widow;
6. Hermits in the forests and ascetics;
7. Kingship and administration;
8. Administration of justice and judicial procedure, eighteen titles of law, theft, adultery;
9. Duties of husband and wife, inheritance, gambling and betting, various punishments, duties of king;
10. Varnas, mixed castes, occupations of castes, times of distress;
11. Penance, ex-communication and re-admission;
12. Transmigration, hell, the supreme bliss.

It was Manu, who for the fist time, gave systematic treatment to legal procedure. He also introduced eighteen titles of law.

Yajnavalkya Smriti. This is the second valuable link in the chain of Smritis. The author of Yajnavalkya Smriti has used *Manu Smriti* as his model. But it is far moie concise and systematic than *Manu Smriti*. It is divided in three broad chapters : The code of conduct; administration of justice and rules of atonement. These three chapters are further divided into various sections such as :

I. The Code of Conduct

(i) Introduction
(ii) Studentship
(iii) Marriage
(iv) Varna and Jati
(v) Householder
(vi) The Sanataka
(vii) Permissible and forbidden foods
(viii) Rules for purification
(ix) Gifts
(x) Sharadhas
(xi) Worship of Planets

(xii) Worship of Ganapati
(xiii) Kingship and administration

II. Administration of Justice

(i) Legal terms and definitions
(ii) Exceptional legal terms
(iii) Debt
(vi) Deposits
(v) Witnesses
(vi) Documents
(vii) Ordeals
(viii) Partition
(ix) Boundary disputes
(x) Disputes between cattle owners and herdsmen
(xi) Sale without ownership
(xii) Invalid gifts
(xiii) Recision of purchases
(xiv) Breach of contract of service
(xv) Violation of conventions
(xvi) Non-payment of wages
(xvii) Gambling and prize-fighting
(xviii) Abuse
(xix) Assault
(xx) Sahasa
(xxi) Non-delivery of sold chattel
(xxii) Partnership
(xxiii) Theft
(xxiv) Adultery
(xxv) Miscellaneous wrongs.

III. Atonement and Penances

(i) Impurity due to death or birth
(ii) Rules of conduct in distress
(iii) Rules for forest hermits
(iv) Rules for yatis
(v) Atonements
(vi) Miscellaneous atonements

Parasara Smriti. **It was written by Vyas Parasara. It consists of twelve chapters. The date of composition of this Smriti is placed between**

the first and the fifth centuries A.D. It is divided into following twelve chapters :

(i) The mythical introduction
(ii) Duties of householders
(iii) The impurities (caused by birth and death) and their purification
(iv) Suicide; punishment for forsaking
(v) The *prayschita* for dog-bites, etc. The performance of last rites on the effigy of an Agnihotra Brahmin.
(vi) The *prayschita* for killing birds, animals, Kshatriya, Vaishya, Shudra or *chandala*; purification for touching impure persons purification of impure foods.
(vii) Purification of different kinds of vessels, marriage of girls before menstruation starts; purification for touching a woman in monthly periods; purification of different impurities.
(viii) 'Prayschita' for killing a cow; formation of Parishad; praise of Brahmin caste; the *prajapatya* penance.
(ix) Different kinds of cow killings and their prayschita
(x) Prayschita for violating woman with whom sexual connection is prohibited
(xi) Prayschita for taking prohibited food and its purification; the Atikrcchra penance.
(xii) Purification after bad dream and vomiting; the five baths; things which should be kept in the house; length of Gokarma-Bhumi and its gift; the prayschita of *mahapatakas* or grave sins; the *tulapurusa* penance.

Narada Smriti. The name Narada is borrowed from Vedic literature. This name occurs in the Atharvaved Samhita in the Vansa of Samvidhana Brahmin. Its text has come down to us almost intact. This is, perhaps, the last Smriti. The classifications and distinctions propounded by Narada Smriti are far more elaborate than found in *Manu Smriti*. The treatment of legal procedure shows distinct advance over the norms laid down by Manu. On many matters, the basic idea seems to be the same as that found in Manu Smriti but it has been worked out in meticulous details. One example of the legalistic approach found in this Smriti is its emphasis on documentary evidence and record. It shows far less faith in oral evidence and verbal procedure. The royal verdict has been considered to be supreme by Narada. The royal verdict can even overrule the Smriti dicta. It seems to have been composed in fourth century A.D.during the classic era. The larger and more authoritative version of the Narada Smriti deals, after a short preface about the creation of world, with legal procedure, plaint, and court of justice. After this, the rules regarding the eighteen titles of law are laid down meticulously. The eighteen titles are: (i) Debt, (ii) Deposits, (iii) Partnership, (iv) Resumption of gifts, (v) Breach of contract of service, (vi) Non-payment of wages, (vii) Sales effected by a person other than the rightful owner, (viii) Non-delivery of sold chattel, (ix) Rescission of purchase, (x) Transgression of a compact, (xi) Boundary disputes, (xii) Mutual duties of husband and wife, (xiii) Inheritance, (xiv) Heinous offences, (xv) Abuse and assault, (xvi) Games, (xvii) Miscellaneous.

Brihaspati Smriti. Like all material codes, Brihaspati Smriti has also taken its name from a famous Vedic seer Brihaspati. The text of Brihaspati Smriti is not available but has survived only in digests and commentaries. The code of Brihaspati is in many ways similar to that of Manu, Yajnavalkya and Narada. It shows fewer diviations from the rules laid down by Manu and Narada. Its composition has been dated in sixth or seventh century A.D. The dicta of Brihaspati relating to law are the following :

Plaints; human and divine evidence; witnesses; documents; possession; eighteen titles of law and *prakirnaka* namely debt; deposit; sale by a person other than the owner; partnership; resumption of gifts, breach of contract of service; non-payment of wages; transgression of a compact; rescission of purchase or sale; boundary disputes; abuse and assault; theft; heinous offences; adultery, duties of husband and wife; inheritance; gambling and betting and miscellaneous. Brihaspati was the first law-giver to distinguish between civil and criminal suits. He declares that the first group of fourteen titles sprang from wealth and the other four from injury. He recognises widow, daughter and mother as heirs. He condemns arbitrariness in dispensation of justice. Emphasising the importance of evidence and procedure, he points out that the right decision cannot be made merely on the basis of Shastras but the evidence and agreements must be examined in each case, otherwise innocents are likely to be punished. In many of these views, Brihaspati comes very close to modern legal norms and at times we think that the modern procedures and norms of law have been carved out of the ancient Smritis, particularly Brihaspati Smriti.

Katyayana Smriti. It presents the legal procedure in a very matured form. He has inherited the terms and style of Narada and Brihaspati. On the basis of the high degree of refinement and elaboration of juristic procedure reached in Katyayana, Kane places this work later in point of time to both Brihaspati and Narada. His prominent feature is the elaborate treatment of Stridhana'. He classifies and defines it and gives absolute right of its disposal to woman. He is the first Smriti-writer, who dwelt with Stridhana elaborately. In many matters, he shows more refinement and elaboration than even Narada and Brihaspati.

Era of Commentaries and Digests

The era of commentaries follows and a bit overlaps the period in which some of the Smritis were composed. Digests were written from the twelfth upto the end of seventeenth century. A commentary covers only a particular text while a digest presents a general synthesis of all the Smriti texts. Generally, commentaries inherited all the tendencies of Smritis and in more concentrated form. They have rejected some old customs and restricted woman's right to property. These commentaries and digests played an important role in the history of legal thoughts. The most renowned commentaries are Asahaya, Visvarupa, Medhatithi, Dhareswara, Bhojdeva, Vijnaneswara, GovindaRaja, Laxmidhara, Jimutavahane, Apararka, Haradatta, Devannabhatta, Kullukabhatta, Candeswara, Sulapani, Madhyavacharya, Visvesavarabhatta, Vakaspati Misra, Pratyaparudradeva etc.

Vyavahara. The term 'Vyavahara' has been used in Smritis and commentaries in the sense of civil law, positive law, legal procedure, litigation or disputes. The ancient Hindu Law is said to be of divine or religious origin. This origin must be sought in the earliest conception of Rta, as we find in the Rigveda, according to which the sages conceived the natural phenomena as God's and invoked them as such. They also noticed an order, uniformity and regularity existing in nature. Varuna was the presiding deity of this Rta order. For their own conduct also, the Rigvedic poets conceived that some orders and rules were implanted by God. Any transgression thereof was to be punished by Varuna through the infliction of the disease dropsy. On the analogy of this moral sovereignty of Varuna, was later on conceived the earthly sovereignty of the king, who was entrusted with the maintenance of law and order in the society on the earth. 'Danda' was to be exercised by the king but he was equally subject to punishment in case of transgression. It was thus believed that Hindu Law was of Divine origin, building the king and the subject alike. Even the judges could not go unpunished on account of wanton and negligent judgement, if any. Since the Hindu Law was based on Dharma, its status was conceived as a bundle, more of duties than of rights. The ancient Hindu kings, therefore, were not only to be responsible for their own deeds but they had to be accountable also for any transgression perpetrated by any other man within their administration.

Reasons and rationality also, therefore, played a very important part in the growth of Hindu Regal philosophy and the provision of Shastras had to be supplemented by and reasoned with reason and principles of justice, equity and good conscience. Both Narada and Brihaspati were one by saying that legal decisions should not be made merely on the basis of the Shastric injunction, when they are devoid of reasoning as such decisions might give rise to injustice rather than justice. Again the philosophical aspect of the early Hindu juristic thought is clearly visible when it is found that almost all their rules are shaped in the form of "should" or "should not". For this, it has been often said that Hindu Law was never actual law in the modern sense of the term but that it was only a moral code giving directions as to what should be done and what should not be done. Thus, from the provision of Smritis regarding the administration of justice in the ancient Hindu society, it was clear that rightly or wrongly, the Smritis were regarded, more or less, like our modern codes. Like the modern advocate today confines himself to the discussion of law as it is, without dilating very seriously about its past condition or future improvement, the kings of the ancient society also treated the provisions of Dharmasutras and Dharmashastras as they were and would try to administer them as such without any comment or deviation. This fact clearly illustrates the analytical way of thinking by the ancient Hindu jurists.

Thus, 'Vyavahar' or adjudication has been a very important source of ancient Hindu Law. The different tribunals, including the king, with original and appellate jurisdiction, used to decide disputes among the litigants. These decisions would have served the purpose of precedents and principles—however, rudementary—for guiding the tribunals in any subsequent dispute of similar or analogous circumstances. According to Dharmashastras and Nitishastras, there were no fewer than six classes of courts in ancient India. Three of them were the royal courts, the highest being with the king and his council; below them was presided over by puisne judges with regional jurisdiction. From the decisions of the puisne judges, appeals lay to the court of chief justice to the king in person. Besides these royal courts, there were three other courts representing the folk element of the ancient Indian judiciary. These were the courts of Pugas, Srenis, and Kulas mentioned according to the order of superiority. Each next higher court was competent to hear appeals from the lower courts. So the heirarchy was Kula's court, Sreni Court, Puga Court, Chief Justice of the State, Chief Justice of the Kingdom and the highest court of justice was the king himself. From this it appears that there was an organised structure of courts and there must have been judgements delivered by various courts, which could have been used as precedents. Although there does not appear to have been a system of reporting but precedents must have been used in deciding future analógous cases. Even at the present time, in deciding a case, the court in reality sees if there is any decided case on the point and if there is a decided case, the judge is bound by the doctrine of *stare decisis and communis error facit jus,* and if there is no decided case, then and then only, he will have to consider as to what law should the case be governed by—Shruti, Smriti, commentry or custom. Hence the actual scope for looking into the shruti, Smriti etc. is limited to those cases only, where there is no decided case on the point and also where there is no custom affecting the point.

Customs. Customs undoubtedly played a very important part as one of the material sources of ancient Hindu Law. It is playing an equally important part even in the present systems of jurisprudence. As a matter of fact, the positive law or *vyavahara* that we find enshrined in the Smritis, is purely secular law—secularly administered by secular courts—though very remotely it might have been of divine or religious origin. Many peculiar usages and customs have been included in the Smritis. Hence there is nothing curious, if in certain parts of the country, certain people observed some rules of conduct which were different from those observed in other parts of the country. The Smritis rightly emphasized the significance of customs as they could realise that suppression of customs would give rise to resentments and rebellions. Customs are hence described as the residual and overriding body of positive law.

Further, only good customs were recognised in Hindu Law. But there was a difference of opinion among the different Smriti-writers and commentators regarding the relative superiorty of landed customs. Thus, Vashistha has said that Manu has declared that customs of localities, families and castes may by followed in absence of the revealed texts. According to Historical School, law is not made, it grows and is to be found in the consciousness of the people. Custom is the true type of law according to this school.

King's Edict. King's edict does not mean any legislative act by the king. It means the law as given rise to by his judicial decisions, as the highest tribunal, with both original and appellate jurisdictions. Therefore, the king always executed and never formulated laws execpt through adjudication.

Dharmasutras

The Dharmasutras are the earliest types of literature in Sanskrit in which some details of the law in the modern sense of the term are available. Many principles in Hindu Law, as conceived by these earliest Sutra-writers, are surviving and being applied even in the modern administration of Hindu Law. It is generally believed that the important Sutra literature was composed between 1000 B.C. and 100 B.C. But as there is no mention of the Arthashastra in the Dharmasutras and as the work of Kautilya was more systematic with exclusive devotion of chapters to civil and criminal laws, it may be presumed that the Dharmasutras were written before Arthashastra, which was undoubtedly written in 300 B.C. It should, however, be clearly understood that the Dharmasutras are not the exclusive codes on civil or positive law. These are treatises written for giving the rules of guidance for the different stages of life and the rights and duties of persons of the different castes in the early Hindu Society. In course of these discussions, something has been spoken of law in the modern juristic sense of the term as much as they were necessary for the regulation of the society as a whole with the king at the head of the administration and the Brahmins at the head of the religious and social regulations.

Arthashastra

Arthashastra of Kautilya throws a flood of light on the material and social and political condition of the ancient Hindus during the third and fourth centuries B.C. Hitherto we had to unfortunately depend mainly upon the meagre account left by greek-writers, whose interest in India was first aroused by the invasion of Alexander. The work of Kautilya, however, removes to a great extent our want in the direction by opening up a mine of information which is as full as it is reliable. Arthashastra narrates the full aspects of governance namely the maintenance of live stock (cows, horses, elephants, etc.) for the Raja; the maintenance of weaponry, soldiers and other army officers; the civil administration; spies system; trade; agriculture; taxation; laws of war and peace; the living style of the king and his palace and people; means of communications, conveyance; roads; river travel; sea travel; medical aid; sanitation; tracing of offenders and punishment to be inflicted on them. For prevention of diseases, adulteration of all kinds was punished e.g. adulteration of grains, oils, alkalies, salts, scents, and medicines. The health of people in cities and crowded places was secured by sanitary measures. Throwing dirt or causing mud or water to collect on roads and highways was punishable. Committing nuisance near temples, royal buildings and places of pilgrimage or in reservoirs of water was penalised. Throwing inside the city the carcases of animals, or human corpses was also punishable with fines. Carrying dead bodies through gates or along paths, not meant for the purpose, as well as the interring or cremation of dead bodies beyond the limits of the prescribed burial places and crematories was also a violation of the sanitary regulation. It is noteworthy that even in those days, there was arrangement for postmortem examination. All cases of violent deaths caused, for instance by suffocation, hanging, drowning, etc., or by poisoning were at once brought to the morgue and the medical officers incharge had to find out, as far as possible, the exact causes of death from an examination of the symptoms, several of which are enumerated in Arthashastra. The whole affair was subjected to a careful scrutiny and if foul play was suspected, evidence was taken and then left to be disposed off by the law courts.

In the city, every householder had to provide himself with the ten remedial instruments to prevent fire. During the summer, the kindling of fire was prohibited during the second and third quarters of the day. All men were enjoined, under the penalty of fines, to run to give help, in case fire broke out in any house. Thousands of vessels filled with water had to be kept in rows, not only in the big roads, but also at the crossings of roads and in front of royal buildings. The masters of the household had to sleep at night at a place near the main gate of their premises, so that they might be easily accessible and come out of their houses to give help without delay. Thatched roofs, made of straws and other materials that readily catch fire, were not allowed within the city. Those, who worked with fire like blacksmiths, etc., had to live in a particular quarter of the city. Persons, wilfully setting fire to a house were severely dealt with. To celebrate the anniversaries of king's birthdays and in commemoration of the birth of a prince, the installation of the heir apparent, or the conquest of a new country, prisoners were set at-large. Generally, on full moondays, such prisoners, as were very young, old or diseased, were let out. Sometimes, the prisoners were set free in consideration of their uniformly good conduct in the jail. Strict rules were made for sale of liquor and heavy fines were imposed on those who violated the rules. A Brahmin, who took to drinking was very severely punished. It is interesting to know that there was some form of census current in India over two thousand years ago. A distinguished feature of census at that time appears to be that it was not periodical but a permanent institution—a department of the state run by permanent officials. The head of the Department was called, Collector General (समाहर्ता), who combined in himself, besides those connected with the census, various other functions such as collection of revenue, checking accounts, land survey and the like. He had districts under him and each district was divided into a number of villages. Each district was placed under an officer and under him were appointed a number of subordinate village officers, whose work was supervised by their superior, the district officer. The functions of the village officers were as under :

1. To number the inhabitants of all the four castes in each village.
2. To count the cultivators, cowherds, merchants, artisans, slaves, the young and the old men and women of each house, and ascertain their character, occupation, income and expenditure; to number the animals in each house (the tax-paying and non-tax-paying houses) and determine the amount of gold, free labour, tolls and fines collected from each house. This work was under surveillance of the spies too and each wrong-reporting was severely dealt with.

Courts of Justice. It goes without saying that the welfare of the public is determined to a considerable extent by the nature of the law of the land and the efficient administration of justice. Laws are unseen agencies as important for popular well-being as the visible agents of the government. The object of this will be to consider in detail, some of the laws of the government, the way they were administered and the contribution they made to the material welfare of the country. There were two classes of law courts—Dharmasthiya and Kantaka-shodhan—each differently constituted. There was also a difference in respect of the nature of the cases that came under their cognizance. Each court was made up of three persons well-grounded in the Shastras or three ministers (अमात्या), who sat together for hearing the cases. As to the jurisdiction of the courts, a court generally decided such cases as arose from the personal grievances of one or a few individuals against another or a few other individuals and the punishments were only in fines; these fines not being very heavy. The cases that came within the jurisdiction of a court generally related either to matters that affected the Government, the king himself, the public at large and large bodies of men, or to such other heinous offences as murder. Though small fines were inflicted by this court for offences that were not so grave, yet the fines for the graver offences ranged upto a very high limit. This distinguishes it from a Dharamasthiya court. Another distinction consisted in the fact that it lay in the power of a Kantakashodhan court to inflict capital punishment, with or without torture, according of the gravity of the offences. Below are given two lists of the kinds of cases that come under the cognizance of the two classes of courts :

I. The Dharamasthiya Courts Tried Cases Bearing on the Following Questions

1. Validity of contracts
2. Violation of service contracts
3. Relation between master and servant
4. Slavery
5. Recovery of debts
6. Deposits
7. Rescission of sale
8. Resumption of gifts
9. Robbery and violence
10. Assault
11. Defamation
12. Gambling
13. Sale of property by other than owner
14. Rights of ownership
15. Boundary of buildings
16. Construction of buildings
17. Sale of house property
18. Damage to agriculture, pasture and public roads
19. Miscellaneous hindrances
20. Duties of man and wife
21. Partnerships
22. Inheritance and succession
23. Miscellaneous offences
24. Rules of Procedure.

II. The Kantakashodhan Courts Tried Cases Relating to the Following

1. Protection of artisans
2. Protection of merchants
3. Measures against national calamities
4. Suppression of wicked
5. Detection of criminals by ascetic spies
6. Arresting robbers on suspicion or in the act
7. Cross-examination
8. Port-mortem examination
9. Discipline in Government servants
10. Fines in lieu of mutilation of limbs
11. Capital punishment with or without torture
12. Improper Social intercourse
13. Punishments for miscellaneous offences.

It should be noted that over and above these courts, the headman and the elders of a village played an important part in the settlement of disputes among the villagers, and the former was vested with the power of summarily punishing certain offenders. It appears that he could 'deport' out of the village under his charge a thief or an adulterator if such a step became neccessary.

The king with his ministers and learned Brahmins formed the highest court of appeal. The courts held their sittings in every town forming the headquarter of villages and in every town that was the headquarter of 400 villages of 800 villages and in every place centrally situated between any two provinces of the empire. It will thus be seen that the metropolis must have had courts of the above two classes besides the royal law courts.

Legal Procedure. The four basic factors that were taken into account in the administration of justice were, (1) Sacred laws or laws contained in the Dharma-shastras, (2) Contractual relation created by the parties, (3) Customary law and (4) Statutory or king-made laws.

In case of conflict between, (1) and (2) or between (3) and (4) the former prevailed over the latter so that a contract could not transcend sacred law or a statute custom. In case of conflict between custom and contract, the injunctions of sacred law should be followed. It is also stated that in the event of conflict between statute and equity, the statute became imperative. When a case came up for decision, the preliminary step taken was the registration of the following, particulars regarding the suit :

1. The exact date (showing the year, season, month, fortnight, and day).
2. The nature of the offence.
3. The place of its occurrence.
4. The amount of debt incurred, if any.
5. The country, village, caste, gotra, name and occupation of the plaintiff and the defendant, both of whom must be competent to sue.
6. The statements of the parties which had to be thoroughly scrutinised by the court.

Each party had to be on guard against any kind of offence termed "Paroktadosha" namely deviating from the question at issue; contradicting previous statement; insisting on the need of counselling the opinion of a third person though his opinion be not worthy of such consideration; breaking off while answering a question though ordered by the court to continue introducing questions other than those already specified; with drawing the statement already made, not accepting what ones' own witnesses have said, holding secret conversation with the witnesses where it was not allowed. The plaintiff had to make his rejoinder the very day the defendant had answered for it was presumed that the plaintiff was ready to go on with the case otherwise he was guilty of Prokta. But if the defendant was not ready for the case, he was allowed three or seven nights to prepare his defence. If he failed to make his defence within that time, he was punished with a fine ranging from three to twelve *panas* and the claim made by the plaintiff set off from his property. If the plaintiff failed to prove his case, he committed the 'Prokta' and was punishable accordingly.

In cases other than strife, violent and direct seizure of property and disputes among merchants, the defendant could not file a counter case against the plaintiff. Also two suits against a defendant for the same offence were not allowed. Regarding the witness, it may be noted that agents were attached to the law courts for secretly ascertaining, if possible, the real facts of a law suit, and for reporting them to the judges. How far the information they furnished would be followed in a particular case depended upon the discretion of the judges. They had to use their discretion with great caution specially in cases like that instanced when the depositions of witnesses were inconsistent and contradictory and consequently in conflict with the statement of the plaintiff and where there was a divergence of the report of the informants from both the statement of the plaintiff and the evidence. The principle check on the discretions of the judges was the punishment they incurred for their laches and iniquity. The report of the informants had to be utilised, therefore, with great care and with its chances of abuse minimised. It was meant to help the judges some times by creating suspicions in their minds which prompted them to sift the evidence more cautiously and sometimes by corraborating the conclusion pointed to by the statements of the witnesses. Further, a suit was not dismissed on the ground that there were no witnesses forthcoming to testify the question at issue. For instance, in disputes regarding the non-payment of wages of a labourer, he could sue his employer even if he could procure no evidence to support his suit. Such a procedure could appear strange, unless we bear in mind that over and above cross-examination of the parties and overt inquiry that could be availed of in such a case, there was another recourse to fall back upon viz. the secret agency for collecting information. Several such instances shall come to notice, when analysed.

In a law suit, three witnesses, either approved by both the parties, trust-worthy or pure, served the purpose best. In a suit for debt, however, two witnesses approved by the parties might be sufficient but never one. The fact of relationship with the plaintiff or the defendant affected the competence of a person as witness. The following persons were not eligible as witnesses :

1. Wife's brother
2. Helpmate
3. Prisoner
4. Creditor
5. Debtor
6. Enemy
7. Dependent
8. Convict
9. The king
10. A person learned in Vedas
11. A village poor
12. Leper
13. An outcast / chandal
14. A person of mean avocation

15. A dogmatist
16. A female
17. A Government servant.

In cases of assault, etc., theft and rape, persons other than the enemy, the wife's brother and the help-mate could bear witness. Any man or woman having secret knowledge of an underhand transaction could be a witness in regard there to.

In case of a dispute between father and son, preceptor and pupil, or master and servant, the words of the superiors were given greater credence. Witnesses had to take oath to divulge the truth before Brahmins, vessels of water and fire. There were set formulas, varying according to the castes of the witnesses by which they were urged to speak the truth. If the witnesses made a concert among themselves and kept back the truth for more than a week, they were fined twelve *panas*. If they continued this for more than three fortnights, they were punished with the payment of the amount used for. When the witnesses gave divergent evidence, the judgement was passed upon the basis of the statements of the majority of pure and approved men among them. Or the judgement could follow a via media if any such were suggested by the diverse statements of the witnesses. Failing these, the Government assumed possession of the article, if that formed the subject matter of the dispute. If an amount were sued for and the witnesses deposed that only a part of the amount belonged to the plaintiff then rest of the amount had to be deposited with the Government. If, however, the witnesses testified to an amount greater in value than what was actually sued for, the excess went to the Government coffer. Those witnesses, who were easily accessible, were called by the parties themselves; those, who were far away or who could not come to court, except under compulsion, were served with summons and the defendant partly had to bear the fees paid to the witnesses. They received a food allowance in which were taken into eight items of food. Besides this allowance, they were given the necessary expenses for and during their journey.

A peculiarity of Hindu Law courts in ancient times was that the judges had to pay a penalty for their iniquity. They were strictly enjoined to decide cases free from all circumvention, steady in all circumstances, impartially and diligently, thus winning the love and confidence of the people but if they were guilty of any laxity, partiality or any such misconduct unworthy of a judge, they could not escape with impunity. If a judge threatened or rebuked or silenced or drove out a party to a suit, he was liable to the lowest amercement and for abusing a party, to a fine of double the amount. If he put irrelevant questions to a party; wilfully omitted to ask a pertinent question; did not note down what he heard in reply to his queries; tutored or provided a party with his previous statements, he was fined the middlemost amercement. If he enquired into unneccessary circumstances; caused delay by such inquiry; postponed work on flimsy pretexts; tired the parties out of court by his dilatorinesses; misled them; helped the witnesses with clues; or resumed the work already disposed of, he was punished with the highest amercement. If he committed any of the offences, a second time, he was fined double the amount and dismissed. For an unjust fine, a Dharmastha was fined double the amount or eight times the excess of the amount over the prescribed limit, according to the nature of the offence. If a corporal punishment was unjustly inflicted, he was condemned either to the same punishment or to the payment twice the amount fixed in lieu of that kind of punishment. The judicial officer, who brought to naught a good case or helped to correct a false case, he was fined eight times its value. The scribe, who took down the statements of the parties, was liable to a punishment for negligence or misconduct if he wilfully omitted to note what was said, or noted down what was not said or left out what was said, or rendered ambiguous or diverse what was well said. He was liable to the first amercement or to any other punishment proportionate to his guilt.

Care was taken to prevent the escape of a culprit from the law court, the *hajat*, or the prison as well as to prevent the abuse of the jailor's authority. The king or his associated judges tried the judges for their misconduct. Certain latitude seems to have been given to the superintendents of the state's departments to summarily dispose of certain kinds of offences committed by their subordinates.

Law of Contract. A contract was a two-sided act, and the parties thereto could be both individuals, as well as groups e.g. a body of persons engaged in a common concern was entitled to be a party to a contract. Secondly, a contract had to conform to some restrictions as :

(a) that the agreemment between the parties should be clearly expressed ;

(b) that it should not be made in secret and ;

(c) that it should be in the presence of witnesses.

Thirdly, it should comply with certain conditions as to time, place, and caste, class, etc. Fourthly, the object for which the contract was made and of the circumstances attending to it must be such as not to offend against law in any way, e.g., there must be none under influence, etc. Fifthly, the consideration must not be illegal and improper and the parties, witnesses and agents must be competent. In short, the contract must conform to all the technicalities of law, i.e., it must be comprehensive, As a rule the following contracts were considred void :

1. Those formed during night.
2. Entered into in the interior apartment of a house.
3. Made in a forest.
4. Formed in any other secret place.
5. The contract should be legally feasible, e.g., if a person, who is being carried away by flood or is caught in a fire, or is in danger from wild animal, be rescued on his promise to give to his rescuer not only the whole of his property but also his sons, wife and himself as slaves, the proposer cannot be made to perform his promise, it being opposed to all justice and common sense and therefore, illegal.

Sale and pre-emption. The first provision in regard to the sale of immoveable property is that the piece of property on sale has to be offered for purchase in the first instance to the kinsmen of the seller. If they donot propose to buy, then the property has to be offered to the neighbours, who can claim such right on the ground of vicinage or participation in the appendage and on their refusal to purchase, the property is to be offered to the creditors of the seller. These rules evidently indicate that something like the 'right of pre-emption' existed in those days. The texts concerning pre-emption are very few in Sanskrit legal literature and even those that exist have been explained away by the later commentators. Some texts also occur in the Mitakshara. This would indicate that the law of Pre-emption, as is generally held, has not come down from Mohammedans only but it existed in our ancient times as well. The fact of the property being on sale has to be announced publicly in the presence of a large number of men, who came from not less than forty neighbouring houses, and who have no personal interest in the sale. An immoveable property includes cultivated land, gardens, enclosed spaces, lakes, and reservoirs. Each of these kinds of property, before being put on sale, has its boundaries accurately defined in the presence of the neighbouring village elders and elderly villagers. Then the crier shouts thrice the following words : "Who will buy at this price?" Thus, announces the price of the property fixed by the seller. The purchaser, who accepts the price then enters upon the purchase if the sale be un-conditional and not objected to by any claimants. A tax is levied upon all such sales and in the event of any increase in price owing to superior natural advantage, the unearned increment goes to the state. The crier is responsible for the collection and the payment of the tax on the sale. Any wrong sale is subject to fines.

Also a tax payer can sell his fields to the tax payers only and a Brahmin can sell his gifted or otherwise owned fields to Brahmins only, who are endowed with such lands and any violation of this rule is punishable with the first amercement.

Sale of Moveable Properties. In the sale of moveables, no elaborate formalites are needed. In such cases the property is passed by the payment of price and delivery of possession. A refusal to perform a contract of sale or a refusal to sell an article put for sale by a dealer was punished with a fine of 12 *panas* unless the purchaser could prove that the article put for sale had defects, that it had been lost, stolen or confiscated by the state or destroyed in flood. The time allowed for rescission of sale is one night for traders, three for cultivators and five for cowherds. Sale of a stolen thing or a thing without proper possession leads to the arrest of the owner by the order of the judge. The stolen or lost articles on being detected by person, other than the owner, are to be deposited at the place for the collection of tolls and if no claimant be forthcoming, such an article is taken by the state.

Loans. The rules regulating loans are firstly recognised to be of great importance. On them depend to a large extent the economic welfare of the country. In those old days, the exploitation by the greedy money-lenders of the necessities of the poor and the needy was checked by a fair rate of interest, which was fixed by the state and which punished all deviations from it. The legal rate of interest for a money-lender, as in Arthashastra, is 1.25 per cent per month, i.e., 15 per cent per year. This rate of interest was charged on secured debts, the maximum rate allowed on unsecured ones being prescribed upto 5 per cent per month. Such a rate is in lieu of the risk to which the investment of the money lent and consequently its realisation. A person claiming interest, when it is not due, or claiming as principal the sum-total of the real principal and interest, shall pay a fine of four times the amount under dispute. False claims were also punishable with four times fines. Some persons were exempted from payment of interest namely :

1. Persons engaged in long-continued sacrifice.
2. The diseased.
3. Those detained in the house of the preceptor for studies.
4. Minors and the indigent.

The repayment of debts is also subject to following rules. The creditor is fined 12 *panas* if he refuses to accept in proper time the sum due, unless the refusal be founded upon some adequate grounds. Moreover, in case of refusal, the sum tendered may be deposited by the debtor with some third person, and no interest accrues upon it for the time subsequent to the date of deposit. The creditor is liable to a penalty for want of diligence on his part to realise his money within ten years next following the due date and after the period the loan is barred by limitation.

The sons of a deceased debtor shall repay the principal with interest thereon. If the deceased have no sons, the debt shall be paid by those who inherit. The property or the debt shall be paid by the surviving joint debtors if it were contracted jointly with them. When their are sureties for payment, they shall be held liable. No suit for debt can be between husband and wife, father and son, and brothers of undivided interests. The wife is not, as a rule, liable for the debt of her husband even if it be acknowledged by her, except in the case of debt due to herdsmen and cultivators. But a husband is liable for the debt of his wife and if he absconds without making provision for the debt, he shall be fined with the highest amercement.

Deposits. There were two kinds of deposits :

1. Sealed
2. Open

A sealed deposit is an article enclosed in a box under seal which the owner delivers into the hands of the depository without saying anything as to its nature and the open deposit is not put under any cover, and the nature, quality, form, etc., of the article deposited are known to the depository at the time of making deposit. The acceptance of the deposit is gratuitous, but the depository is responsible for its safe-custody and if he puts it to his own use, he has to pay a compensation fixed according to the circumstances of the case, in addition to a fine of 12 *panas*. Also the deposit must always be returned to the actual depositor, otherwise the depository is answerable.

Pledge. Kautilya does not expressly mention the rules to be followed when the article pledged is used, sold, pledged, lost or misappropriated, but leaves them to be inferred from the allied rules laid down in connection with the deposit. The pledged article is to be returned within the time-limit fixed with the interest that accrued for the period. A pledgee, who refuses to return the pledge, when duly demanded backed by the pledger, is fined 12 *panas*.

Mortagage. A piece of mortgaged immoveable property may be of two kinds viz :

1. Yielding income without any labour.
2. Yielding income after labour being spent on it.

When the money lent, as well as its interest, has been realised from the income of the mortagaged property, it shall be returned to the mortgager with its value undiminished. If the mortgagee enjoys the mortgaged property without the sanction of the mortgager, then it shall be returned with compensation for such enjoyment after the capital lent is realised.

Adesa (Bill of Exchange). Two other forms of contract next engage our attention viz. Adesa (आदेश) and Anvadhi (अन्वाधि). An *'adesh'* is literally an order, and it seems to mean an order to a third person to pay up a sum of money on behalf of the sender of the order. It is akin to the modern bill of exchange in its simplest form. Anvadhi is a 'bailment' for delivery. If a person, entrusted by a merchant with an article for delivery to a third person, does not reach the destined place, is robbed on the way by thieves, breaks the article or abandons it, the merchant shall not be responsible nor the kinsmen of the carrier if he dies on the way. The rules of open deposit apply to these two forms of contract as far as possible.

Contract of Service. People near at hand should be called to witness the nature of the contract between a master and a servant. The contract should indicate the person engaged, his caste, qualification, rate of wages, period of engagement, etc. If no wages have been fixed then it will be in proportion to the time spent and the quantity and quality of work done. A cultivator shall generally obtain one tenth of the crops growns. A factory worker shall get one-tenth of the business transacted. A servant neglecting or not doing work for which he has been paid, is fined 12 *panas*. If an employer does not accept the services of a workman, who, according to contract, presents himself for it, the latter will be deemed to have done his full duty and is entitled to his wages.

Partnership. Traders or cultivators, who engage in work after joining partnership, shall apportion among themselves, the profits after the performance of the work in hand and before entering on a fresh one. The traders shall have shares of profit of the partnership business after the commodities in stock are sold out. The losses sustained by goods during transmission are to be borne by the partners equally. A partner deserting his work is fined 12 *panas* as he cannot withdraw from the business at will after it has been commenced. The shares of profit of the partners may be equal or otherwise according to the contract among themselves.

The priests officiating at a sacrifice shall share the earnings equally or as agreed to, over and above what may be specially due, to each for his portion of work.

Contracts of common interest. If preparations are made for a public entertainment, an individual may help it up at will, either by subscription or otherwise, but in case he does not join it, then he and his dependents lose the right of enjoying it. Seeing or hearing stealthily at the place of entertainment is punishable with fines.

Arthashastra is mainly secular and is as such virtually divorced from all sorts of religious or sacerdotal elements. In other Shastras, there are two chapters on law—one is known as the chapter on Dharmasthiya and the other is known as the chapter on Kantak-Shodhanam. The former deals with civil law and the latter deals with criminal law. Books III and IV of *Arthashastra* deal with administration of law—description of location and the constitution of courts, formation of contracts or agreements by different parties, the grounds of invalidity, punishment for fraud and the principle of agency in contracts, trials, the different parties with details sufficient for the identification, plaint, the written statements, the office, witnesses, prohibition of counter-suits, adjournments and the different means or sources of administration of justice even with the help of spies. Chapters II to IV (Book III) deal with marriage, its different kinds, Stridhana, compensation on husband remarrying for the second time, duty of wife, her maintenance, cruelty to her, favours shown to others, her vagrancies and development of husband's sojournments of different durations. Kautilya says that marriage is at the root of all disputes, perhaps he refers to personal law of property, etc., are due to the institution of marriage. He also refers to eight kinds of marriages. Widows were allowed to remarry. No marriage tie could be dissolved without mutual consent, though mutual enmity also could dissolve it.

Chapters V, VI and VII (Book III) deal with partition, its line, special shares, different shares and discrimination between the different kinds of sons regarding their status and right in inheritance. Partition was based on local customs. Self-acquired property or gains of learning were not liable to be partitioned. Partition was to take place, when all heirs had attained majority. Partition was to take place after death of parents. If father was alive at the time of distribution of property, he was not to make any discrimination between the different sons nor shall any son be disinherited without sufficient reason. King was the ultimate heir in case of failure of other heirs.

Chapter XI (Book III) deals with recovery of debts and the character of witnesses to prove those debts. All transactions between debtors and creditors were subject to severe scrutiny by the state as the very welfare of the realm depended on those transactions, greatly responsible for the prosperity of the country on account of encouragement of trade and commerce. The usual rate of interest was a *'pana'* and a quarter per cent per month, i.e. 15 per cent per annum. No interest could accrue to debts due by students, minors, too poor persons or persons engaged in performing sacrifices for a long time. A transaction of debt had to be proved by three or atleast two witnesses.

Kautilya makes a general provision that never shall an Arya be subjected to slavery. A man who is not a born slave and who has not attained majority when sold or mortgaged by his kinsmen will make them liable to the punishment with fine varrying from 12 to 48 *panas* according to his caste. Slaves could also be emancipated on paying ransom or otherwise.

Recision of Contracts and Resumption of Gifts. Kautilya has enumerated the conditions under which contracts for purchase and sale and marriage contracts could be rescinded and the different rights and duties of the different parties concerned. Marriage contracts could be rescinded whenever there was any *suppressio veri* regarding any material factor. All cases of resumption of gifts were to be adjudged by an assembly convened for this purpose. Thus, gifts of everything, including ones own life, wife, children, gifts or charitable subscirptions to the wicked or for unworthy purposes, gifts of momentory helps to the cruel or for malevolent persons could naturally give rise to suspicion and as such were liable to be resumed. Any property robbed or stolen, which could not be recovered by the king or his officers had to be made good from the king's treasury.

Crime. Last four chapters of Book III deal with crime such as robbery, defamation, assault and gambling and betting along with other miscellaneous offences—which are clearly topics of substantive criminal law. Kautilya conceives a truly criminal element in robbery when he says that the fine or punishment shall be proportional to the gravity of the offence rather than to the value of the articles involved. He also describes various kinds of fines, first amercement, middle-most amercement and the highest amercement. For abetment of robbery, an abetor has to be fined twice or four times according to his connection i.e. whether he causes another man to commit the robbery or employs a hireling for that purpose. Within defamation, Kautilya includes calumny, contemptuous talk and intimidation. Defamation of one's own nation or village was to be punished with the first amercement; that of one's caste or guild with middlemost; and that of gods and temples with the highest amercement. Fines were to be imposed according to caste and rank of the person defamed. The crime of assault is committed by touching, striking and hurting. Here again the fine was to be imposed according to caste and rank of the person assaulted. Hurts were distinguished as those causing bloodshed, and those causing no bloodshed. Beating a man to death without causing bloodshed, breaking the hand, leg, etc., was to be punished with first amercement. No offence could be affected by limitation or passage of time.

Kantak Shodhanam. In Book IV of *Arthashastra*, Kautilya deals with Kantak Shodhanam, which is wrongly supposed to deal with criminal law exclusively. The word 'Kantak' means artisans. There is hardly any discussion of substantive criminal law proper in Book IV. Whatever little criminal law has been dealt with herein is merely concerned with Police functions or preventive measures along with some means employed for detecting crime and some methods of punishment and almost all the usual topics of substantive criminal law as have already been discussed in the last four chapters of Book III. Chapters I and II deal with selling, mortgaging or letting out for hire the clothes of others. Washerman shall be fined 12 *panas* and physicians shall be guilty of negligence when the patient dies or disease aggravates. To prevent merchants from practising deception in weights and measures, they shall be punished. In chapter III, there is discussion about different kinds of national calamities and the persons carried away by floods, persons neglecting rescue shall be fined 12 *panas*. Chapters IV to VI deal with suppression of the wicked living by foul means; detection of youth of criminal tendency by ascetic spies; and arrest of criminals on suspicion or on the very act of committing crime. Chapter VII deals with examination of sudden or unnatural deaths. Chapter VIII deals with the different methods of trial and torture for eliciting confession. Persons charging innocent men with theft or any other crime shall be punished as having committed the same offence. Women were to be subjected to half or no torture at all. Chapter IX deals with the penal measures, which could protect people from being oppressed at the hands of public servants under the colour of their authority and office appertaining to the different departments of the administration. As a matter of fact, very stringent rules had been provided, for the punishment of Government servants, who on account of their very office, were subjected to additional liability to be more careful and considerate in dealing with the people at large; reason for this being high standard of honesty and integrity on the part of the Government servants. Chapter X provides for alternative fines in lieu of mutilation of limbs.

Any person selling human flesh was to be condemned to death. Chanakya makes a very comprehensive provision for inflicting different kinds of punishments taking into consideration all the relevant facts and circumstances of the case including the social status, the antecedents of the family, the occassion and the time and place of the offence. Chapter XI deals with certain offences which must be punished with death with or without torture. Different methods of inflicting capital punishments were by hanging, by burning, by drowning, by shooting and by tearing with the help of bulls. Mutilation of limbs could also be imposed depending on the gravity of offence. Chapter XII provides that no man shall have sexual intercourse with a woman against her will. The women yielding themselves for the offence are also to be punished and lastly that all abettors in such offences are to be punished equally with the principal offender.

Special Responsibility of the King and the Rule of Law. It has already been seen that if a theft could not be detected or the stolen properly could not be recovered, the king was to compensate the aggrieved person out of his treasury. Sometimes the villagers and sometimes the officers concerned were to make good the loss. This was the rule not only enjoined by Kautilya but also more or less by other writers of Dharmasutras and Dharmshastras. Narada has also stated that wherever the foot prints of the thief go, the inhabitants or the owners of that place must make good the loss unless they can satisfy that the footmarks got out of that place again.

Kautilya also made elaborate provision regarding the conduct and character of judges so that they might readily inspire the confidence of the litigants. Thus, if a judge browbeats or unjustly drives out or silences any of the litigants in his court, he shall first be punished with the first amercement. If he defames or abuses any one of them, the punishment shall be double.

As regards the recognition and application of the rule of law, it was quite clear that nobody was held above the law. The king himself, not to speak of the other members of his family, was equally subject to the law of the realm, along with the ordinary subjects. The courts in ancient India were held in great esteem and judges were highly paid king's officers. According to Kautilya, the salary of the chief justice was forty eight thousand *panas* per annum. The chief justice was assisted by puisne judges who were not so highly paid. The trials were held openly, where all members of the public could have access. It was specifically enjoined that no trial should be held privately.

4

PROVISIONS OF LAW IN SMRITIS AND MITAKSHARA

The Provisions of Manusmriti

Manu devotes the eighth chapter of his Smriti mainly to the treatment of law, consisting of 18 topics. For the purpose of deciding, the king should enter the court house with learned Brahmins and experienced councillors preserving a very dignified demeanour. The 18 titles of law should be divided according to usage and the institute of sacred law. The cases were decided on the basis of evidence—witnesses or documents. On a conflict of witnesses, the king or the judges shall accept as true, the evidence of the majority, if the conflicting witnesses were equal in number to that of those distinguished by good qualities and on a difference between the equally distinguished and meritorious witnesses, that of the best among the twice born. Evidence shall always be direct.

Civil Law. In civil law, the topics discussed by Manu are pledge, deposit, adverse possession, Damdupat and exceptions to the application of the principle of adverse possession. A chatel is lost by ten years of possession. A man, who becomes surety for a debtor must pay from his own pocket but his heirs are not liable to pay any immoral debt, etc.

Criminal Law. The entire law of defamation was mainly heard on the variation of caste. Obviously the heaviest punishment was reserved for the Shudras, specially when they defamed the Brahmins. A Shudra insulting a twice-born class with contempt, shall have his tongue cut off. Like defamations in case of assault too the law was based on caste. Manu also provides for criminal punishment in the shape of fines for those who hurt trees, plants, animals and even inanimate goods. In cases where hurt is caused to men and animals through the negligent driving of carriage, the driver and the owner are to be fined. As per Manu, one of the most fundamental duties of the king is to protect the subjects against theft and other crimes. It is the duty of the king in reciprocating the receipt of taxes to carefully restrain the criminals by imprisonment, by putting them in fetters and by corporal punishment, the nature of punishment being determined according to the nature of the crime committed. Adultery was regarded as one of the most heinous offences for which exemplary and deterrent punishments were provided for, so that these might create awe and fear in the minds of the people at large. A Shudra, guilty of adultery with a woman of twice-born, was to be given capital punishment.

Gains of Learning, Gambling and Betting. Manu also recognises the principle of "gains of learning" according to which, what one brother may acquire by his labour, without using the paternal property, shall not be liable to be shared by other brothers, unless the earner himself agrees to do so.

The Provisions of Yajnavalkya

On account of the paramount importance of the Mitakasara in modern Hindu law, as administered by the British Courts in the whole of India, the Smriti of Yajnavalkya has indirectly become the guiding work for the whole of India. It richly deserves this position by its concise but clear statement of princples, its breadth of vision and its comparative impartiality of the claims of both sexes and the different Varnas. His work being a purely scientific book, the scientific attitude and freedom from prejudice made the work acceptable throughout India. According to Yajnavalkya, the king is primarily responsible for the administration of justice with the help of learned and virtuous assessors. In case of unavoidable preoccupation, a learned Brahmin should replace the king. Any judge or assessor doing any deliberate injustice should be punished by the king to the extent of double the amount in dispute. The allegation of the plaintiff shall be recorded and treated a plaint which will be followed by written statements, which also should be recorded similarly. Then will follow the proof and the last stage shall be judgement. These precisely are the stages even today. The different means of proof are document, possession and witnesses. Ordeals are to be resorted to in their absence only. The king was required to replenish the property stolen or robbed but not recovered. Yajnavalkya refers to rates of interest chargeable on debt, which was different for different castes; Brahmins paying the minimum and the Shudra the maximum.

Means of Proof. Witnesses, Documents and Ordeals. There should be three witnesses but one witness may also suffice if he be extraordinarily virtuous and reliable and if he is approved by both the parties. The qualifications and disqualifications of witness/ witnesses have been enumerated in detail. False evidence is a heinous crime. It is equally sinful not to give evidence on a fact known to a man. Documentary evidence is taken at the top of the proof but if it is forged then the procedure is sentence of twice the complaint or the plaint. Possession is full proof of ownership unless a proof to the contrary is produced by the other party.

Partition and Inheritance. The father may divide the property among his sons equally or unequally giving at his discretion the best thing to the eldest son. But if the division takes place after the death of the father, then sons divide it equally amongst themselves. Gains of learning are not subject of partition among the brothers. The conception of joint tenancy of the Mitakshara school is based on the provision of Yajnavalkya.

Boundary Disputes. A boundary dispute should be decided by internal as well as external marks and witnesses, specially consisting of elderly nighbours. Yajnavalkya also refers to the construction of embankments and wells around and in one's fields for the benefit of many.

Sale, Gift, Services, Contract and Non-payment of Wages. When a man claims a thing as purchased, he shall be apprehended and detained until he can produce the person from whom he purchased and the actual owner demands that this property was lost or stolen. When the seller is found out, the real owner shall get the thing. No gift of property should be made without already having made adequate provision for the members of the family. A slave should be released by paying ransom or if he has saved the life of his master. The labourers should be paid their wages fully on the completion of their work and on the basis of *quantum meriut* "when it is done partially and reasonable remuneration be paid by every employer if not already stipulated.

Partnerships, Gambling and Betting. Partnership associations could be formed by traders, sacrificers, agriculturists and artisans. The members could adjust their profits and losses according to capital and agreement. A member shall compensate others in case of his negligence and shall be entitled to special compensation for his specially meritorious service. Gambling and betting were recommended to be organised under the state control by a superintendent, who was also to be appointed from among the gamblers.

Crime. Abuse, assault, *sahasa*, theft and adultery were the different types of crimes, as enumerated by Yajnavalkya. Abuse or defamation was to be adjudicated chiefly with reference to the question of castes of the different parties. For assault also, the fine is to be imposed differently for people of different castes. Punishment has also been prescribed even for assault to animals and trees. A *sahasa* or a heinous offence is committed when a common or another's property is taken away by force. For *sahasa,* the fine shall be double the value of the thing taken away by force and four times when the offence is denied. Yajnavalkya enumerates several other offences such as cheating, criminal misappropriation, criminal breach of trust and their punishments. The most important group of offences comprises those in connection with trade and commerce. The King is required to fix the price of commodities and any breach of the same was severely punishable. In cases where theft cannot be detected or the stolen property cannot be traced, the king's officers and villagers concerned are to be blamed and they are to compensate for the unrecovered stolen property as it is the duty of the king to protect the life and property of his subjects. In case of murders, investigations should be conducted according to the suspects' inclination and antecedents. Burning was the punishment for those who would burn a thrashing floor or a house. For adultery, punishment is very severe. A non Aryan committing the adultery with an Aryan was to be put to death like a man defiling a maiden of the higher class.

The Later Smritis

Provision of Narada Smriti : Narada refers to the original code of Manu, which underewent at least three abridgements at the hands of Narada himself. He also refers to the different topics dealt with by Manu and himself. He discusses general principles of legal procedure which was neccessitated on account of the transgressions of mankind and its deviation from duty. The king was appointed to decide disputes with the help of oral and documentary evidence.

Court of Justice. While inside the courts of justice, no one shall speak without being duly authorised for the purpose, an authorised person can speak only when he can point out the true provision of law which is not otherwise clear to or going to be administered by the judge and the assessors. A man delivering a strange opinion in the court of justice, is like a man who eats fish alongwith the bones. Justice is deemed to be done when all members of the judicial assembly are absolutely convinced that the truth has been fully ascertained and justice has been clearly administered.

Topics of Law. Narada deals one by one with the 18 different topics of law mainly based on Kautilya and Manu and accepted by Yajnavalkya like law of debt, property, adverse possession, witnesses and evidence including ordeals. Possession, according to Narada, is the most important mode of proof. In spite of documentary title, a property can be lost by adverse possession. He deals with gifts, pledges, or purchase, surety, rate of interest, etc.

Evidence. Nårada refers for the first time to circumstantial evidence where no witnesses are necessary. He has enunciated certain circumstances which speak for themselves but in most of the cases the criterion insisted upon by the modern courts of justice for establishing guilt beyond reasonable doubt is not satisfied.

Deposits. Narada's second title of law deals with deposits which must invariably be made with persons of respectable families and those who are virtuous, dutiful, veracious, wealthy and honourable as these transactions are absolutely based on confidence. The return or re-delivery must take place in the very manner of deposit.

Gifts. Narada has enumerated seven different kinds of valid gifts and the sixteen different kinds of invalid gifts. The most important condition of a valid gift is that what is left after the expenses of maintaining the family have been defrayed may be given, giving away anything more than this is to be morally censured.

Sales Without Ownership. It is one concerning sales by persons other than the real owners. Clandestine sales, as contrasted with open sales, make both the vendees and the vendors equally liable for theft of the things concerned.

Boundary disputes. The term boundary disputes is used in a wider sense and practically it includes all disputes relating to field. In all possible cases of boundary disputes of lands, tanks, etc., on the one hand and villages on the other, the opinion of the neighbours and other members of the community should be taken into account laying emphasis on the opinions of the elderly persons.

Inheritance, Partition and Stridhana. In 13th title, Narada deals with inheritance, including the rules of partition, Stridhana, gains of learning, the guiding principles for sons to be entrusted with the management of the family, exclusion from inheritance, presumption of separation, the different kinds of sons, their order of superiority and the order of succession among the different kinds of heirs. Partition can take place on the death of father or in his life time as per his own will.

Crimes. 14th, 15th and 16th titles in Narada deals with crime. The later the Smriti, the more systematic is the law of crimes and more exclusive is the treatment between civil law and criminal law. It discusses the heinous offences called 'Sahasa' which consists of man-slaughter, robbery, an indecent attack on another man's wife and the two species of insult. For a *sahasa* of highest degree, the punishments are not less than thousand *panas*, corporal punishment, confiscation of the entire property, banishment from the town, branding and amputation of the offending limbs, indiscriminately for people of all the castes excepting the Brahmins, who are not to be subjected to corporal punishments and who are only to be banished being branded on the forehead with a mark indicating the crime committed. Theft is a special kind of *sahasa* and admits of three-fold classification according to the value of the subject matter of theft. Possession of stolen articles, luxurious mode of living, indulgence in extravagances and presence in the company of the wicked raises assumption of theft. Persons giving shelter to thieves are equally guilty as thieves. The 17th title in Narada deals with games including gambling and betting which must be regulated by the state. The 18th title deals with miscellaneous topics like treating of public law of the law or the kings; private law being treated in the 17 other titles of law.

Brihaspati

Brihaspati Smriti exhibits the latest and the most perfect specimen of juristic speculation and the most systematic and methodical treatment thereof. The book is divided into 27 chapters. The first two indicate the constitution of a court of justice and the general rules of procedure; the next four are devoted to treatment of the plaint, the answer, the trial and the judgement—the four stages of legal proceeding; next four explain different mode of evidence and the last seventeen are devoted to the treatment of the topics covered by 18 titles of Manu, Yajnavalkya and Narada.

Judicial Proceedings. These comprise of four stages. The first is the plaint which should be free from all defects, susceptible of proof, provided with good and strong arguments, precise, reasonable, brief in words, rich in contents, unambiguous, free from confusion and devoid of improper arguments. Plaints not correctly written may be impossible, unmeaning and purposeless. If the defendant cannot fully meet the allegation in the plaint, he will lose the suit, but he may be allowed adjournment for preparing his answer. The answer may be confession, denial, special plea, etc. The most important part of the actual trial is the evidence by means of which each party will try to establish its case. The judge should after examining the plaint and the answer, determine as to on which party the burden of proof will lie. Evidence may be human and divine. Human evidence may be oral, documentary and inferential. Oral evidence is adduced by witnesses, who are of various kinds; documents may be of ten kinds and inference is also of several kinds. Divine tests or ordeals are also of several kinds. After examining the evidence, the judgements is delivered, which contains the findings of the judge with his reason. The judgement could be appealed against and king is the highest court of appeal.

Debts and Deposits. Brihaspati begins by saying that debts should be contracted by either pledges or documents. Interest charged is of six kinds. When the amount of debt has doubled and the debtor is dead, the creditor may sell the pledge in presence of witnesses. The liability of debt does not involve the great grandson and the heirs are not liable to pay immoral debts.

Sale without Ownership. There are six kinds of sales without ownership. If the vendor, when produced, cannot explain his ownership, he will have to return the price of the property to the pruchaser and shall pay a fine to the king and the property shall be returned to the real owner. The responsibility of the purchaser ceases when he can produce the vendor. Similarly, the gifts can be invalid. The most significant category of invalid gifts is the gift of the entire property of a man.

Master and Servant : Wages. Brihaspati deals with the relation between the masterand theservantand non-payment of wages in chapter xvi. These are based on the terms of agreement between them and suits arise in case of any violation. All such agreements should, therefore, be in writing, giving the wages payable, period of employment, jobs to be done by the servant, etc.

Criminal Law. Brihaspati uses the word 'Sahasa' (or violence) in two distinct senses—wide and narrow. In its wide sense, 'sahasa' virtually comprises all criminal acts such as defamation, assault, homicide, theft, (including robbery) and sexual offences and in narrow sense it means any of the last four offences. The punishment for the crimes generally has been provided for in terms of variations—sometimes direct and sometimes inverse—of the castes. Rank also played an important part in determining the punishment not only for defamation but also for assault. It is no offence to inflict an injury including even death, in exercise of the right of private defence. Cruelty to animals is also stated as offence punishable with fines. He has dealt with various kinds of heinous offences, or offences involving violence such as homicide, theft, robbery, and so on, and provides for different kinds of punishments beginning with mutilation of limbs and ending with infliction of capital punishment, which might be by hanging, drowning, burning, etc. Adultery has been narrated as being of three kinds namely forcible, fraudulent and sensual. Even winking or smiling at a woman is stated to be adultery. Punishments for various kinds of adultery have been stated. Heavy fines have been indicated for adultery on rich persons.

Relation between Husband and Wife. Brihaspati says that woman should be kept under strict guard through constant occupation in domestic duties and by never failing vigilance by other members of the family. He advocates early marriage and refers to sati rites too emphasising also the right to property of the widow in husband's property, specially in absence of sons and daughters.

Gambling and Betting. Gambling and betting have been recommended by Brihaspati to be practised under state control and suprintendance for the purpose of revenue inter alia.

Other Smriti Works. Katyayana's Smriti is not fully available. His treatment of 'Stridhana' and explanation of different kinds thereof have attained classical rank. The other Smriti writers, who have dealt with law inter alia were Pitamaha, Prajapati, Marici, Yama, Samvarta, Vyasa, Harita, Angerin, Ris Yasringa, etc.

Nibandhas and Commentaries. The *nibandhas* and commentaries played a very important part in the development of Hindu Law, so much so, that in many cases greater importance was attached to the commentators and *nibandhakaras* than to the original text writers themselves. The reason would be that legal experts would have been consulted in deciding cases even at the time of the Smritis themselves. The Smriti texts were there but their interpretations differed and the meaning of the text also was not known equally to all the people and only a small fraction of the people had mastered the texts, who could offer their legal opinion on account of their learning and eminence.

The commentaries and *nibandhas* served a very useful purpose in preserving and giving accounts of the different texts as they existed in their respective times. As a matter of fact heavy texts would have been absolutely lost to us had they not been referred to or quoted by different commentators. The commentaries and *nibandhas* differ from each other—both in conception and execution. The former contemplates explanations or interpretations—philological or otherwise—as it is seen when Narada Pandita in his *Dattaka Mimansa* advocates the adoption of daughters on the analogical principles of the instituion of the adoption of sons, or when different authorities in Bombay, Madras, Varanasi ascribe different shares to sons born after the adoption of a son or when the Mitakshara and the Dayabhaga explain in different ways the selfsame texts or the word 'Pinda' and then on this explanation they base their theories, which are diametrically opposed to each other. According to Narada Pandita as there may be twelve kinds of substitutes for the legitimate son, so substitutes of daughters also can be made in an identical way. Asahaya was the earliest commentator regarding whom some reliable information is available. Visvarupa, Bharuchi, Srikara, Meohatithi, Bhojadeva, Vijnanesvara are other commentators on various Smritis.

Mitakshara is the best known commentary by Vijnanesvara on Yajnavalkya. It occupies unique position in the history of Indian legal literature. Mitakshara applies to the whole of India particularly from the time of British administration. For this wide prevalance and almost universal acceptance, the very nature of the Yajnavalkya Smriti, which has been commented upon must be largely responsible.The intrinsic merit of the Yajnavalkya Smriti attracted commentators, who in their turn made the contents of Smriti in question easily understandable and acceptable to the people. In this respect, a very instructive antithesis is to be found between the two most important Smritis of Manu and Yajnavalkya. *Manu Smriti* was, no doubt, regarded as the greatest Smriti, particularly by the foreigners. The Smriti-writers themselves also extolled the *Manu Smriti*. The Mitaksara was composed in the last quarter of 11th century AD or the first quarter of 12th century AD and it was not only a commentary but it is in the nature of a digest of Smriti material. It brings together numerous Smriti passages, explains away contradictions among them by following the rules of interpretation laid down in the Purvamimansa system, brings about order by assigning to various dicta their proper scope and effects—a synthesis of apparently disconnected Smriti injunctions.

Mitakshara and Dayabhaga

Mitakshara is applicable to entire India except Bengal and Dayabhaga is applicable to Bengal. Mitakshara was the earliest of these two most important commentaries on Hindu Law. It was composed around the close of 11th century or the beginning of 12th century A.D. Regarding ancestral property, Mitakshara recognised the right by the very birth. Thus, a son is regarded as a co-owner with his father from his very birth. According to this school again a father has got only a restricted power of alienation and a son can claim partition even against the father. The Mitakshara makes a distinction between "Apratibandha Daya" and "Sapratibandha Daya", the former applying to ancestral property and the latter applying to self-acquired property. Regarding Sapratibandha Daya, the position of Mitakshara father is exactly same as that of a Dayabhaga father. The interest of a member of a joint family property passes by the doctrine of survivorship to the other members. Regarding alienation, members of a Mitakshara family cannot dispose of their shares while undivided. The principle of inheritance in this school is consanguinity or propinquity or blood relation. In the Dayabhaga on the other hand, right to property accrues by death of the last owner. Hence a son cannot have any share in the ancestral or self-occupied property until the death of the father. There is no distinction herein between the "Sapratibandha Daya" and the "Apritibandha Daya". In all cases, Sapratibandha is independent of the question whether the property is ancestral or self-occupied. A father, therefore, has got an absolute power of alienation and a son cannot claim partition or even maintenance as a matter of right. The interest of every member would pass on his death to his own heirs like the widow, or daughter according to the rule of inheritance. Even an undivided member of a joint family can sell or give away his share. The principle of inheritance is based on the theory of *pinda* or spiritual efficacy. The doctrine of *factum valet*, is fully recognised in Dayabhaga school whereas, it is partially recognised in Mitakshara. More important difference in the two schools is regarding Stridhana. Mitakshara derives the meaning of the term Stridhana from Yajnavalkya that which was give by the father, by the mother, by the husband or by a brother and that which was presented by the maternal uncles and the rest, at the time of wedding, before the nuptial fire and a gift on second marriage or gratuity on account of supersession and property obtained by inheritance or purchase, partition, seizure (adverse possession) and finding are all Stridhana according to Manu. In Dayabhaga, Stridhana has a technical meaning viz that it means the absolute estate of a woman. Over the property inherited by a widow from her husband, the wife has got only a limited interest. The latter interest is called woman estate. That only is Stridhana which she has power to give, sell or use independently of her husband's control.

Judicial Institution and Procedure

Vedas do not speak much about the judicial institution. Two terms we get in Rigveda are Sabha and Samiti. Samiti was a larger body than Sabha. King administered justice with the assistance of Samiti, which included a Purohita. According to Yajurveda too, king is the chief judge. Dharmasutras, which are the most ancient law books, provide that king assisted by Brahamanas, should administer justice in accordance with the Vedas, sacred law and the usages or customs of the country, caste and family, which are not opposed to the sacred law. The members of the courts were supposed to have learnt the specific customs of cultivation, traders, herdsmen, moneylenders and artisans in order to decide their suits. In the Dharmasutras, the law-courts acquired a shape which is more clean and regular than that found in Vedas. Kautilya's Arthashastra does not speak of the presence of Sabhyas in the court. Justice is administred either by the king himself or by the judges or Dharmasthiyas appointed by the king. The courts of the Dharmasthiyas consisted of three judges. The status of the judges was equal to an *amatya* (minister). These courts were to be established at Janapadasandhi or a frontier post. The Sangrahana or the headquarters of ten villages, one hundred villages, or the chief city in eight villages. In the Smritis, the judicial procedure is more crystallised. A gradual development of code of justice had taken place in this era. The *Manusmriti* was the first to introduce it. Yajnavalkya Smriti presented a more concise and systematic law code. But both of these Smritis do not give judicial procedure as elaborately as it developed in later Smritis. Brihaspati Smriti elaborately deals in judicial procedure and courts of law.

Narada Smriti is an independent work on law. Its treatment of legal procedure is far more elaborate and technical. Katyayan Smriti has further elaborated the legal dicta. Kautilya, Yajnavalkya, Brihaspati, Narada, and Katyayana call 'Vyavhara' as 'Chatuspada' or 'quadraped'. They specify the four stages as : the plaint. the reply, the proof and the decision. They say that Dharma is the Satya or truth and through right decision, Dharma is achieved. The judge should have various qualities such as he should preferably be a learned Brahmin. A Kshatriya or Vaisya can also be a judge provided he is proficient in law. He should be vigilant and born of good family; should be impartial; should not cause disgust to the people; is incorruptible; is afraid of the next world; and is most devoted to the observance of sacred rules of conduct, assiduous, and free from irascibility. He should not be a cruel person but should rather be sweet tempered, kind and belonging to a hereditary line of judges. He should be clever, energetic and not greedy. Besides, the chief justice, there should be three, five or seven other assessors in the court. They should also have the same qualifications as the chief judge. The court should be held in open. The chief judge and assessors should not hold a conversation in private, while the case is undecided and if they do so, they should be punished. Kautilya lays down that some merchants should be included in the court. These merchants are appointed to listen to the commercial causes and to look to the administration of justice. Disputes within a tribe, guild or sect were not to be decided by the king but were decided by the residents of the same country, Panchayats etc.

As already indicated, every trial has four stages. In the first stage the facts of the dispute are received. In the second stage the title of law should be ascertained; in the third stage the pleadings and evidences should be examined, and only after these, the decision should be given. There are elaborate rules, how the plaintiff should enter the court bowing before the king; how king asks about the complaint, the examination of witnesses, etc. On receipt of the plaint, the defendant is summoned. He is required to come in person or he could send his deputy, put another person as defendant or the plaintiff may accept another person as defendant. This is more or less like the present system of defence through lawyers. Persons busy in performing religious rites; who are under influence of intoxicants and women are exempted from appearing in courts.

Plaint. Plaint has been referred to as 'Purvapaksha'. 'Vadin' and 'Prativad' are also used for plaintiff and defendant. A person, who first approaches the court with his complaint is plaintiff. There are four kinds of plaints. It can be founded on suspicion; founded on fact; regarding the recovery of a debt or a fresh trial of a cause tried earlier. The plaint should mention the year, month, fortnight, day and names of castes of the parties. It should be free from defects; capable of proof; provided with good arguments; precise and reasonable; brief in words; rich in contents; unambiguous; not self-contradictory; devoid of opposite arguments; and capable of meeting opposite arguments. The plaint, once filed, could be amended within a specified time and afterwards no amendment is allowed. The plaints can be defective as being contradictory to the prevailing principles of law; being ambigous; do not present correct and necessary facts. Law suits between teacher and student ; father and son; husband and wife and master and servant are prohibited because they are considered to be undesirable.

Defence. After the plaint has been tendered, the reply should be given by the defendant which should correspond to the tenor of the plaint. The defence is called 'Uttara' or 'Pratipaksha'. Where the defendant cannot remember the transaction mentioned in the plaint, he can ask for suitable period in order to collect the evidence. If he is not able to file reply even during this period, then he is considered to have been defeated. A reply by the defendant can be of four kinds : denial; confession or admission; special plea; one which is based on a plea of former judgement or 'Resjudicata'. Ancient law givers do not allow a counter claim in reply except in case of abuse, assault; *sahasa;* theft, bribery, adultery and urgent matters.

Sandhi or Compromise. Once a plaint has been filed, the litigants cannot compromise their disputes privately without the order of the court. If they do so, each of them would have to pay a fine double of that imposed on a defeated party because they have cheated the court by depriving it of its fees. But if the king is informed of the compromise, then there is no fine. With such mutual understanding, uncertainty and suspense regarding the approaching declaration of the witnesses and judges come to an end.

Proof. After the answer has been produced before the court, the court would call upon one of the parties to establish its claim according to the reply. The defendant has to prove his assertion before the court. Thus, the burden of proof is on the defendant. In case of a denial, the burden of proof is on the plaintiff. He has to prove the contents of the plaint. The means of proof can be two-fold—human and divine. Human means of proof or ordeals. When human means of proof are available, the plaintiff should not depend upon ordeals, and if he does so he becomes a losing party. Further, for the different kinds of cases, different means of proofs should be adopted namely when there is any dispute about usages, of *'puga'* or association of traders, a guild of artisans and of a 'Gana' or group, the document is the only means of proof. Such cases cannot be proved by ordeals or witnesses. In disputes about things given or promised to be given but not given; in decisions of disputes of servants and their masters; in matters of taking back a thing after it has been sold, etc., witnesses are to be employed. Document as a means of proof occurs indirectly in *Manusmriti*. It mentions a document that is got written by force and declared as void. Three types of documents are mentioned. Documents written before the king; documents, attested by witness; documents without any attestation. The royal documents shall be written by the scribe of the king having the signature of the royal official. The 'Laukika' document should mention the origin of the parties; the transaction; the caste, the names and the amount of money and year, month, fortnight, etc.; the rate of interest, with the signature of debtor; atleast three witnesses and the scribe. A document is invalid if it has been executed by a person who is intoxicated; one charged with crime; by a woman or by a child or is written by forcible means; by intimidation or by deception; by one dying ; by one deceased or by a lunatic or by those who are defendants.

Though possession was recognised as a means of proof, yet long possession alone cannot be a mode of ownership. Various modes of possession are, through inheritance, through purchase, through partition, through seizure or finding. Seizure is in the forms of trees in forests. When there are no owners and findings refer to the appropriation of lost property, the owner of which was unknown they are like treasure-trove. Valid owners need both title and possession. Title without possession has no strength though title is stronger than possession, in case possession is not inherited. If an owner silently watches and raises no protest when his property has been enjoyed by a stranger for ten years, he loses his ownership over the property if the owner is not a minor or an idiot. This is like the present day provision of easement. Subsequently the period of ten years had been extended to three generations. A property without title, if enjoyed for thirty years, becomes the property of the possessor.

Witnesses. The institution of witness is well established since ancient times. The word 'Sakshi' means one has seen. The Dharmasutras discuss this subject at length and also speak of awarding supernatural punishments for giving false evidence according to the gravity of the sin committed. The Smritis provide that witnesses should be atleast three in number. A single witness is not considered enough to decide a matter.

Householders, father of a male issue, and indigenous persons of all the four castes, who know their duties and are free from covetousness are competent witnesses. Law treatises give a long list of incompetent witnesses. According to Manu, there are those who are interested in the suit, friends, enemies, men convicted of perjury, severely ill, fainted by moral sins, the king, the mechanic, the actor a dependant person, one having a bad name, a *dasyu*, a follower of forbidden occupation, an aged person, an infant, a single man, a man of the lowest caste, one deficient in organs, one extremely grieved, intoxicated, mad man, one tormented with hunger and thirst, desire, a thief are incompetent witnesses. Narada divides witnesses into two types : (1) Krta or appointed by the litigants and (2) Akrta or not appointed by the litigants. These are further divided into several types. The Smritis prescribe that judge should bind witnesses by an oath firmly and examine them separately. This system is still in vogue. The witnesses should be inspired by the judge with deep awe by quoting sacred texts for extolling the excellence of truth. If a witness does not give evidence, he should be punished eight times the amount in dispute.

Oaths and Ordeals. As already indicated, taking oath is a very common method of proving oneself cleared from a certain sin. It is resorted to not only in judicial proceedings but also in everyday life to prove the purity of one's character. Narada says that taking of oath even by gods and sages is on record. But Smritis say that when evidence (witness, document, and possession) or circumstantial evidence is available, ordeals should not be depended upon. King should administer ordeals in the case of heavy crimes, whereas in light cases, the offender shall swear with oaths.

Decision. Decision or '*Nirnaya*' is the last stage of a trial. Narada says that at the time of decision, both parties should be removed from the court of justice by the Sabhy as. When a party is defeated due to confession on wrong conduct or after judicial investigation, the judge declares the defeat and the successful party receives a 'Jayapatra' couched in appropriate language. Jayapatra contains an accurate record of the plaint, the reply, judicial investigation together with the signature of the judge and the royal seal. When a suit has been completed, a fine has to be inflicted with the sanction of the king. In ancient India, in civil cases, the execution of the verdict was done by the successful party itself, But without the help of the king it is difficult to get the judgement executed.

Law of Inheritance. According to Rigveda, a son born of body does not give the paternal wealth to his sister. This statement clearly reflects the norms prevalent at that time. Changes in law of inheritance follow an interesting course since Vedic times. While Rigveda prescribes partition of family property after the death of the father, in later Vedic literature, it could take place even during his life time. Smritis allow and even recommend partition while the father is living. The Manusmriti provides division of property after the death of the parents when brothers should divide the property equally amongst themselves. Alternatively the eldest brother takes charge of the whole paternal property and treats his younger brothers like a father. Smritis say that partition during father's life time can take place only if he permits it. Father can distribute property among his sons in equal, less or greater shares and all the sons have to abide by such arrangement. Brihaspati and Katyayana prescribe equal share for all sons but the sons have no right over the self earned property of the father.

Joint property can be ancestral property or that which is actually earned but poured into joint account according to Mitakshara school. The joint family consists of all males lineally descended from a common male ancestor, including their wives and unmarried daughters. The daughters after marriage become members of their husbands' families. But separate property can be owned by any member of the joint family. It can be gained by valour, gift, received at the time of marriage, wealth acquired by learning a service or Vidyadhan and what is given by father through love. This individual property is not subject to partition. Wealth acquired in this manner can be recognised as individual property only in case no paternal wealth was used for acquiring it. According to Smritis when an ancestral property, which had been lost to the family, was recovered by the father himself by his own effort without using money from the common fund, the father would own it as his individual property. The Vidyadhan or gain of learning are not divisible with the coparceners in case the acquirer has not used the money of the joint family in acquiring the same.

Stridhana. Dharmasutras define 'Stridhana' as the ornaments and wealth received by a woman from his relations. Kautilya puts a ceiling of two thousand *panas* for the money to be given in dowry but puts no restriction on the amount of ornaments, which are worn by the bride, to be included in dowry.

Manu Enumerates Six Kinds of Stridhana

What is given before the nuptial fire ; what is given as a token of love ; gifts; received from brothers, gifts from mother and gifts from father. Yajnavalkya adds presents of husband on marrying another wife and money given by cognates or maiden after the marriage. Katyayana recognises the sole ownership of woman over Stridhana. He ordains that neither the husband, nor the son, nor the father, nor the brothers have authority over Stridhana for the purpose of taking for themselves or for giving it away to others. Even the husband has not been given dominion over his wife's Stridhana. However, husband can spend it with wife's consent if he be afflicted with disease or in calamity or when harassed by creditors but afterwards he should return it.

According to Dharmasutras, only daughters are regarded as heirs of Stridhana. It can be inherited by unmarried daughters and on their failure by a poor married daughter. Manu, like Kautilya, includes sons also among the heirs of Stridhana. He provides that the mother's property is to be divided among brothers and sisters after her death. According to Mitakshara school,the order of succession of the Stridhana is as follows :

(i) Unmarried daughters.
(ii) Married daughters, who are destitute of wealth or without issue.
(iii) Married daughters, who are provided for.
(iv) Daughter's daughter.
(v) Daughter's son.
(vi) Son.
(vii) Son's son.
(viii) Husband, if she was married in approved form.
(ix) Husband's heirs in the order in which they inherit his property

Inheritance of a Sonless Man. When a person is dead without a son, Dharmashastras provide that *sapindas* or the blood relations within six degrees and *sagotra* relations bearing a common family name and the wife shall share the property of a person died without son. *Manu Smriti* also provides for *sapindas* to inherit in case of sonless father. Brihaspati and Yajnavalkya make wife the first heir. Daughter can also inherit in case of mother's death. Narada provides that if among several brothers, one issueless brother dies or becomes an ascetic, the others should divide his property leaving Stridhana. The wife of the dead brother receives maintenance till death in case she is chaste.

Law of Contract. Dharmasutras contain little material of legal value compared to the Smritis. Manu Smriti for the first time introduced eighteen titles of law. These titles were adopted and elaborated by the later law givers. Smritis laid down certain rules about the persons incompetent to enter into valid transaction. The first category includes persons, who are mentally not sound such as intoxicated, the insane, the diseased persons. Second category covers persons, who are incompetent due to their over age or under age. In the third category come those persons who are not authorised by the party. Yajnavalkya adds that contracts made at a wrong place or at an unearthly home should be treated as null and void. Contract made through force is also invalid.

Recovery of Debt. Debt and its recovery are ancient problems. The liability to pay off the debts of the father and ancestors is considered the holy duty of the son. Dharmasutras also ordain that heirs shall pay the debts of the deceased person. The rate of interest to be charged on debt had also been prescribed in Smritis. There is one-eightieth part of the capital, when nothing has been prescribed as pledge for. Rate of interest also depended on the Varna of the debtor. Brahmin to pay two per cent, Kshatriya three per cent, Vaisya four per cent and Sudra five per cent. Manu and Narada ordain that two per cent monthly is the proper rate of interest.

Five means of recovery of debts have been prescribed. These are ***dharma*** or moral persuation; legal proceedings; artful management; customary, such as sitting down at his door or compulsion to do work or confinement. Moral persuasion is by advice of friends and kinsman; artful management is that when the creditor with a crafty design borrows something from the debtor for his own use or withholds a deposit and thus enforcing payment of debt. Mode of compulsion is by beating the debtor. The customary mode is that in which the debtor is made to pay by confining his wife, son, or cattle or sitting down at his door. A creditor can compel to work only those debtors who are of equal or lower caste and not persons of higher castes. When there are many creditors, the debtor should pay that debt first which was incurred first except that debt to a Brahmin should be paid first. When a debtor makes payment of the debt—whole or in part, he must get receipt for it. If the creditor does not give receipt even on being reminded, he loses the balance debt. The descendants are considered liable to pay the debts of their ancestors. The son is not expected to pay the illegal and immoral debt even of father. Such debts are gifts for illicit love to a wife of another person or the balance of a fine or toll. Conversely, the debts contracted by son and wife are not to be paid by father or husband normally. But in case son has incurred the debt by the order of his father or for the maintenance of the family or in the precarious situation, the father is liable to pay the debt.

Partnership. Narada and Katyayana declare that when several persons for example, traders, artisans or unseparated brothers, carry on a business jointly, it is called partnership. A person should carry on business jointly with persons who are of noble parentage, clever, active, intelligent, familiar with coins, skilled in revenue and expenditure, honest and enterprising. In partnership, the percentage of gains and charges should be in accordance with the share contributed by each partner.

Smritis ordain that the loss, expenses, profit and labour of each partner would be equal, more or less, in proportion to the capital invested by them as their shares.

Payment of Wages. Yajnavalkya provides that when wages are not settled, a servant will receive one-tenth portion of the profit earned through trade, cattle and agriculture. But when a servant gets food and clothing, he would take less and when he does not get food then he would take more. Yajnavalkya further says that the wages of a servant may be more or less according to the profit he earned for his master. He provides that a servant should keep the instruments entrusted to him and when some goods entrusted to the servant are damaged by his fault, not by fate or by the king, he has to make good the loss. Manu provides that if a servant is ill, he may perform the work after recovery and he will receive his wages even after a long time. Smritis also provide rules about the servant employed for looking after cattle, etc. A herdsman can milch one cow out of ten cows as his wages. A breach of contract exists when a person fails to render certain services which he had promised.

Slaves. There is also mention of slaves in *Manu Smriti*. He speaks of seven kinds of slaves. These are : One who is made a captive under a standard; one who serves for one's daily food; one who is born in the house; one who is bought; one who is given; one who has inherited slavery; one who is enslaved by way of punishment. A slave who has been captured and sold by robbers, becomes free if he saves the life of his master or pays back the money spent on him with interest. But an apostate from ascetic life cannot become free till his death. When a master has intercourse with his female slave and the latter then gives birth to a son, the master should then make her free from slavery due to the fact that she has conceived from him and if he does not free her, his own son will be a slave. However, a person of higher caste cannot be a slave of a person of lower caste because slavery is not permitted in reverse order. The Smritis do not recognise a slave as a full legal person. He can neither give evidence nor be a surety. A slave is declared to have no proprietary rights. Whatever property he acquires, would become the property of his master.

Boundary Disputes. Disputes about land are a very ancient problem. The *Manusmriti* suggests various ways to make the boundaries between villages, fields, houses, etc. Katyayana points out six causes of land disputes : Claiming more land; to claim that a certain man is entitled to possess less than what he possesses; claim for a share; denial of a share; possession, when there was no possession or boundary before. The making of boundary is :

1. By growing big trees along the boundary.
2. Building a tank, well, fountain and temples to mark the boundary.
3. Burrying stones, bones, cows-horns, chaff, ashes, potsherd, dry cowdung, bricks, cinder, pebbles, sand and other things, which the earth cannot corrode even after a long time, along the boundary.

Besides these visible marks, there should also be invisible marks which should be deposited under ground, such as things which cannot be destroyed by earth, at the extremities of the boundary. These should be deposited in vessels and be told to sons, grandsons, etc. The fruits and flowers, which grow on the boundary between two fields, should be considered joint between the owners of the two fields. But when a tree, after growing in the field of a person, spreads over another man's field, the owner would be that person in whose field the tree has taken roots. The roads, houses, drains, fields, etc., which having been used by a person since the establishment of the village, must not be taken away from him or demolished or altered. Similarly, a window, a water-course, a balcony, a shed, or square of four buildings, a drain for the exit of water after the rainfall, base of the wall and dwelling house of another should not be transgressed. But these things should not be added after the construction of the building so as to cause obstruction or annoyance to anyone else. Similarly, the window in the interior of another person's house, or a watercourse of another's house should not be obstructed. This is like present day law of right of easement.

Criminal Law. The growth of criminal law in India went hand in hand with the growing requirements of the social system as a whole. The contents of legal texts bear ample testimony to the pattern of their development. Dharmasutras, which are the earliest texts dealing with legal matters, contain no elaborate dicta on criminal law. ***Manusmriti*** laid the foundation of the restructured Hindu society after the advent of Buddhism and it is in this work that we find the specific mention of certain works pertaining to criminal law. But the zenith of sophistication of the traditional Indian system of criminal law was reached in the era of later Smritis, when the society attained a high degree of complexity as a result of the growth of trade and industry. This is shown by the elaborate treatment given to various kinds of crimes and the intricate provisions of dealing with them in various Smritis.

Like all provisions of Indian Law, the rules pertaining to abuse were deeply influenced by the caste hierarchy. Dharmasutras provide that a Shudra, who, intentionally reviles twice-born man by abuse, shall be deprived of his tongue. If a Vaisya abuses Brahmin, he was to pay a fine of one hundred and fifty *Karsapanas*; the Kshatriya has to pay only one hundred *Karsapanas* for the same offence. But a Brahmin has to pay only fifty Karsapanas if he abuses a Kshatriya; for abusing Vaisya he has to pay only twenty five and if he abuses a Shudra, no fine is to be imposed on him. These rules had been inherited by Smritis too.

Dharmasutras provide that if a Shudra criminally assaults twice-born persons, he shall be deprived of the limbs with which he offends. One, who breaks the skin of an equal caste person, shall be fined hundred *panas*. If he cuts a muscle, six Nisakas and for breaking bone, banishment should be given. Smritis also say the same thing. They say that hurting the limbs of another with hand, foot, weapon, or otherwise or defiling him with ashes, etc., would come under this title of law. The assaults have been divided into three kinds—mild, middle and heavy. The gravity of offence depends both on value of the objects involved and on the nature of the action of the offender. They have laid down rules about abuse and assault. The mild assault is like throwing ashes or mud on someone for which a fine of ten *panas* is there.

The middle amercement is when two angry persons use weapon against each other and a wound has been inflicted. The punishment would be decided by experts corresponding to the severity of the wound. The heavy punishment is imposed when an injury has been caused to someone with brick, stone or a wooden clink. For cutting flesh, causing blood oozing pecuniary punishment is generally given and the highest fine for killing is capital punishment.

Smriti writers usually put theft under the title 'Sahasa' or heinous offences. Manu distinguishes theft from 'Sahasa' by saying that the latter is that offence which is commited in the presence of the owner with violence, while theft is done during his absence. Narada says that theft is taking away one's property while he is asleep, careless or intoxicated. He also speaks of three kinds of thefts according to the value of the article stolen, viz. trifling articles such as earthen wares, a seat, a couch, bone, used leather, grass, grain and prepared food; articles of middling value such as clothes made of other material than silk, cattle other than cows, and metals other than gold, rice and barley;

articles of superior value as gold, precious stones, silk, women, men, cows, elephants, houses or property of Brahmin or temple. There are two kinds of thieves—patent and secret. Patent are traders, who forge measures and weights. gamblers, quacks, public prostitutes; those, who offer bribe to *sabhyas*; receivers of bribe, robbers, persons pretending to know how to interpret good or bad evils; non-Aryan; wearing the marks of an Aryan. The secret thieves are the house-breakers, highway men, robbers of bipeds or quadrupeds, thieves of clothes, etc., and stealers of grains. They roam in forests or other concealed places and attack and rob an unaware person. The King should, therefore, employ trustworthy persons as spies, who mingle with them after disguising themselves in assembly houses; houses, where water is distributed; brothels; cross-roads; festive assemblies; play houses, etc., to detect these thieves. After detection, the property should be recovered and they should be punished. When a thief confesses his crime, it is for the king to punish or pardon him. Different kinds of punishments—pecuniary and physical—have been prescribed for different kinds of thieves and on persons of different Varnas.

Dharmashastras donot contain much material on 'Sahasa' but Brahmins and twice-born were given priviliged position. Murdering a Brahmin by a lower caste person is considered as a crime of violence and capital punishment is awarded, while a token punishment is awarded to Brahmin for killing a person of lower caste. In Manusmriti, this title of law is specifically mentioned. The later Smritis treat it elaborately. They prescribe various punishments according to the crime. They explain 'Sahasa' as an act which is done by violence and prescribed accordingly. Manu says that criminal of *sahasa* must be punished by the king. Brihaspati and Narada speak of four types of crime of violence, which include all aspects of criminal law—manslaughter, robbery, and indecent assault on another man's wife and two kinds of 'Parusya'. They also classify crime of violence under three categories—lowest, middling and highest. When, several persons in passion beat a single individual and kill him, the responsibility for his death shall be charged to him, who strikes the fatal blow, while others be given lighter punishment.

Adultery. Adultery or unlawful relationship of a man and woman has been considered a serious offence. The Dharmasutras and Smritis prescribe severe punishment for adultery like beating by hot iron. If a woman commits adultery with a man of lower caste, the king shall cause her to be devoured by dogs in a public place. As per Dharmashastra, the adulteraters should be put to death. If a Shudra defiles an Aryan woman, his organ be cut off and all his property be confiscated. Vasistha says that if a person of Kshatriya, Vaisya or Shudra Varna approaches, a woman of Brahmin caste, he should be burnt alive, while the Brahmin woman should be paraded along the highway without clothes on a donkey after getting her head shaved. He provides many penances even for a woman who is mentally faithful to her husband. Similarly, cohabitation with forbidden relations is punishable according to caste and the degree of offence, and relation involved.

Deposit

Deposit is a contract, whereby one person delivers a movable thing to another for gratuitous safe custody. In Sanskrit, important synonyms for the word 'deposit' are *'niksepa' 'upanidhi'* and *'nyasa'*. There is literally small difference in their meanings.

Open Deposit **(Niksepa).** It is unsealed deposit handed over to the depository in the presence of the owner.

Sealed Deposit **(Upanidhi).** A chattel, property (*dravya*), which being placed in a box or a pot or hidden in another thing or under a seal or covered with seal or cloth without being described or known, is sealed deposit.

Secret Deposit **(Nyasa).** This was a deposit which was entrusted to a member of the house in the absence of the owner and without being shown to him with the mandate to be handed over to the owner of the house.

Mutual Deposit **(Pratinyasa).** This is one agreement of a re-deposit or a mutual deposit held to be understood, where both parties exchange deposits with one-another with the words "You should keep this thing of mine and I shall keep that thing of yours". So two contracts of deposit take place at one time.

Deposit with an Artisan. This is a deposit given to an artisan in order to perform a particular piece of work like giving gold to goldsmith in order to make ornaments.

Property of a minor. This kind of contract of deposit took place when a man took a wealthy minor, who has no guardian into his house. Then the property of minor was subjected to the rules of deposit like in the case of death of father and mother, a child was deposited by the king or on his behalf with a man, who had to take care of the orphan, and the guardian had to take his proper care.

Law of deposits. Almost all the essentials of the contract of deposit, which consisted in the delivering of a moveable thing by one person to another for safe custody constitute the law of deposit. The depository, according to ancient Indian law, possessed the thing deposited in subordination to the depositor. Therefore, the thing deposited was in his detention only. The depository could not alienate the thing deposited and even the person to whom the thing deposited was transferred would not become the owner of this thing as he could not prove the title. The depositor, therefore, had to chose a right man and a right place, a place where the thing deposited was safe, and if the depository was at fault, he was responsible for every loss, destruction or damage of the object deposited even if it was caused by 'vis major'. The rule was that the depository had to restore the object deposited when asked for and if he failed to restore it, he was at fault and if there 'vis major' occured, the depository was responsible for the object desposited and had to restore it, when lost or destroyed or damaged. But if the depositor knew that the loss of the object deposited was probable, and still deposited it, then the depository was not responsible for any loss, damage or destruction. Otherwise the object deposited had to be returned in the same condition in which it was delivered. It is in the very manner and to the very man. The deposits given to a depository without agreeing on the term of deposit, had to be returned immediately after the depositor asked for its return and when any agreement for return has been made then the deposit has to be returned in terms of agreement. The object deposited must be returned to the depositor himself, if not, the depository had to be punished. In case of any default of the depository, the depository should be made to pay a fine equal to the deposit and the deposited could not be used by the depository without the consent of the depositor.

According to Manu and Brihaspati Smritis, a wise man could deposit an object after duly considering the case with persons who were :

(a) Born of good family.
(b) Endowed with good character and qualities.
(c) Truthful.
(d) Well acquanted with Dharma.
(e) Honourable.
(f) Wealthy and powerful.
(g) Who had many relatives.

All these considerations were advisory only and the non-juridical sources dealing with deposits have shown that in all cases mentioned there, the deposits were not placed with persons having the attributes enumerated above.

Pledge

In Sanskrit its equivalent is 'Bandha' or 'Bandhaka'. Pledges were of eight kinds as moveable and immoveable; to be kept; to be used; with no time limit and with time limit; stipulated in writing and stipulated before witnesses. The first six are from legal point of view and last two are from the formal point of view. An object given by the pledger into the possession of the pledgee could have been kept but not used. If the pledgee used the pledge, such an act caused legal consequences regulated in the Smriti. Such a pledge lost all the interest due to him or part thereof and sometimes was under obligation to pay compensation for the use of the pledged article. Therefore, the pledge cannot be used without the authorisation by the pledger. The pledge could even be in the shape of the fruits of labour obtained by the use of the living pledge but the pledgee could not insult or injure the pledge or living being otherwise he shall have to pay compensation.

Duties of the Pledger. The first duty of the pledger consisted in giving the pledge and afterwards in repaying the debt. The repayment of the debt has to take place at the time and place agreed upon by both the parties and the person causing breach had to compensate the other party. In ancient India, the permitted interest could amount up to 240 yearly if unsecured by pledge and when secure by pledge, it could be 24 per cent annually.

Duty of the Pledgee. The duty of the pledgee consisted in the giving of loan and the restoration of the pledge as soon as the debt was discharged. Secondly, he had to preserve the pledge carefully and where damaged due to carelessness, the pledgee had to compensate the pledger for that except when the damage was caused by 'vis major'.

Sureties

Surety is the guarantee to be offered to a creditor by another person to create confidence. This could be a surety of a pledge. Pledge has already been discussed. In case of surety, the loan is given on personal surety of a person who is of confidence to pledgee and in case of default of the pledger in repayment of loan, the surety is responsible. The suretyship consisted in the obligation of the surety to produce the debtor at the time and place agreed upon between the creditor and debtor. If the surety failed to do so, he was obliged to pay to the creditor the debt contracted by the debtor or to pay the fine determined. In the case of more than one sureties, their obligation towards the creditor could be either a solitary obligation or a pro-rata part obligation depending on the text of agreement. Mostly they were bound jointly and severally.

Legal Position of Physician in Ancient India

It is generally accepted that the origin and growth of science of Ayurveda and the rise of the early schools of medicine in India were as follows :

1. ***Primitive Medicine.*** It was in Indus Valley Civilisation and much material is not available.
2. ***Early Vedic Medicine.*** Gods such as Rudra, Soma, Varuna, Aditya, etc., had as one of their numerous attributes the power of causing or revealing diseases. Rudra was best physician. Indra was restorer of limbs and life. Varuna was owner of drugs, etc.
3. Celestial Physicians were incarnations of Dhanvantri to propagate knowledge of Ayurveda among the mortals. Ayurveda was attributed to Vishnu, who was a teacher of medical science. He was also called Sudhapani or the carrier of nectar in his hands.
4. Indian sages besought divine beings or incarnation of Dhanvantri to teach them Ayurveda for the relief of ailing mankind.
5. Bhardwaj, Atreyi, and colleagues of Susveta wrote learned treatises based upon the lectures they had heard and propagated the theory and practice of medicines among the learned classes of ancient India. These centres were at Taxila and Kasi (Varanasi). A physician treated the human beings according to these provisions. He was one, who could discover the nature of diseases by a study of their causes and symptoms and one who gave remedies and tried prescriptions after ascertaining whether the diseases were curable or incurable. A physician had to be well-behaved, brave, clean in habits, modest, bodily sound, intelligent, learned and possessing good memory. The students had to study the subject and there was indications about how the study had to be conducted. During apprenticeship, the pupil had to give up lust, anger, avarice, folly, vanity, pride, envy, rudeness, deception, falsehood, idleness and all other reprehensible conduct. He had first to study various Shastras. Then he started treating diseases, and resorted to study of surgery. The physician and surgeon used to be the same man. He had detailed practical training. Therefore, the principle qualifications of physician were mastery of scriptures, experience, cleverness and purity.

Moral ethics were clearly described in ancient India. Not everybody could be treated by physicians. The physicians were ordered not to treat hunters, fowlers, outcastes, sinners. They could not act for self interest.

After ascertaining the nature of disease, the physician had first to test the longevity of the patient and apply carefully selected medicines. He then had to commence the treatment with full knowledge. Proper diagnosis was necessary for appropriate treatment. The physician, who undertook perilous medical treatment had to inform the respective authorities otherwise in case of any eventuality, he could be fined. Some spies could also be sent in the guise of a physician by one king in other's kingdom as the physician could be a person of trust of the king.

As already stated, in ancient India, it was necessary for a physician to obtain permission of the king for starting medical practice. Non-licensed and ignorant physicians were called "companions of diseases". They could be punished if something untoward happened or detected as such by the spies of the king. However, when the treatment was by a licensed physician, the patient received no indemnity in the case of improper medical treatment causing any harm. However, a physician, who acted improperly prima facie, was liable to punishment. For such punishment, details have been given in Smritis, different from caste to caste, man to man, etc.

Remuneration of Physician. It was accepted in ancient India that physicians should receive remuneration for their work. The mention is that a physician did not go from his patient empty handed because otherwise his visit would have been ineffective.

It is mentioned in Rigveda that a physician got remuneration for his work in the shape of a horse, or a vestment from his patient. Kautilya has said clearly that physicians, who worked on their own, had to earn as much as persons employed in the similar fashion elsewhere usually would. It was a fixed salary of 2,000 *panas* per annum. The physician was held responsible for his wrong (*mithya*) action due to false conception, misapprehension or wrong diagnosis due to his ignorance or lack of medical knowledge. The degree of penalty depended upon the result of *mithya* medical treatment particularly upon degree of wrong done i.e. whether treatment led to death, increased illness or proved uselessness. It was also dependent upon social class of the patient. Such rules were not for the safeguard of the patient but for safeguarding good administration of the state. There is mention of the patients' right to an indemnity; the penalty being imposed by the state and paid to the state (king). The physicians were, however, held in high esteem in the society.

Specially Protected Beings

Legal, fiscal, social and penal privileges were accorded to infants, aged, diseased, helpless and distressed persons according to ancient Indian law in the Dharmashastras and Smritis and in particular according to *Arthashastra*, and such persons were considered as being under the special protection of the state. Not only such people, we find special rules which concerned the prohibition of killing or torturing animals, protection in their old age and in case of disease. Even some kinds of natural parks were provided. There was also prohibition against catching, killing or injuring deers. Although the mention is of deers but such protection must be to all animals.

Forms of Marriage

The ancient Indian Law recognised eight forms of marriage namely Brahm Vivah, Daiva Vivah, Arsa Vivah, Prajapatya Vivah, Asur Vivah, Gandharva Vivah, Raksasa Vivah and Paisacha Vivah.

Raksusa Vivah. This form of marriage was a marriage by capture. It was based on forcible abduction of a maiden. Nearly all Dharmashastras prohibited forcible abduction and considered such an act as crime and there were punishments laid down for such marriages. For kings, however, such marriage was permissible.

Paisacha Vivaha. This was a marriage based on deception of the girl. The deception was determined like that it consisted in deceitfully and fraudulently carrying off the girl when she was asleep. Such marriage was not by force but was a crime accept in the case of the king. Such marriage was also based on the seduction of the girl, most probably on sexual intercourse against the will of the maiden. Such sexual intercourse was a great crime and punishment for it was capital penalty.

Asura Vivaha. In such a marriage, the girl was sold to the bridegroom. In other words such marriage was based on the purchase of the maiden by the suitor. Though we do not find the exact amount to be paid for the purchase of maiden but such amount had to be paid according to the ability of the suitor. There is mention that the bridegroom had to give wealth for his future wife not only to her kinsmen (who had authority over the maiden) but also according to his own will to the bride herself in the form of jewels, vestment, gold, etc. If after the nuptial fee had been paid for a maiden, the giver of the fee died, the girl, if she consented, had to be given in marriage, to his brother. Some Smritis discouraged such marriage as it amounted to selling of the child which was a crime. Despite this, such marriages were very much in vogue.

Arsa Vivaha. This form of marriage was concluded by the gift of a bull and a cow. Such a marriage was considered as not a purchase and was considered praiseworthy and an orthodox form of marriage.

Brahma Vivaha. In this marriage, the girl was voluntarily given in marriage to an honourable man after having decked her up with ornaments. Here the giving away of the girl took place after going round the fire three times and after having pronounced the name of the *gotra* or after pouring out a libation of water. The sons born of such marriage were endowed with Brahmanic glory and were respected by cultured persons.

Daiva Vivaha. Here the girl was given away to *ritvij*, while he was officating at a sacrifice in consideration of his finishing the sacrifice, which could last for several days. Therefore, giving away a girl to the *ritvij* was in consideration of his fees. This is also an orthodox form of marriage, wherein the girl had no influence in the choice of her husband and the choice depended upon the will of the father or the guardian. Such a marriage was lawful and righteous for the upper castes.

Prajapatya Vivaha. The giving away of a girl to a suitor by a saying that both should perform together their duties was the Prajapatya vivah. According to this form of marriage, the father or he, who had authority over the girl, had to give away the girl to a suitor, who solicited her hand by saying a formula such as "May both of you perform together your duties". This form of marriage was considered as lawful and righteous for the upper castes.

Gandharva Vivaha. The union of a willing maiden and a lover constituted Gandharva vivaha. Here a young man behaves in public towards a girl, who has been courted by him and is entirely his, as if she were his wife. He obtains consecrated fire from a Brahmin, strews the ground with holy grass, makes oblation before the fire and thus is married according to the religious regulations relevant to this form of marriage. This was considered as a low way of marriage and was below the three forms of Brahma, Arsa and Daiva vivahas.

Swayamvara. There were three kinds of Swayamvaras. One was when the girl had absolute freedom of choosing her husband like Savitri had. Second form was where the bride was to be won by a feat of prowess as in the case of Sita and Draupadi. Third was a festive Swayamvara like that of Nala and Damyanti, where the girl chose the husband having heard of his praise, etc., even without having seen him. Here the girl's choice of husband has been recognised.

Dowry. From marriage by purchase or a symbolic marriage of purchase in which the price paid for the girl did not correspond to the real value of the girl, we come to the practice of dowry, which is apparently the very reverse of marriage by purchase. But whilst the marriage portion partly derives its origin from the purchase of wives, it is not so in every case. Here the money is given by the bride's father to groom's father for having accepted the girl in marriage. It was in fact not a consideration but an amount settled for use of the bride to enable her to establish her new house and the money was paid not by any force or consideration but of his own volition.

Polygamy or monogamy. Polygamy was not as a rule permitted but kings were allowed to have as many marriages as they liked. Rama did not marry even a second wife which would indicate that by and large there was monogamy rule.

Post-Smriti Period

In the history of Hindu Law, creative and critical periods succeed each other and it was the post-Smriti period during which Hindu Law and jurisprudence reached a remarkable stage of progress and assimilation. The Smritis, though accepted as revelations remembered, were themselves partially based on usages and practices and did not profess to comprehend every aspect of Vyavahara. The salutary rule that in course of time had come to be accepted and emphasised by the Smritikaras themselves was that cases were also to be decided agreeably to such usages and customs as were approved by the conscience of the virtuous and followed by the people. This contributed to the growth of Hindu Law by introducing innovations and modifications in what was in theory attributed to divine percepts, otherwise unattainable owing to their emanation from the deity.

The History of the Development of schools of Hindu Law

The process of interpretation of law and through that process the declaration and exposition of law went on for a long time and naturally helped the rational development of law. There were established courts but there was no system under the Hindu Law of reference to authoritative or persuasive judicial precedents. Instead, a very large number of commentaries and digests were, from time to time, written during the post-Smriti period but the commentators did not at any time arrogate to themselves the position of law-makers. But in course of time, these commentaries appear to have acted with ever increasing force to give an impulse to the systematic building up of the law. These opinions and conclusions became law by acceptance.

An account of the origin and development of the schools of Hindu Law was given by the Judicial Committe of the Privy Council in Collector of Madurai vs Mootoo Ramlinga : "The remote sources of Hindu Law are common to all the different schools. The process by which those schools have been developed seem to have been of this kind. The Mitakshara, which is universally accepted by all the schools except that of Bengal as of the highest authority and which in Bengal is received also as of highest authority, yielding only to Dayabhaga in those points where they differed. The Dayabhaga prevails in Bengal and the Mitakshara school prevails in rest of India".

Mitakshara is sub-divided into four minor schools :

(i) Benaras School
(ii) Mithila School
(iii) Maharashtra or Bombay School
(iv) Dravida or Madras School

Benaras school covers practically the whole of Northern India with the exception of Punjab, where the Mitakshara law has on certain points been considerably modified by custom. Mithila school prevails in Tirhut and some districts of Northern Bihar. The Bombay School covers Western India and Dravida School covers Southern India.

Mitakshara has for more than nine centuries been accepted a place of ascendency and authority, unique and unrivalled in the annals of legal literature. Vijnaneshwara was one of the greatest of the juristheologicians, who contributed to the making of Hindu Law. Even though his treatment of certain matters is exhaustive and sometimes elaborate, he is mostly concise and precise and true brevity designated in the title of the work. In his Mitakshara, he produced a juridical work, which is an institutional treatise. His treatise had, from a very early time, a large degree of practical influence on many branches of Hindu Law.

Personal Law of Hindus

Wherever the laws of India admit the operation of personal law, the rights and obligations of a Hindu are determined by Hindu Law that is his traditional law subject to the exception that any part of that law may be modified or abrogated by statute. The Hindus are divided into four castes namely :

(i) The Brahmins
(ii) The Kashatriyas
(iii) The Vaisyas
(iv) The Sudras

The Hindu Law as administred by the courts of India is applied to Hindus in some matters only. Throughout India question regarding succession, inheritance, marriage and religious usages and institutions are decided according to Hindu Law except in so far as such law has been altered by legislative enactment. Following are the Acts which made fundamental and radical changes in Hindu Law in 1955 and 1956 :

(i) Hindu Marriage Act 1955
(ii) Hindu Succession Act 1956
(iii) Hindu Minority and Guardianship Act 1956
(iv) Hindu Adoption and Maintenance Act, 1956

The Hindu Law had prior to 1955 been modified and supplemented in certain respects by the following Acts :

(i) The Caste Disabilities Act 1850 removed disabilities on renouncement of religion.
(ii) The Hindu Widows Remarriage Act 1856 legalised marriage of Hindu widows.
(iii) The Indian Succession Act 1925.
(iv) The Native Converts Marriage Dissolution Act 1866 enables a Hindu convert to Christianity to obtain dissolution of marriage.
(v) The Special Marriage Act of 1954.
(vi) The Transfer of Property Act 1882.
(vii) The Indian Majority Act 1875 fixes the age of majority on completion of 18 years.
(viii) The Guardians and Wards Act 1890, where guardian had to be appointed by the courts.
(ix) The Hindu Inheritance (Removal of Disabilities) Act 1928. It limits the disabilities which excluded a Hindu from inheritence and share on partition.

(x) The Hindu Law of Inheritance Act 1979. Repealed by Hindu Succession Act 1956.

(xi) The Child Marriage Restraint Act of 1929.

(xii) The Hindu Gains of Learning Act 1930. It makes all acquisitions by means of learning the separate property of the acquirer.

(xiii) The Hindu Women's Rights to Property Act 1937. It gives rights to inheritance to widows and strikes at the root of Mitakshara coparcenary. Since repealed by Hindu Succession Act of 1956.

(xiv) The Hindu Married Women's right to Separate Residence and Maintenance Act 1946 was repealed by Hindu Adoption and Maintenance Act 1956.

Sources of Hindu Law

The main sources of Hindu Law are Shrutis, Smritis and customs. The law of Smritis was empiric and progressive and in course of time several commentaries and digests were written on it, and then arose the schools of law which are operative in different parts of India. Juridical decisions in Hindu Law are also source by law and supersedes the commentaries.

General Principles of Inheritance

Prior to Hindu Succession Act 1956, there were two systems of inheritance amongst the Hindus in India namely the Mitakshara system and Dayabhaga system. Dayabhaga prevails in Bengal and Mitakshara in other parts of India. The Mitakshara recognises two modes of devolution of property namely survivorship and succession. The rule of survivorship applies to joint property and rule of succession applies to property held in absolute severalty by the last owner.

Order in Inheritance of Males According to the Mitakshara Law. The rules of inheritance laid down in the Mitakshara are followed by Bombay, Madras, Benaras and Mithila Schools but the rules in all states are not the same and differ to some extent. In determining the mode in which the property of a Hindu male governed by the Mitakshara law devolves on his death, the following is to be noted :

1. When the deceased was, at the time of death, a member of a joint and undivided family, technically called coparcenary, his undivided interest in the coparcenary property devolves on his coparceners, by survivorship.

2. Even if the deceased was joint at the time of his death, he might have left self-acquired or separate property; such property goes to his heirs by succession and not to his coparceners.
3. If the deceased was at the time of his death, the sole surviving member of a coparcenary property, the whole of his property, including the coparcenary property, will pass to his heirs by succession.
4. If the deceased was separate at the time of his death from his coparceners, the whole of his property, howsoever, acquired, will pass to his heirs by succession.
5. If the deceased was re-united at the time of his death, his property will pass to his heirs by succession.

Female Heirs. Before the Hindu Law of Inheritance Act 1929, the only females recognised as heirs were : 1. The widow 2. The daughter 3. The mother 4. The father's mother and 5. The father's father's mother. According to Hindu Law of inheritance 1929, the son's daughter, the daughter's daughter and the sister rank as heirs in Mitakshara Law.

Woman's Property (Stridhana)

The word 'Stridhana' is derived from 'Stri', woman and 'dhana' is property. It means woman's property. Manu has enumerated six kinds of Stridhana :

1. Gifts made before the nuptial fire.
2. Gifts made at the bridal possession, i.e., while the bride is being led from the residence of her parents.
3. Gifts made in token of love, i.e., those made through affection by her father-in-law, mother-in-law and other elders.
4. Gifts made by father.
5. Gifts made by mother.
6. Gifts made by brother/brothers.

The Stridhana is woman's absolute property and she has power to sell or give it away as she pleases even though it consists of land or house. Neither the husband, nor the son, nor father nor brother has power to use or to alienate the legal property of a woman. Every female, who succeeds as an heir, whether to a male or to a female, takes a limited estate in the property inherited by her. A widow or other limited heir is not a tenant for life, but is owner of the property inherited by her, subject to certain restrictions on alienation, and subject to its devolving upon the next heir of the last full owner upon her death. The whole estate is for the time being vested in her and she represents it completely. Where a widow sells the entire property left by her husband and from the sale proceeds acquires new property, the property so acquired partakes of the nature of her husband. To uphold an alienation by a widow or other limited heir, of the corpus of immovable property inherited by her, it should be shown that there was legal necessity or real necessity that existed or there was consent of the next reversioners to the alienation as would raise a presumption that the transaction was a proper one or it was a surrender of her whole interest in the whole estate in favour of the nearest reversioner at the time of alienation otherwise a widow or other limited heir cannot in any case dispose of by will, property inherited by her or any portion thereof, whether the property is movable or immovable.

Joint Hindu Family Coparceners and Coparcenary Property

A Joint Hindu Family as per Mitakshara Law, consists of all persons lineally descended from a common ancestor and includes their wives and unmarried daughters. A daughter ceases to be a member of her father's family on marriage and becomes a member of her husband's family. The joint and undivided family is the normal condition of Hindu Society. An undivided Hindu family is ordinarily joint, not only in estate, but also in food and worship. When there is a joint estate and the members of the family become separate in estate, the family ceases to be joint. However, mere severance in food and worship does not operate as a separation.

Coparcenary. A Hindu coparcenary is a much narrower body than the joint family. Generally speaking, it includes only those persons who acquire by birth an interest in the joint or coparcenary property. These are the sons, grandsons and great grandsons of the holder of the joint property for the time-being, in other words, the three generations next to the holder in unbroken male descent.

Ancestral Property. All properties, inherited by a male Hindu from his father, father's father or father's father's father are ancestral properties. The essential feature of ancestral property is that the sons, grandsons and great grandsons of the persons, who inherit it, acquire an interest in it by birth.

Separate Property. Property acquired in any of the following ways is the separate property of the acquirer. It is called "self acquired" property.

(i) ***Obstructed Heritage.*** Property inherited as obstructed heritage that is property inherited by a Hindu from a person, other than his father, father's father or father's father's father.

(ii) ***Gift.*** A gift of small portion of ancestral movable property made through affection by a father to his male issue.

(iii) ***Government Grant.*** Property granted by Government to a member of a joint family is the separate property of the donee unless it was intended for the benefit of the family.

(iv) ***Property Lost to Family.*** Ancestral property lost to the family and recovered by a member, without the assitance of joint family property.

(v) Income from separate property and purchases made from such income.

(vi) Share on partition by a coparcener, who has no male issue.

(vii) Property held by a sole surviving coparcener when there is no widow in existence who has power to adopt.

(viii) Separate earnings of a member of a joint family.

(ix) All acquisitions made by means of learning are declared by Hindu Gains of Learning Act 1930 to be separate property of the acquirer.

Separate Earnings. Income of a member of a joint family is his separate property if it has been obtained :

(i) by his own exertions; and

(ii) without any detriment to the father's estate that is without the aid of a joint family property.

Rights of Coparceners. No coparcener is entitled to any special interest in the coparcenary property nor is he entitled to exclusive possession of any part of the property. There is community of interest and unity of possession between all members of the family.

Who may Alienate Coparcenary Property. The following persons alone have power to alienate coparcenary property so as to pass a good title to the alienee :

1. The whole body of coparceners, when they are adults.
2. The manager under entertain notified circumstances.
3. The father to the indicated extent.
4. A sole surviving coparcener in indicated circumstances.

Debt. When son/sons are joint with his their father and debts have been contracted by the father in his capacity of a manager and head of the family for family purpose, the sons as members of the joint family, are bound to pay the debts to the extent of their interest in the coparcenary property. Like son, the grandson is also bound to discharge the debt contracted by grand father when there is no son living. The son's liability ceases when the debt had been contracted by father for his personal use. But the father of a joint Hindu family may sell or mortgage the joint family property, including son's interest therein, to discharge a debt contracted by him for his own personal benefit as such alienation binds the sons provided that the debt was antecedent to alienation and it was not incurred for any immoral purpose.

Partition and Reunion

The only property that can be divided on a partition is coparcenary property. Separate property cannot be the subject of partition nor can property which by customs descends to one member of the family to the exclusion of other members, e.g., a Raj or Principality.

In order to determine what property is available for partition, provision must first be made for joint family debts, which are payable out of the joint family property; personal debts of the father, not tainted with immorality; maintenance of dependant female members and of disqualified heirs and for the marriage expenses of unmarried daughters ; expenses on funeral ceremonies of the widow and mother of the last male holder when the property is partitioned between sons. After this is done, an account must be taken of the joint family property in the hands of the manager and other members of the family as per rules laid down in this regard.

Every coparcener is entitled to a share upon partition between the members of a joint family. Shares are allotted as under :

1. On partition between father and his sons, each son takes a share equal to that of the father.
2. When a joint family consists of brothers, they take equal share on partition.
3. Each branch takes per stirpes.
4. On the death of a coparcener leaving male issues, his right to a share on partition, is represented by his male issue provided such issue be within the limits of the coparcenary.

A father has the power to divide the family property at any moment during his life provided he gives his sons equal shares with himself and if he does so, the effect in law is not only a separation of the father from the sons but a separtion of sons *inter se*. Consent of sons is not necessary for the exercise of that power. A reunion in property so called can only take place between persons who were parties to the original partition. The effect of reunion is to remit the reunited members to their former status as members of the Joint Hindu Family.

Gifts. Gift consists in the relinquishment (without consideration) of one's own right (in property) and the creation of another man's right is completed on that other's acceptance of the gift but not otherwise. A Hindu may dispose of by gift his separate or self-acquired property subject in certain cases to the claims for maintenance of those whom he is legally bound to maintain. A female can gift away her Stridhan. The transaction of a gift is giving away of the property, possession by the person to whom gifted and acceptance of the gift by him.

Wills. Every Hindu, who is of sound mind and not a minor, may dispose of his property by will. A Hindu can not, however, gift property which he can not alienate by gift. For wills, a Hindu can dispose of by will his separate or self acquired property. The ancestral property can not be given by will.

The will made by a Hindu is required to be in writing, signed by the testator and attested by atleast two witnesses. No will can be revoked except in the prescribed manner.

Religious and Charitable Endowments. A Hindu, who is of sound mind and not a minor, may dispose of his property by gift or by will for religious and charitable purposes such as establishment and worship of an idol, feeding Brahmins and the poor ; performance of religious ceremonies like Shradha, Durga Puja, and the endownment of a university or a hospital. (The list cannot be exhaustive).

No writing is necessary to create an endowment except when the endowment is created by a will, in which case the will must be in writing, and witnessed by two persons. A Hindu may only express his wish and purpose and endow it. The dedication of property to religious or charitable uses may be complete or it may be partial. If complete, then a trust is created in favour of the charity.

Marriage. Marriage, according to the Hindu Law, is a holy union for the performance of religious duties. It is not a contract. However, a marriage brought about by force or fraud is altogether invalid. The ancient Hindu Law recognised eight forms of marriage of which four were approved forms and four un-approved. The approved forms were Brahma, Daiva, Asha and Prajapatya. The unapproved forms were Asura, Gandharva, Rakshasa and Paushacha. The only forms of marriage now recognised are Brahma and Asura. The marriage where father or other guardian of the bride gives the bride in marriage without receiving any consideration to the groom for giving the girl in marriage is Brahma marriage. But when he receives some consideration then it is 'Asura'. A Hindu could have any number of wives although he has a wife or wives living except where anti act had been passed.

Then while her husband is alive except on divorce. A remarriage of a Hindu Widow is expressly by legalised by Hindu widows Remarriage Act 1856. A girl can be given in marriage by following persons in order mentioned below :

(a) Father
(b) Paternal grandfather
(c) Brother
(d) Other paternal relations of the girl in order of propinguity.
(e) The mother.

The marriage of a male minor is not prohibited and his lawful guardian may consent to his marriage.

Marriage in Same Gotra. A marriage between persons belonging to different sub-divisions (Gotra) of the same caste is not invalid.

Prohibited Marriage. No marriage is valid if it is made between persons related to each other within the prohibited degrees unless such marriage is sanctioned by custom. Marriage, with a girl in his 'Sapinda' is prohibited. A man cannot marry a girl, if their common ancestor, being liased through his or her father, is not beyond the seventh in the line of ascent from him or her or if then common ancestor being liased through their mothers, is not beyond the fifth Line of ascent, from him or her. The marriage should be by invocation before the sacred fire, and *satpadi*.

Divorce. Divorce is not known to the general Hindu Law. The reason is that a marriage, from the Hindu point of view, creates an indissoluble tie between the husband and wife. Neither party can therefore, divorce, unless divorce is permitted by custom. The wife is bound to live with her husband and to submit herself to his authority and the husband is bound to live with his wife and to maintain her. He is also the lawful guardian to his minor wife.

Adoption. Adoption is not recognised by Mohammedan Law or Parsi Law but recognised by Hindu Law but here also at some places it is prohibited by customs. Ancient Hindu Law recognises five kinds of adopted sons. The modern Hindu Law recognises only two namely Dattaka and Kritrika. Dattaka is used throughout India and Kritrika is used in Mithila only. The object of adoption is religious to secure spiritual benefit to the adopter and his ancestor by having a son for the purpose of offering funeral Shradha and the second is secular, to secure an heir and perpetuate the adopter's name.

Who may Adopt. Every male may adopt provided he is otherwise competent to do so. A wife can also adopt to her husband but no other female can adopt. The man should be of sound mind and has attained the age of discretion, even though he may be minor and should have no son, grandson or greatgrand son, natural or adopted, living at the time of adoption. A wife can adopt to her husband after his death only.

Who may give in adoption. The only person who can lawfully give a boy in adoption are his father and mother. The persons giving in adoption must have attained the age of discretion and must be of sound mind.

Who may be Adopted. The person to be adopted must be a male; must belong to the same caste as his adopting father and must not be a boy whose mother, and the adopting father could not have legally married. A deaf or dumb cannot be adopted. The adoption must be before upanayana.

Ceremonies on Adoption. There should be physical giving and taking by Datta 'homam'. The adoption has the effect of transferring the adopted boy from his natural family into the adoptive family and confers on the adopted son the same rights and privileges in the family of the adoptee as the legitimate son. When a son is born after adoption to the adoptive father, the adopted son does not on a partition between him and the after born natural son share equally with him as he could have done if he were a natural son. The share differs in different states.

Minority and Guardianship

There is difference of opinion among the Hindu writers as to the age of majority under Hindu Law. Some think minority terminates at the completion of 15th year and according to others at the completion of 16th year. Guardians are of three classes.

1. Natural Guardian like father or husband.
2. Guardian appointed by father by a will.
3. Guardian appointed by District Court or High Court.

Maintenance

The aged parents, a virtuous wife and an infant child must be maintained even by doing a hundred misdeeds (Manu).

A Hindu is under a legal obligation to maintain his wife, his minor son (sons), his unmarried daughters and his aged parents, grandparents, grandsons and granddaughters. Section 23 of the Hindu Adoption and Maintenance Act 1956 lays down rules to the quantum of maintenance to be allowed interalia to a widow taking her position of living and Stridhana into account.

PART—II

HINDU PERIOD

5

AWARDING OF PUNISHMENT AND PROCEDURE OF JURISPRUDENCE

Dharma

Law is nothing but one's conduct according to the laid down rules that is the rules which have necessarily to be followed and whose breach would be punishable in one way or the other. In ancient India, the follow up of such rules was one's Dharma. This was subsequently called Jurisprudence and the present laws were narrated in the religious books in ancient India although religion was not only law but laws were a part of the religion. Dharma is one that leads to the development of mankind and their protection. Any society can work properly only if it conducts itself according to set rules of Dharma and restraint. Dharma covers all incidences of one's life. The ancient India, following the good conduct rules, was within the ambit of Dharma. Even the governance and rules of polity were based on Dharma. In fact Dharma inspires a person to conduct himself well. Dharma, therefore, involves two things—belief and action. Manu has indicated that God has provided that Raja should act as per Rajdharma and punish the guilty as punishment of guilty protects the other people. In fact it is not Raja but the Dharma which rules a country. It is one's Dharma only which accompanies one even after death whereas all other materialistic things are left over in the universe only although the present day concept of jurisprudence is based on one's conduct in this universe only and does not speak of Dharma or salvation in the context of following the laws as following of the laws is must and their breach leads to punishment. There is no place of religion or ethics in the present day laws as according to Dharma, one has to respect and bring up the parents but according to law it is not binding on anyone. As per Dharma, one has to devote oneself to the cause of almighty for attaining salvation but according to laws it is not essential. In our Shastras the indication is that Varuna (the emperor) conducts everyone according to righteousness, truth or laws and justice. The Smritis narrate these laws in detail and the place of Varuna and Divine has been taken over by jurisprudence. Here the justice starts from truth or Dharma and ends with punishing the guilty of the breach of the same. According to Vedas, justice has three ingredients—first is knower of laws, the second is laws themselves which are logically correct and the third is following of these laws.

Imparting of Justice

Brihaspati has said that the disputes should not be decided only on the basis of principles enunciated in Shastras but logic and common sense should also find place in it. Such logic and common sense is derived from Shastras. For example, there are four stages in deciding a crime—charges, defence, examination of defence and judgement. It is at the stage of examination of defence that one has to take the assitance of spirit, righteousness and Dharma to reach to the conclusion and decide the matter. During examination of the matter, the circumstantial evidence too has to be taken into account. Where evidence—documentary and oral—is not available then the judge has to decide the case on the basis of the common sense. Therefore, common sense usage is also an essential part in imparting justice in any given case and it is Dharma and usage, which found place in legislating laws and Rajshakti (Royal power) was used for enforcing the same. The Raja, therefore, has to have a legislative wing, which is Sabha/Samiti as per Vedas. That Sabha/Samiti formed laws keeping Dharma/usage into view and the Raja's men enforced these laws on the criminals with a view to provide protection to his people.

Awarding of Punishment

Once a crime has been established then the criminal has to be punished. In fact, it is to determine the punishment only that any criminal case is produced before the court and the Raj Shakti/Royal power is there to execute the punishment awarded. The punishment or 'Dand' has come from the word 'Stick' (Dand)' by which the Raja beats the criminal. Therefore, 'Dand' has become synonymous to punishment. Further, the present day 'polity' is synonymous to the words 'Raj Dharma', 'Raj Shastra', 'Dandniti', 'Rajniti', etc. Manu has called it Raj Dharma. According to Kautilya, 'Dand' is the source of protection of people. 'Dand' or punishment is a part of law. According to 'Shukra', punishment converts a person from bad conduct to good conduct and it is by punishment only that the crime is eradicated. Manu has indicated that various people in the country follow their respective Dharmas and it is by punishment, that the persons not following their Dharma are brought to the correct path. It is, therefore, punishment, which inspires a person to leave the path of wrong and adopt the path of righteousness. Kautilya too has stated that punishment is necessary for the well- being of the people and their protection from the criminals.

Purposes of Awarding of Punishment

Now for awarding a punishment for the crime, it has to be seen that it is commensurate with the crime—neither more as it shall be injustice to the criminal, nor less, lest the criminal is not dissuaded from repeating the crime. Punishment, therefore, involves three purposes :

1. First is to monitor the feelings of revenge in the human beings and to afford satisfaction to that feeling. When a person does wrong to another, the person, to whom wrong has been done, desires to have revenge for the same and such a desire continues to arise. Therefore, it is considered necessary to control such feelings. As a result of the same, the person to whom wrong has been done is not authorised to take revenge himself but he is granted justice by the court. Therefore, it is for the court to kill the feeling of revenge amongst the people directly and with a view to avoid repetition of the crime, to punish the criminal. But according to Brihaspati in some cases such authority for revenge has been bestowed in the people themselves too, for example, if a person of lower caste rebukes the person of an upper caste, then the upper caste person could punish the lower caste person and such punishment was not considered as a crime. But then it leads to many undesirable aspects coming up such as the punishment by the upper caste person may be stricter than the guilt or there shall not be uniformity in such punishment in the country. Therefore, the correct way is to keep all punishments in the hands of the Raja only.
2. The second purpose for grant of punishment is to avoid recurrence of such crimes in future. It was considered that because of the fear of punishment or seeing the punished person, people would avoid committing any crime and shall lead a moral life. If the criminals are not punished, then the strong person would make

the life of the weaker one difficult. In fact, it was only to avoid such happenings that the establishment of the state (*rajya*) came into being and the Raja was an elected person, whom everyone respected and who could control all others. The punishment, for the crimes is fixed by the Raja commensurate with the crime involved and such punishment could be even death. Kautilya has propagated amputation of parts of the body of the criminals so that the others could have a lesson and avoid causing such crimes. Moreover, such criminals find it difficult to live in society and such feeling shall force them not to commit such crime again and shall be deterrent for others.

3. The third purpose of imposition of punishment is self-reformation. Ancient Indian thinking had always pleaded for self-reformation. Manu has written that a criminal, after having undergone the punishment, becomes a person of good conduct like other such persons and becomes eligible for salvation as punishment washes off the sin of the crime. This is also called 'Self-repentence.'

This would show that the concept of imposition of punishment was with a view to eradicate immorality/crime from the society and to protect the people from such criminals. Since punishment (Dand) has been considered to be 'Dharma'. Only a person who is follower of Dharma can impose punishment (Dand). Therefore, only Raja has been considered as the proper authority for this purpose as he is above any temptation, non-biased and without any vested interest. But then the Raja has to be one, who acts as per Rajdharma. He has to accept the advice of the Sabha/Samiti; has to be truth-lover; pious with good advisers and law-knower and law-abiding. Also he is given the power of imposing punishment because he is all powerful and is able to prosecute the culprit and make him undergo the imposed punishment.

Types of Punishments

Although there are many kinds of punishments imposed on the criminals but in shastras, these have been included in following five kinds :

1. Pecuniary;
2. Physical;
3. Imprisonment;
4. Expulsion from the state, including his retention in a separate island under the Raja; and
5. Death.

Before imposing any punishment, Manu has indicated that the Raja should at first orally warn the criminal not to repeat the same. After which he is outcasted; on the levelling of more serious charges pecuniary, punishment is imposed on him or physical punishment that is amputation of some parts of the body or death sentence awarded depending on the degree of crime.

1. ***Pecuniary Punishment.*** This was imposed on the criminal in the shape of monetary payment to royal exchequer or as compensation to the person to whom wrong has been done. Such a punishment is imposed keeping in view the paying capacity of the criminal and should be commensurate with the crime involved. Primarily the amount of monetary punishment was deposited in royal exchequer and out of the same the Raja gave a part (as considered adequate) to the person to whom wrong had been done and the rest was retained in the exchequer and subsequently distributed amongst Brahmins. Such imposition was mainly in the cases of thefts, robbery, rape, etc. Even Kautilya has considered pecuniary punishment as a source of revenue to royal exchequer.

2. ***Physical Punishment.*** There are many kinds of physical punishments as amputation of each part of the body is connected with the crime involved. This includes flogging, hanging in upside-down condition, amputation of hands, feet, nose, ears, injuring the sensitive parts of the body, etc. Kautilya has pleaded strict punishment of amputation of various parts of the body.

3. ***Imprisonment.*** Imprisonment has been indicated as a punishment at very few places in the Smritis. This punishment involves hand-cuffing and foot-cuffing of the criminal and putting in the prison and then beating according to the crime involved. Such prisons were constructed on roads and highways, so that the travellers could watch the severe punishments being granted to the criminals and restrain themselves from involving in such crimes. Katyayana has indicated that when the Raja finds that a person cannot pay the pecuniary amount fined on him then such person should be put in prison and made to do work equal to the amount of punishment. Kautilya has described in detail the location of the prison; the design of the prison; who should man the prison; their duties and powers; the rules of the prison; what should be the punishment to be imposed on prisoners if they misbehaved with the imprisoned persons. The women prisoners should be kept separately in prisons. There was also the provision for keeping juveniles in the prisons. The prisoners had to live as per rules of the prison in

discipline and any breach of rules was severely taken. Ashoka's inscriptions indicate that the Dharma Mahapatra had to visit the prisoners and help their families in case of need. They also made the punishment milder if the incumbent was not able to stand it. According to historians, Hazrat Usman (700 A.D.), for the first time indicated that the prisoners should be kept in prison for varying periods depending on the crime involved and the hardened criminals should be physically tortured during this period so that when released on completion of the periods of prison, they got out duly reformed out of fear or otherwise and do not repeat the crime. Ashoka's inscription that the prison and prisoners should be visited by the Dharma Mahapatras also confirms that the imprisonment during ancient Hindu Periods too was for specified periods. Shukra also mentions about time-bound imprisonment.

4. ***Expulsion from Rajya.*** Expulsion from Rajya was also a kind of punishment imposed in ancient times. This punishment was imposed mainly by affluent Rajas so that the criminals going out of the Rajya lost the benefits of living lavishly in his Rajya. Such punishment was also imposed on Brahmin criminals, who, according to law, could not be put to death. This expulsion could be just where the incumbent be asked to go out of the rajya or was sent to an isolated part/island within the same Rajya with no facility of meeting his people. English had also made Andaman and Nicobar islands as prisons for the political offenders. Shukra has given a long list of the offenders on whom punishment of expulsion from Rajya could be imposed.

5. ***Death Sentence.*** Generally death sentence was not imposed even on hardened criminals, unless the criminal was beyond reformation and had been repeatedly committing crime. According to law, no risk could be taken in keeping such people in society as they only caused fear in the society and were of abuse only rather than of any use. Even now, according to law, the death sentence is granted in rarest of the rare cases. Although the matter has come time and again before the supreme court about the advisability of retaining such a provision in law, the court has held the necessity of this sentence. In Vedic era too, as already indicated, the first sentence was only warning; then pecuniary punishment; then physical punishment; then expulsion from the state and death sentence came only as the last resort. In crime against the Rajya, death sentence was a must. During Maurya period and immediately before that, the punishment to criminals was rather severe as a result of which there was hardly any crime.

Immunity from Punishment

1. The minors (below 15 years of age) were not awarded any punishment. Such persons were sent to reformatories for being reformed rather than making them hardend criminals by punishing them and keeping them with other seasoned criminals.
2. The relatives of the criminals were not punished for their crimes as crime is considered to be individual's fault which should be faced by him only and not others.
3. The crime committed in self-defence was excused.
4. The Brahmins were not sentenced to death.
5. The representatives of other countries, like ambassadors, messengers, etc., were not punished and were allowed to convey their master's message without any fear. In *Ramayan*, Vibheeshana had advised Ravana not to kill Hanuman, although he had killed his son and others, in view of his being an ambassador of Ram—

   नीति विरोध न मारिये दूता।

6. In some situations, the individuals themselves used to punish the guilty such as a money-lender could punish a money-taker on his inability to repay the money.
7. The Varna of the culprit was seen before a punishment could be imposed. For the similar crime, the Brahmin, Kshatriya, Vaisya or Shudra were punished differently viz for theft a Shudra was punished to pay eight times the loss, a Vaisya sixteen times, Kshatriya thirty two times and Brahmin was required to pay sixty four times. This was based on the fact that the knowledge of crime involved in theft was less to a Shudra compared to other three Varnas; to Vaisya less than the other two Varnas; to Kshatriya less than a Brahmin and a Brahmin knows it most and still committed the crime. However, in case of death sentence, Brahmin was not killed and was only expelled from the Rajya. Even Brahmins have been given less punishment in the first instance only. In case of repetition of crime, the death sentence could be imposed on Brahmin too.

Repentence. Repentence too was a kind of self-imposed punishment. This is in two kinds of sins—degradation in the Varna like theft of gold, to block the process of education, and intercourse with prohibited relations, etc. Then there are two kinds of sins—one having been done intentionally and the other having been done unknowingly.

The punishment is more in the cases of crimes done intentionally and one is left with warning when the crime has been committed unintentionally or repentence is considered adequate in the latter case. Repentence is done when one accepts having committed crime and undertakes not to repeat the same. Once Balram had killed a Shudra sitting on the seat of a Brahmin. Now for a Kshatriya to kill such a person is not a crime as he was not following the Varna Dharma of the Shudra but in this case the Brahmin had himself authorised him to occupy his seat in his absence. So Balram was found to be guilty of having killed him without checking up the full facts and he had to repent for the same. It has been indicated that the Raja could punish a person when the guilty did not repent for the crime done.

Law Courts

The courts of modern times had been differently called in different Smritis. Manu, Shukra and Yajnavalkya have called it Sabha and the judge hearing the case has been indicated as Sabhasad. Katyayana has called it Dharmadhikaran as the crime was nothing but breach of canons of Dharma and a tribunal hearing such cases was Dharmadhikaran. Dharmasthan, Dharmasan, Adhikaran, etc., have also been used for courts. There were two kinds of courts —one was where the Raja acted as the judge whereas the others were at regional or local levels where Raja's men heard the cases. The court of the Raja was the supreme court. In this court either the Raja himself was the judge or when he was not able to attend the same, another person of his confidence was asked to act in his absence and he was called Chief Justice. The location of such court, the qualities of the chief justice, the cases which could be heard there, what would be the duties and powers of the Raja to disburse justice, etc., are discussed ahead.

Qualities of the Raja as a Chief Justice. The Raja sits in the court as chief justice to check the crime in the Rajya. With a view to see that he imparts justice correctly, he should be truth-loving, religious-minded, God fearing, pious, non-greedy, rageless, intelligent and learned, knowing the law fully. He should treat everyone equally and should not have vested interest in anyone. His judgements should not only be non-biased but appear to be such too.

Powers of the Chief Justice. Since the court of the Raja as chief justice was supreme and no appeals lay against the judgement of the chief justice, the Raja had to impose punishment after going into the case thoroughly. Although the Raja was supposed to be doing no wrong, he was tied down with certain checks, such as he had to consult the learned persons meant in his council for this purpose. He could not go against the provision of the Dharmashastras and where he did so, he had to give reasons for the same. For this purpose, the Raja was supposed to be adequately learned. The Raja had to hear the case in the court and not in isolation as in isolation he could be tempted to be biased. The Raja, as chief justice, had appellate jurisdiction too and the decision of the Raja was final. Such a court was located in the capital of the kingdom so that the Raja could easily attend it. The bell arranged by Jehangir to hear any complaint is ideal for the Raja to listen to the complaint and award his judgement then and there. The emperor had small Rajas under him. These Rajas were autonomous in their *Rajyas* but in case of their judgements, appeals lay in the court of the emperor. Where the Raja, not being in a position to attend the court appointed a chief justice to hear the cases, there he used to appoint three learned persons to act as bench of the court and the decision of majority was considered as correct decision. These judges were generally Brahmins as they knew the Dharmashastras perfectly compared to the persons of other Varnas but the persons of other Varnas (other than Shudras) could also be appointed if they were considered learned enough by the Raja. Even where the Raja attended the court, he was assisted by three other judges. At times, the number of these assistants could be five or seven too but they were in odd number so that the decision of the majority could be accepted by the Raja. These judges had the same qualities as the Raja as a chief justice. Besides the Raja and the assistants, the Law Minister and the Purohit used to attend the court of the Raja and could guide the Raja where such guidance was sought.

Proceedings of the Court. The court was generally held in the morning after the Raja was free from his daily chores. The proceedings of the court were also based on Dharma. The Raja used to come to the court fully dressed. He had to pay respects to the Purohit, etc., in the court. The Raja had to be religious, capable, praiseworthy, respectful to people, conquerer, treating everyone equally, etc.

In the proceedings, there were four parts as per Narada— First the receipt of complaint; second to place it under one or more provisions of laws ; third hearing both the parties (the petitioner and the defendant) and fourth to award the judgement. In the entire proceedings, the petitioner and the defendant were given chance to produce written and oral evidence in support of their case. Some categories of persons like minor, invalid, busy in religious jobs, etc., were exempted from personally appearing in the court. The case could be reopened too if some new evidence became available to be produced. There was also provision for the pleading of the case in above cases and other cases through a pleader and his fee was fixed according to each case which was equal of one-fifth, two-fifth, one-tenth, one sixteenth and one-twentieth of the amount of the case. Such persons had obviously to be well-versed with Dharma and usages. Anyone demanding higher fees than above was punishable. The judgement given in the case was, however, applicable to the plaintiff and defendant only and not to the pleader.

Local Courts. For deciding the personal matters there were local courts and were primarily decided by the judge as a mediator. There were also courts—Civil and Criminal—at regional levels. The cases in these courts were decided by the judges appointed by the Raja.

Other Courts. The courts, other than the court of the Raja, were of various kinds like those established in villages and towns and mobile courts, which held the proceedings in turn in various villages to whom the cases pertained. These were courts established by the Raja. Such courts issued the judgement under the seal of the Raja. Such courts were established at District and Regional levels. The decisions in such courts were generally based on local usages. There were also courts called family courts, which decided cases of disputes between various families. Then there were courts dealing with the cases pertaining to traders, craftsmen and persons of other vocations. The decisions in these courts were taken on Dharma and usages pertaining to particular vocation. These courts were held by judges appointed by the Raja. There were courts for ten villages, hundred villages, four hundred villages and eight hundred villages. In these courts, there were three ministers and three judges and they decided cases as per procedure laid down for the Raja's courts based on Dharma and usage. It appears that these courts being for the collection of ten, hundred, four hundred and eight hundred villages, would be having appellate jurisdiction from smaller courts to higher courts and the last appeal lay before the Raja.

Procedure of Jurisprudence (Maurya Period)

By the start of the Christian era that is during the Maurya period, the procedure of jurisprudence and evidence had fully developed in India.

I Petition and Defence

The first step in the proceedings of any case in local courts, regional courts or Raja's court was the presentation of the petition. The petitioner bowed before the judge and then the judge asked for the plaint to be narrated without any fear. After examining the viability of the plaint, the same was admitted. Utmost sanctity was placed in the correctness of the plaint as on its having been proved, the defendant was punished otherwise the plaintiff was taken to task for filing a wrong plaint. All plaints arise as a result of desire, rage and greed. The plaint could be wrong or right depending upon the production of proof for the same and the examination and conclusion by the judge. The plaint indicated the plaintiff's name, father's name, village and caste to which he belonged, and the date of filing the plaint. The plaint had to be brief and to the point. This also indicated the place of occurrence of the complaint, the defendant responsible for the guilt, his name, father's name, address, etc. Then the complaint was indicated. After considering the plaint, it was noted down on court papers in open. The plaint was necessarily filed in the correct court—vocation court, regional court, local court or Raja's court. It would indicate that jurisdiction—original or appellate, etc.,—had been clearly defined for all courts. In case the plaintiff was not able to produce evidence —oral or documentary—in support of his continution, the same was dismissed. The plaint should be correctly made out as per subject matter. It should not be ambiguous; should indicate clearly the claimed amount involved in civil cases; the complaint was covered by existing laws; the plaint should not include irrelevant matters; it should be legibally narrated. The plaint could be supplemented before the defendant projected his defence. Afterwards the signature of the plaintiff were obtained and the plaint was put in a sealed cover in the court. If the defendant did not raise any objection on the plaint, then the same was treated to have been accepted by the defendant.

II Defendant

Then the defendant was summoned by the court. The defendant was told about the plaint and he was required to reply to the points raised in the plaint. These replies were given in the presence of the plaintiff. The reply was to the point and not very long. It was in the language which could be understood by the plaintiff. If after being summoned, the defendant did not appear before the judge or was not able to offer his defence, he could be punished. The replies of the defendants were of four kinds :

1. Acceptance of the plaint by the defendant.
2. Non-acceptance of the plaint by the defendant.
3. The defendant accepeted the charge but projected his defence for the occurrence of the charge levelled against him.
4. The defendant stating that the matter had already been considered and he had won it in that case.

According to Kautilya, the defendant had to submit his defence within three fortnights after which he was considered to be having no defence and the case was decided against him. Persons, who were mad without mental balance; down with intoxication; infirm; minor and hardened criminals were not considered fit to submit defence. Further, the replies not to the point; irrelevant or too brief or too long; or ambiguous were not entertained. Otherwise the defence was noted down. The provision of *res judicata* (Filing a plaint which had already been decided) was there in ancient time. This procedure exists even today.

During the arguments of the case by the plaintiff and defendant, proofs—documentary and oral—in support of the case or against the case, were produced. These proofs were of four kinds—written; possession of the property involved; witnesses and circumstantial evidence. The first three were, however, generally relied upon.

III Evidence

(i) Documentary Evidence. Out of these also written documentary evidence was given top priority. The prudent people always believed in written documents and not on any oral assurance as the oral assurance could be available till the witness lived whereas the documentary evidence always held good. In case of written documents, however, it was seen that the same had not been got written under duress; had been written without deception, without telling lie and after making the position known to the signatory fully. Such documents were also got witnessed. This is exactly the position even today. Also such documentary evidence could not be made by mentally deranged, mad, infirm and minors. In case of old documents (including the documents granted by the Government), their bonafide (genuineness) was got ascertained before a decision could be arrived at on the case at the time of filing of case.

(ii) Defacto Possession. Possession of the property was considered more forceful even to the documentary evidence such as if a property was being used by the occupier for the last over twenty years and its real owner had not objected to the same, then the occupier was considered to be the owner of the property. Similarly in case of movable property, one lost the ownership in ten years period. Such a provision is available even today and is called the right of easement. Such right did not, however, pass to the occupier in case he was keeping the property as a pledged one; the property belonged to a minor, or the property belonged to the Raja. In case of immovable property, the occupier did not get the right of easement if it was educational, bonded, won, got in dowry, got as a result of will as also the property belonging to the people without offspring.

(iii) Witnesses (Oral Evidence). The third type of proof is oral evidence. According to Panini, the witness is one who had himself witnessed the factual position. Where the documentary evidence and defacto possession were not available, then the court had to depend on the oral evidence produced by the two sides. The witness had to be a man of confidence, a man of character, God fearing, meditator, belonging to high family, truth speaker, without any suspicion, without any greed, should be having son, should be a donor, intelligent, frank, religious-minded and acceptable to both sides. Brahmins had been accepted as reliable witnesses by both sides. Women, minor, old (above 80 years), gambler, drunkard, mad, sinner, forger, dumb, deaf, killer of Brahmins friend, enemy, thief, robber, out caste persons, etc., were not accepted as witnesses. If the witnesses spoke contradictory to each other then such witnesses were discarded or the evidence of the more confident person was taken into account. In the case of crimes pertaining to rape, robbery, (in house or out of house), etc., any person could be a witness. This was in view of the fact that such persons, as were available on site, could only offer themselves as witness and not others. The witnesses, however, were required to be more than one and were to be in odd number viz five, seven, three so that the evidence of the majority could be relied upon. Even a single witness was entertained, if acceptable to both the sides. The witnesses were interrogated by the other party as also by the judge. The witnesses were summoned by the judge and they spoke under oath as is being done even today. Before the start of the evidence, the opposition party could question the bonafides of the witnesses. Such question could not be raised after the evidence had started. Also the bonafides of the witnesses could not be questioned on irrelevant grounds.

Before starting to project evidence, the witness had to take oath before a Brahmin, water, or fire as per Kautilya. The evidence was obtained in open court before both the parties and questions were mostly asked by the judge/Raja only. In case of telling lie by the witness, he was punished for the same. The witness was not allowed to talk keeping his head downwards, talking irrelevant things or replying to questions not asked. Such person also became punishable. This punishment could be pecuniary as also physical. Self-contradiction by the witness was not accepted and such witness was treated as liar and punished accordingly. In case all witnesses spoke the same facts, then the evidence was accepted. The names of the witnesses had to be mentioned by both the parties before the arguments started and new witness could not be produced after the arguments had started unless such evidence was very important for the case. The matter was not decided on the basis of the witness alone, but all other evidence—documentary, defacto occupier and circumstantial—was also taken into account.

(iv) Circumstantial evidence and godly evidence. Godly evidence was taken to prove a case if someone jumped in fire and came out alive, then his evidence was accepted. The circumstantial, evidence was taken in case of murder, the finger-prints at the place of murder and the criminal, any proof of his belonging left by the criminal at the place of crime, etc. The circumstantial evidence was taken into account when the other forms of evidence—documentary, defacto possession, or oral evidence—were not available.

IV Decision and Appeal

The next (fourth) and the last part of any case is to give a decision. The decision is arrived at after having considered the documentary evidence, defacto occupation, oral evidence, usages, conduct of the parties, acceptance and rejection of evidence by the opposite party, oath, circumstantial and Godly evidence. This is also called 'judgement'. If the plaintiff is able to prove his point, then he is considered to have won the case and where he is not able to make his point, the judgement is notified against him. Where the case could not be decided by any of the evidences, then the order of the Raja was only accepted as 'king can do no wrong'. This decision was conveyed to the victorious party and was, therefore, called 'victory order' also. This judgement contained the plaint, the defence by the defendant, the evidence produced by both the parties and the reason for arriving at the decision and was signed by the judge under his seal. Vashishtha has indicated that the judgement should also mention the previous decision given in similar cases. Now-a-days too the cases are mostly decided on the basis of case-laws or precedents.

Appeal. There was a provision for filing appeal against the judgement of the court in higher courts. The last appeal lay in the court of the Raja. When the case originated in Raja's court itself, then there was no scope for any appeal and the decision of the Raja was considered final. In some cases no appeal could be filed but an application for review by the high court could he made. In such appeal, only point of law was looked into and the facts of the case were not re-examined as such examination had already been done in the lower court and it was accepted by the higher court too. The Raja could also review the decisions given by the former Raja. If the decision appealed against was found to be against the canons of law or Dharma, then the judge, who delivered that judgement was also taken to task. Although there is no specific mention of the level of the courts in which the original or appellate jurisdiction lay, yet from the fact that there were courts for 10 villages, 100 villages and 1000 villages, it can be presumed that these were the levels of appeals in various courts.

Court Fees. It is noticed that no court fee was required to be paid for approaching the courts with plaints. There was, however, a provision for the payment of fines by the parties. This would only amount to the pecuniary punishment and not court fees. The Raja used to charge the per cent from the money taken and five per cent from moneylender in case of suits pertaining to non-payment of loan taken and decreed for payment by the court. Further, the defendant had to pay fine if he did not appear in the court on having been summoned. This encouraged the people to approach the court for redress of their grievances and not to disobey the court when summoned or when decree awarded.

6

CIVIL AND CRIMINAL CASES ACCORDING TO THE SMRITIS

Laws

In Satyayuga, there were no disputes as all people were resourceful, content and of good character but when pollution started creeping in, necessity of formation of laws to deter the guilty arose and so laws were framed. Then for the enforcement of laws the royal power was required and in this way the Government came into being. Manu has indicated that in this universe, there is small number of gentlemen and there are plenty of people with greed, rage, desires and love, and it is these people, who with a view to fulfil their desires, harassed the gentlemen and to eradicate such people only that laws had to be framed. Contrary to present thinking, the Indian view was not restricted to materialistic life only but the spiritual well-being was also taken into account. Therefore, Dharma has been made the basis of following the laws and even in committal of crime. The Raja, the Purohit, the law minister and all judges were supposed to be learned in Laws. Law was based on usages apart from Dharma although Dharma was inherent in usages too. In our Smritis, laws, procedures and punishments have been narrated in the same book. The aggrieved party had to approach the court or Raja with his grievance. This was called plaint (व्यवहार पत्र अथवा विवाद-पत्र). These plaints arose out of pecuniary loss caused to a person or some violence caused against him or breach of civil and criminal laws. This clearly indicates that our Smriti writers were well-versed with the nature of plaints being either civil or criminal.

Criminal Cases

The criminal cases included calling abuses, rebukes; causing insult to a person; causing physical harm to a person by beating, etc, ; theft, and rape.

Abuse. In abusing a person, if only one has been abused then the abuser is punished and when two persons have entered into abusing each other, then both are liable to punishment if it is not possible to ascertain who abused first. Then the punishment differed from Varna to Varna; whereas Brahmin was not punished and Kshatriya could be punished selectively, the Vaish could be punished mildly but Shudras were punished rigorously.

Physical harm. A reading of the chapter on causing physical harm by another would indicate that the present Indian Penal Code (Sections 319 to 377) has been copied from the Smritis only. According to Kautilya, the physical harm to one person by another is from touching him to injuring him by hand or arm/weapon. Narada has put the physical harms into there categories—first, second and third. The first kind of harm is to raise hand or weapon to harm anyone; the second type of harm is to attack by surprise and to injure someone is the third type of harm. Then these harms have been given in detail and the punishment to be given for each harm is prescribed too. The punishment is different from harm caused by Varnas of different persons and to persons of different Varnas. For small harms like spitting on a person or for raising hand or weapon to cause injury, pecuniary punishment has been prescribed. Death sentence is prescribed for causing death of another person. If in causing someone's death, several persons are involved then all the persons are punished by death sentence. Harming an animal like cow, goat also led to pecuniary punishment according to the cost of the animal. Similarly, cutting the others' trees also was punishable and commensurate cost had to be paid. In case no evidence was available for such crimes then the Raja/judge used to impose punishment on the basis of circumstantial evidence. In cases of pecuniary punishments, the money had to be paid to the aggrieved party as also an equal amount to the Government exchequer.

For self defence or defence of animals, etc., force could be used and the harm caused to the other person in such use of force, was not punishable but such force had to be commensurate with the crime likely to be caused viz. if a person wants to kill another person then the other person could kill him but if one person had been *gheraoed* and not attacked then the person could not be killed by the *gheraoed* person. The killing of Brahmin was not allowed even if he caused death of the other person unless the Brahmin had been killed under the right of self-defence. A person defaming the Raja was to lose his tongue as punishment.

Theft. In case of thefts, pecuniary punishment was given and on repeated thefts the hands were amputated. There is however, a big list of the kinds of thefts and in some cases like the theft of Government treasury, even death sentence could be imposed. In other theft cases, at first pecuniary punishment was imposed. On repetition of the same a hand was cut and again on repetition he was punished with death sentence. In death sentences, there was provision for killing by gibbetting, hanging, throwing in river, burning in fire or by axing. Short measurement, short weighing, misappropriation of money by Government inspectors, less return by gold-smith, etc., were punishable by pecuniary punishments. An alien committing theft was expelled from the Rajya after snatching the stolen as also his other belongings. Any one giving refuge to a thief was also punished like the thief.

Rape. Rape has been defined in Smritis as having illicit relation with other's wife. Such rape is of three kinds—by force, by cheating and by inspiring the woman to have sex. When a man has sex with a woman against her desire in isolation or rapes a woman, while asleep, or mentally unsound, then it is rape and is punishable accordingly. Inviting a woman by a man in his house, intoxicating her and then having sex with her is also rape by deception. When a man invites a woman by signals to quench the thirst of sex then it is third kind of rape. When a man had sex with an unmarried woman with her consent, then it did not amount to rape but then such person had to accept such action and compensate such lady by paying money or giving ornaments, etc. A person having illicit relation with an unmarried girl against her desire, was punishable by amputation of his fingers and on repetition amputation of hand and on third repetition a death sentence was imposed. A man could have sex with prostitute, maid servant, etc., but such sex with a maid servant by force was punishable by pecuniary punishment. Illicit relation with a 'keep' who is other's wife, was also treated as rape. In some cases sex was not allowed at all viz. with mother, mother's sister, mother-in-law, maternal aunt, father's brother's wife, friend's wife, sister, sister's friend, pupil's wife, guru's wife, daughter-in-law, daughter, refuge seeking woman, *sanyasin*, *ayah*, and the woman of higher caste. In case of illicit relation with any of the above women, the genital was amputated and the person was killed on repetition. In case of homosexuality, pecuniary punishment was imposed. A bad character lady having illicit relation with a person by going to his house, was treated as prostitute and no punishment was imposed on the man having illicit relation with such a woman.

Forcible Crime. Forcible committal of sex (rape) or kidnapping, or harming other by force is punishable. Such crime can be killing a person, robbery, kidnapping another person or harming another person by force in any manner. Destroying other's harvests, etc., is also crime and punishable according to laid down punishment. A group of persons committing such crime were individually held punishable for such crime and all were imposed sentence according to the crime involved such as in case of murder, all such persons were punished with death sentence, and so on. Even anyone causing abetment in such crime was punishable equally.

Civil Suits

Civil suits are based on the breach of contract agreement, etc., and includes non-payment of borrowed money, non-fulfilment of contracts and agreements. Sale/purchase by force or by manipulation were illegal. Similarly, snatching money by intoxicating a person or from intoxicated person, patient, person shocked by a close relation's death, minor or from a person, who is not the owner of the property, is illegal.

Debt. Repayment of debt or borrowed money comes first in this category as in ancient times money lending and borrowing was on personal basis from the money lenders, and there were no banks, etc. Such cases included non-payment of borrowed money, asking for repayment of money without having paid it, and breach of agreements entered into for this purpose came in this category.

Such cases indicated :

1. Which borrowed money was repayable.
2. Which other borrowed money was repayable.
3. Who has to repay the money.
4. How to repay the money.
5. Where to make payment of such money.
6. The conditions of agreement to be followed while taking money and while repaying the same.

In case of death of the father, the sons or grandsons had to repay the money borrowed by the father / grandfather. All sons, who were heirs to the father's property, were liable to pay debt of the father in proportion to the property owned by them.

Interest. Manu has mentioned four kinds of interest payable for the borrowed money :

(1) Compound interest, (2) Fixed amount of interest payable after certain period, (3) Through labour, (4) Through bonded labour.

Charging interest was, however, never looked upon as an honourable practice. Then some rates of interest chargeable were fixed by the Government and charging interest higher than that, or charging more than double the amount lended or continue charging the amount of interest for long periods were considered as mean jobs. Vashishtha has specified 1/80th of the principle per month as the reasonable rate of interest. This rate, however, applied when something was pledged in consideration of borrowing money. In case of non-pledging of anything, the rate of chargeable interest was to be 2 per cent from Brahmin; 3 per cent from Kshatriya; 4 per cent from Vaisya and 5 per cent from Shudra, per month. These rates of interest were generally fixed but were changeable according to the usage prevalent in certain countries or locally or in varied situations. The persons involved in performing Yagyas for a long period, ill persons students studying in gurukulas, minors and infirm persons were exempted from making payment of interest and were required to return the principal only. Similarly, interest was not charged from a friend. Pledging property for borrowing money has been prevailing since long. These pledgings were in the shape of immovable and movable property. In case of repayment of the principal with interest, such pledged property had to be released and in case it was not released then the money-lender was treated as a thief and sentenced accordingly. In case of death of the borrower, his heirs could repay the amount with interest and get the pledged property released.

Surety. Production of a surety while borrowing money was very much in prevalence in ancient times. In case of breach of surety, the court used to get the borrowed money repaid. In case of the death of a surety, his heirs were not responsible for fulfilling the surety and surety was considend as a personal bond only. The moneylender could get the landed money back by persuading the borrower on religious ground ; by threatening him; by use of force (not injuring the persons); by manipulations; by resorting to filing suit in court of law. The money lending and borrowing had to be brought in black and white, giving the rate of interest and the period within which the debt could be discharged. On repayment of the borrowed money, such document had to be returned to the borrower. If a borrower had to pay back borrowed money to several persons then it was returned on the priority on the basis of Varna, i.e. first to Brahmin, then to Kshatriya and then to Vaisya. Within the persons of same Varna, the borrowed money was returned first to the person from whom it was taken earlier, and so on.

Mortgage. Several words like 'निक्षेप', 'उपनिधि', 'न्यास', 'धरोहर* etc., have been used in this regard. This is in the shape of animals, ornaments, property, etc, pledged to the moneylender to assure him of the bonafides of the borrower. In case of loss of the pledged article, its cost with interest thereon is returned to the borrower.

Partnership. When two or more persons enter into an agreement to start a business by investing money, it is called partnership. The profit or loss is distributed in proportion to the shares of the individuals. Such partnership should be amongst people having trust in each other, who should be honest ; intelligent and hardworking. All terms of investment, working persons, their shares, etc, are incorporated in the 'Partnership deed'. All policy decisions should be jointly taken with the consent of all partners. In case of breach of the conditions of partnership, the person causing breach could be sued in the court of law.

Industrial Disputes. These disputes arise out of non-payment of salary. An agreement is entered into between the employee and the employer specifying the salary to be paid, the date on which salary be paid each month, whether salary is to be paid in cash or kind, the job required to be done by the employee etc. Both have to respect these conditions and any breach by either party could be brought to the notice of the court for decision for enforcing the conditions of employment. If the payment of salary is not predetermined then the employee is entitled to take one-tenth of the earnings of the employer from production— in factory and from field—, milk, etc. This could be varied in case food and clothes are provided by the employer. A labourer had to make up for the loss caused due to his negligence. Smritis prescribe various kinds of jobs undertaken by the employees such as labourer, writing work, milching the cows, work in farms, etc., but the employees could not be minor.

Sales and Purchases Disputes. Manu has indicated that in case of any wrong committed and detected within ten days of the sale or purchase of a thing, then the same could be returned within ten days of such sale or purchase. Some Smritis, however, prescribe different periods in respect of different commodities such as seeds, iron and steel, clothes, animals, diamonds, maid servants/servants, etc. This period ranges from one day to one month. Some Smritis also prescribe return of money for the commodities sold at full rate if returned on the same day or with 1/30th and 1/15th deduction, if returned after two or three days. The metals could be tested by putting in furnace about the base content. A seller, who did not deliver the commodity after having obtained the cost of the same then the court arranged the delivery with interest. The sale/purchase of an immovable property was not considered final till the approval of neighbours or near relations of purchaser/seller had been obtaind. It means that like present time, in ancient times too the right of pre-emption was in existence.

Kautilya has included marriage too in such sale/purchase contracts and in case of any deception in marriage such deception was punishable by court. In case of Brahmins, Kshatriyas, and Vaisyas no case lay for any change after the marriage having taken place. In the case of Shudras, however, the marriage could be dissolved before consummation. In the case of Brahmin, Kshatriya and Vaisya, the marriage could be dissolved in case of any shortcoming found in either of the spouses on first consummation. In case of sale of a commodity by a person, who is not its actual owner like mortgaged property, stolen property, commodity taken on loan, the court can punish such person by pecuniary punishment payable to the real owner, as also to Government exchequer or after compensating the purchaser and Government exchequer to arrange for the return of the commodity to its real owner. In case a stolen commodity is sold at very low rate compared to its cost in the market, then the purchaser is also treated as a thief and punished. If the real owner of a stolen commodity finds his commodity in the possession of a person, he could approach the court and get him apprehended and in case the property is found to be belonging to the complainant, then the property is got returned to him and the purchaser is not held guilty but the seller is apprehended and made to compensate the purchaser and the Government exchequer. In case the seller too names someone else then that someone is caught and the seller is acquitted, and so on.

All such cases are in present times included in civil matters. All such matters involve execution of contracts or agreements in one form or the other and in case of any deception in the transaction, the punishment was generally pecuniary payable to the decepted as also to the Government exchequer.

Other Matters. The matters pertaining to categories other than criminal and civil are other matters such as donation. Narada has divided such matters in four parts :

1. What can be donated;
2. What cannot be donated;

3. Legal donation;
4. Illegal donation;

Yajnavalkya has clearly indicated that the extent of donation should be such as may not effect the running costs of the donor's own family. In a family comprising of sons and grandsons and others, all donation of all householders or the donation of son/grandson or wife is not permitted. Narada has also agreed with this provision. The mortgaged belonging to the owner jointly with others or the property already given in donation cannot be further donated. The property once donated could not be taken back except where the same had been given to a non-deserving person taking him as deserving such as the cow to be donated to a Brahmin if by mistake is donated to a person of another varna, it could be taken back and then given to the deserving person that is a Brahmin.

Disputes about Boundaries. In such matters generally disputes pertaining to boundaries of farms are included. Encroachment in others' land, not parting with the land belonging to others and not giving the proper share of land to others in case of division of ancestoral property, etc., fall in this category. Such matters are generally settled by the village Panchayats and in case the Panchayat is not able to settle then the matter is brought to the court. The boundaries of the land are of various kinds such as by trees, by canal, pond, etc., by walls made of bricks or as settled by the concerned parties and as settled by the Government. Such boundaries should be brought to the notice of the successors too so that the persons in each generation could know it and is not disputed in future. The boundaries of personal understanding are alright so far as the present dispute incumbents are alive but could be disputed by the successors. It is, therefore, better to provide other boundaries in life-time of the incumbents. The disputes of boundaries are decided by the local panchayats as they are generally familiar with the correct situation otherwise such disputes are decided on the basis of documentary evidence, oral evidence, circumstantial evidence or on the basis of the defacto occupier of the property like the other cases pertaining to properties. The disputes of boundaries amongst the people of two villages are settled by the Panchayats of the two villages and if they are not able to settle such disputes then the court decided on the basis of documentary, oral or circumstantial evidence keeping in view the defacto occupier of the same. In case no evidence is available then the court decided under its discretionary powers. In the matters pertaining to boundaries, a person offering false evidence is liable to punishment. A person destroying the existing signs of boundaries is punishable by snatching the property from him. Snatching others' property under duress is also punishable but the proof of agreement under duress is to be produced by the complainant. There were rules pertaining to provision of windows, doors, drainage, sewerage, construction of wells, etc, and these were generally according to customary usage. Kautilya has indicated in detail the rules pertaining to construction of houses / buildings. For example, if a person causes harm to others by opening the window of his house towards other's, he could be checked and if he does not agree then court could punish such a person. This would indicate that there were detailed bye laws about construction of houses in ancient period, perhaps more exhaustive than what they presently are.

Matrimonial Matters. Such matters have generally been indicated in our Smritis as pertaining to morality and not legality as the marriage once having taken place was treated as sacrosanct and could not be dissolved except in cases of deception about the consummating capacity of either spouse detected on first consummation of marriage. Kautilya has, however, given legal colour too to such matters. Such matters pretain to matrimonial relation of the spouses; impotence, matrimonial Dharma; love making and divorce. Narada recognises a marriage held with the mutual consent of the boy and the girl. Kautilya has narrated in three chapters of Arthashastra the rules relating to the relation of husband and wife, and marriages. Their duties, physical relations, remarriage, widow marriage and divorce. The issueless widow can have son from her brother-in-law or near relation of the husband with the permission of the guru and the relations. After having got a son, the widow could not have physical relation with such a person.

In regard to divorce, we do not get much material in Vedas and initial books as the dissolution of marriage was not allowed after the *saptpadi.* We, however, have to understand the difference between the divorce and legal dissolution of marriage. As already indicated, the husband or wife could dissolve the marriage on the other spouse being impotent, etc. Otherwise even when the husband or wife goes away from the other spouse, the marriage is not dissolved. Kautilya has, however, indicated in *Arthashastra* that the marriage could be dissolved with the mutual consent of both husband and wife and not with the desire of either of them. There were, however, some specified conditions under which the marriage could be dissolved even by mutual consent.

Division of Property. (Law of Succession) The law of succession was known as Dayabhag (दयाभाग) division of ancestral property. In this case the ancestral property becomes the property of some relations of the owner. According to Smritis, the father's property could pass to sons only. Smritis also provide for the proportion in which the property could pass to the sons / grandsons, etc. The succession of property could be by will of the owner; by purchasing the same; by division amongst the successors; possession by force and by appropriating to oneself the movable property. The succession has been recognised as from birth itself. A wife or a son does not own a property when father is alive. Manu has, in addition, prescribed servant too, who cannot own a property.

The succession to property could be during the father's life-time, with his consent, or after the death of the father. The male could become major at the age of sixteen and female at the age of twelve. The minor could also succeed to father's property but it was kept under custody of any old man till he became major. The property could be movable or immovable. The movable could be in the shape of bullion/cash and any other. The movable property created by a person, dowry obtained in marriage, or the money obtaind as gifts from friends, etc., was not divisible amongst the successors in life time of the owner. Further, the clothes, utensils, food, wife were also not divisible.

The immovable property was of two kinds—one which was received in succession and the other which was created by himself. The property received in succession could only be divided amongst the successors. The adopted son succeeded to the father's property like his own son. However, in case the father after adopting a son, had his own son then the share of the adopted son was comparatively less. In case of father having no sons, the daughters could succeed the father's property. They, however, had no right of succession rights in case sons were there. Wife had no right of succession except what had been willed by the husband or when they had no offspring. The impotent; blind by birth; mental; suffering from chronic disease were not entitled to succeed to father's property but had a right of maintenance. Although the father is supposed to be impartial in the division of property amongst his sons in his life time, yet he had a right to give more to any of the sons. The eldest son had a better right compared to other sons. At some places, there is mention of the eldest son succeeding to entire property of the father but in such a case he had to own the maintenance of younger sons. The Stridhan could not be owned by anyone till the lady is alive. Stridhan is the property obtaind by the lady from her relations as gifts, etc., or the one obtained in marriage. This is even now accepted as the property at the sole discretion of the lady. Even husband had no right over such a property. There are detailed rules about the Stridhan in our Shastras. Daughters have been recognised as successors to Stridhan of the mother.

Gambling. Gambling has been continuing in India since ancient times. Gambling is played by dices on stake. It includes the quarrel between cocks, pigeons, wrestlers and sheeps. Manu has prohibited gambling. This has been treated as theft and is not taken even as a source of enjoyment. Kautilya has, however, allowed it under Government monitoring but has specified a certain part of the money won being deposited in Government exchequer and supervisor was to be appointed by the Government for the maintenance of gambling dens. Even after having been permitted by the Government, the gamblers were not treated with respect. Katyayana has even permitted use of force by the winner to extract the money lost by the loser. This shows that the gambling had been monitored by the Government personnel and use of force for recovering the lost money was also allowed in the presence of such personnel. The dices were properly checked to see that there was no deception in their making, etc. The persons involved in gambling were not allowed to use any force/ deceptive tactics in the play and in case of such use, they were punished by court of law. Such punishment was generally pecuniary and an equal amount was also deposited in the Government exchequer. The rules applicable in gambling by human beings were equally applicable in case of gambling through quarrels of animals. The inclusion of above matters in the list of justiciable matters would indicate that our rishis in ancient times had exhaustively studied the matter and no matter was left uncovered by them which could take place and could not be brought to the court of law. These laws were more exhaustive even compared to modern laws as these contained punishment for law breaking even on moral and spiritual grounds as well.

Application of Hindu Law by Hindu Rajas

The principles of Hindu Law, as enunciated by Vedas and supplemented by Smritis, anubandhas and commentaries by various writers, had been fully applied to by the Hindu Rajas in pre-historic period and thereafter.

The Buddha Period

The pre-historic period in India is based on assumptions only and real documented historical period starts after Buddha or Alexander's invasion, as known from Greek writers. Bimbisara is considered to be the first king, who acceded to the throne of Magadha in about 545 B.C. Under him, Magadha became a flourishing kingdom, which attracted the most enlightened men of the age. Jain and Buddha Dharmas were widely preached during his reign. He was succeeded by Ajatsatru followed by Darsaka, and Udayi after whom the history of Magadha is obscure. Then came Nandas and then Mauryas.

The most important feature of the administrative development of the period was the rise of a class of high officials styled 'Mahamatras'. In the administration of justice, the king played an important part. It was his duty to give decisions in accordance with the special laws of the districts, castes and families. But much of the judicial work was entrusted to 'Vyavaharikas' or judges. The process of law in certain localities was according to Buddhist tradition. There were various tribunals, set one above the other, from the court of the Vinischaya Mahamatra to that of the *rajan*. Judgements were pronounced according to the book of customs. In criminal law, the use of ordeals was recognised. This shows that the legal structure was several tiered like the present day. In villages the system like that of Panchayats prevailed.

With Chandragupta Maurya, started Maurya dynasty from 4th Century B.C. or in 312 B.C. with the downfall of the Greek rule established by Alexander. He was helped in securing kingdom by Chanakya (Kautilya), who became his Prime Minister too. Hereafter the governance was as per *Arthashastra* of Kautilya. Chandragupta was followed by Bindusar and then Ashoka. We do not know much about the reign of Bindusar and early days of Ashoka. It was after the Kalinga war, when Ashoka adopted Buddhism, that he came in to prominence. He preached and practised the virtues of concord, tolerance and non-violence. Ashoka was followed by his sons Kunal, Jalav, etc. They were followed by Sugas, who preached Brahmanism and then again came a Buddhist king Kanishka in 120-16- A.D. then the Gupta (320-455 A.D.) and the last Hindu king was Harsha (606-647 A.D.).

The Maurya kings did not lay claim to Divine rank and looked upon their people as their children and assigned their care to his officers. *Arthashastra* says, "Whatever pleases himself the king shall not consider as good, but whatever pleases his subjects he shall consider as good". The king had the assistance of a council of Advisors styled the 'Parishad' or the 'Mantri-Parishad', who were specially consulted in all important matters. At the head of the judiciary stood the king himself. But there were special tribunals of justice—both in cities and the country partys—presided over by Mahamatras and Rajukas. Petty cases in villages were decided by the headman and the village elders. Ashoka introduced many reforms in judicial administration and procedure. While preserving a certain amount of uniformity, he is said to have allowed considerable discretion to the Rajukas so that they could discharge their duties unperturbed. Judges in the outlying provinces do not appear to have done their work to the satisfaction of the emperor. Greek writers testify to the severity of the penal code. To check maladministration, the emperor or his viceroys sent forth in rotation every five years or three years, such officers as were of mild and temperate disposition and regardful of the sanctity of life. The empire was divided into provinces and subdivided into districts called 'Aharas', 'Vishyas' and 'Predesa'. Each province was placed under a viceroy or a governor, who was either a prince of the blood or an official of the crown. Like the king being at the head of judiciary, the viceroy was head of judiciary in the province. The districts had the district officers responsible for administration and judicial pronouncement.

In judicial administration during the reign of Hindu Rajas, there was general honesty in the people and there was efficient administration of criminal law. In Chandragupta's camp of 4,00,000 persons, the total of thefts reported in any one day did not exceed 200 *drachmai* or about 8 pounds sterling. Crime was repressed with terrible severity, ordinary wounding by mutilation of the offender, in addition to the amputation of his hand. If he happened to be in the royal family, then death was the punishment. Judicial torture for the purpose of extorting a confession was recognised and freely used. In case of theft not having been traced, the aggrieved party was compensated and the local headman was held responsible for such thefts as could not be solved. The canons of *Arthashastra* were followed in all administrative and judicial matters. Impartial justice was granted. The King was the fountain head of justice but law was held superior to him even. There were civil courts for contracts, agreements, gifts, sales, marriages, inheritance and criminal courts decided cases of thefts, robbery, murders, etc. In the capital, there was Supreme Court.

Fahien visited India during the period of Chandragupta Vikramaditya (375-413 A.D.) He has said,

"The people were rich and prosperous and seemed to him to emulate each other in the practice of virtue. It may be doubted if any equally efficient foundation was to be seen elsewhere in the world at that date. The Indians had not to register their house-holds or attend to any magistrate and rule meaning thereby that there was no crime. Most crimes were punished by fines according to the gravity of the offence and capital punishment was unknown. Person, guilty of repeated rebellion, suffered amputation of right hand but such a punishment was exceptional. Judicial torture was not practised. Throughout the country, no one killed any living being or drank wine, or ate onion or garlic; no killing of cattle; no butchers' shops; no distilleries. No religious torture or bias was seen. Hindus had no tendency of harassing any one believing in other religion. For breach of social morality and filial duty, the penatly was mutilation or exile—a punishment which struck one as unduly severe. For the remaining offences, the penalty was only a money payment."

Division of Law

The great works of the Hindu period form a triumvirate in the realm of Hindu law and procedure. The administration of justice was as per *Arthashastra*, and Smritis of Brihaspati, Narada, Katyayana, Vyas, Parasara, and others. Law was in three heads:

1. Court of justice
2. Judicial Procedure
3. Civil and Criminal Law

Court of Justice. King's court was the highest on land called Sabha, Dharmasthana and Dharmadhikarna. We have full account of its contribution in Katyayana, who requires the king in one place to decide suits in association with the learned Brahmins, elders and ministers, well-versed with statecraft and in another place to do so in the company of judges, the ministers, the Purohit and the assessors, the scribes, the bailifs, the investigators, etc. The king awarded the punishment, the assessors examined the disputes, the scribe wrote down the pleadings, dispositions and the bailifs summoned the defendant, the witness, the assessors etc. The king was to abide by the decision of the judiciary, although he had overriding powers, being fountain head of justice. The king had original and appellate jurisdicton. Under him were the courts in provinces and Districts and then at village or town levels. Appeals lay from lower Court to higher on upto the king as per above hierarchy.

Judicial Procedure. This period marks the climax of Hindu jurisprudence. In the first place, the transaction of legal business has four stages—receiving information from a person ; finding out under what title of law the information fell ; the consideration of the pleadings of the parties and the evidence and lastly the decision. The burden of proof was to lie on the plaintiff in a reply of denial and on the defendant in the reply of special plea or of former judgement. Proof was humane and divine. Former comprised witnesses, documents and possession and the latter consisted of ordeals. The judgement was given in the form of a written document, called 'Jayapatra'. This indicated summary statments of parties, dispositions of witnesses, deliberation of the court and the decision.

Civil and Criminal Law. In the penal law of the late as of the early Smritis, the punishment of crime occupied a more important place than compensation for wrongs. It is, in other words, a law of crime in the strict sense of the term, while the law of torts held the subordinate position. Under the head law, called abuse and defamation both Narada and Katyayana have indicated fines for these offences depending upon the distinctions as well as the castes of the parties. The idea of the compensation to the person injured was reflected in the clause that, "He, who kills an animal must provide another animal of the same type or pay its value to the owner". Thefts were of two kinds—Patent and Clandestine. Patent thieves were traders employing false weights, measures and balances and clandestine were gamblers and quacks, those, who counterfeited articles and those, who lived by magic or palmistry by forfeiting good fortunes or portents. Punishment for thefts comprised mutilation, imprisonment, confiscation of property, exile and death.

As already indicated, many Smritis, *nibandhas* and commentaries had come in during the reign of Hindu Rajas and the justice was granted as per provision of these Smritis etc. The law, therefore, was as per these Smritis. These Smritis gave various kinds of crimes, procedure to be adopted for final decision on the punishment to be awarded, i.e., at first there is the report, then the examination of defence and witnesses, and then the decision. This is what is precisely being followed even now. There were two kinds of crimes—civil and criminal—and punishment for each offence had been duly prescribed. It means there were the codes like the present day Indian Penal Code, Criminal Procedure Code, Civil Procedure Court, Evidence Act etc., which system is considered to be the best. So, India too had the best systems in those days although English had condemned these systems as barbaric and rather appreciated the Islamic system. But none seems to have understood or else the English did not want to appreciate this system although it is not only akin to what British had brought out in I.P.C., Cr.P.C., C.P.C., etc. but more elaborate and comprehensive as the modern legal system does not consider religious or moral sins as punishable whereas in our Smritis, these have been described as sins and punishments prescribed for the same.

For civil cases, generally monetary punishments were awarded and for criminal cases too, monetary compensation was awarded in Gupta Period, whereas corporal punishment was awarded during Maurya and Harshas' rule. On rebellion against the state, death was the penalty. In view of this detailed civil and criminal law management, English were wrong in saying that there was no proper administration of law in Hindu period and in fact it was better administered than through the present Indian Penal Code, C.P.C., Cr.P.C. etc.

PART—III

MOHAMMEDAN PERIOD

7

ISLAMIC JURISPRUDENCE

Mohammedan Law was applied by Muslim rulers in India. This law was based on Islamic jurisprudence. Before, therefore, embarking upon the application of law during Mohammedan Period, we have to see what Islamic Jurisprudence is ?

Law in every society aims at the maintenance of social control. It is a system which is primarily established to protect the rights of individuals as well as of society. The legal system in every society has its own nature, character and scope. Similarly, Islam has its own legal system, known as 'Fiqh'. Islamic Law is not purely legal in the strict sense of the term, rather it embraces all the spheres of life— ethical, religious, political and economic. It has its origin in the 'Divine Revelation'. These revelations determined the norms and basic concepts of Islamic law and in many respects initiated a break in the customs and the tribal legal system of pre- Islamic Arabia. The scope of Quranic Laws encompasses rules of human conduct in all spheres of life, ensuring man's well-being in his mundane life as well as in the hereafter. The enforcement of Islamic Laws contained in Quran is the duty of an Islamic state. Muslim Society is supposed to be under the obligation according to Quran to enforce the application of rules of moral behaviour as divine commandments. Thus, the Quran, by making the observance of the rules of the 'Shariat', a matter of human conscience, has dignified the concept of law and the ethical values of its teachings which could constitute the noblest and most perfect basis of universal laws. The first available systematic work on the theory of Islamic Law is 'Al-Shaf-i', Risalah. The Islamic Law is based mainly on the works of Malik, Ab-uf yusuf, Al-Shaifbani and Al-Shafie.

Quranic Expressions

The word 'Fiqh' was originally used by the Arabs for a camel expert in covering, 'He, who distinguishes the she-camels that are lusting from those that are pregnant'. From this expression, it is believed the meaning of deep knowledge and understanding of anything has been derived. Hence Fiqh al-Lughah (understanding of the science of language) is the title of a work produced by 'al th a a bibi', The Quranic expression shows that in the Prophet's time the term 'Fiqh' was not applied in the legal sense alone but carried a wider meaning covering all aspects of Islam namely theological, political, economic and legal. The Muslim society became more diversified and complex with the association of Muslims of the conquered territories. Prophet's 'Kalam' had been 'O God, give him understanding in religion'. It did not quite mean exclusive knowledge of law but rather a deeper understanding of Islam in general. So, it is to be noted that 'Kalam' and 'Fiqh' were not separated till the time of 'Al mamun'. It appears that 'Fiqh' embraced the theological problems as well as legal issues till the second century of Hijrah.

Shariat and Fiqh

Alongside the term 'Fiqh', the term 'Sharai' was also current among the early Muslims. Newly converted Muslims, who had come to the Prophet from different parts of Arabia, requested him to depute someone to their locality to instruct them in the 'Sharai' of Islam. The term 'Shariat' was used to carry the specific meaning, i.e., 'The laws of Islam', at a later date. Literally the word 'Shariat' means a "Course to the watering place" and a "Resort of drinkers". The Arabs applied this term particularly to a course leading to a watering place, which was permanent and clearly marked out to the eye. Al-Shafii uses the term 'Shariat' in the sense of institution. Today the term 'Shariat' covers all aspects of Islam. It combines 'Fiqh' and 'Kalam' both. A contemporary author defines 'Shariat' and distinguishes it from 'Fiqh' in the following words :

"Shariat is the wider circle, it embraces in its orbit all human actions; 'Fiqh' is the narrower one and deals with what are commonly understood as legal acts. Shariat reminds us always of revelation, that 'Ilm' (knowledge) which we could never have possessed but for the Quran or Hadith, in 'Fiqh' the power of reasoning is stressed and deductions based on it are continuously cited with approval. The path of 'Shariat' is laid down by God and his Prophet; the edifice of 'Fiqh' is erected by human endeavour. In the 'Fiqh', an action is either legal or illegal, permissible or not permissible. In the 'Shariat' there are various grades of approval or disapproval. 'Fiqh' is the term used for the law as a science and 'Shariat' for the law as the divinely ordained path of rectitude."

It is, however, difficult to draw a sharp line of distinction between them as they are generally used interchangeably. It may, however, be noted that 'Shariat' constitutes law and tenets both, while 'Fiqh'deals with law alone.

During the time of Prophet there was no such science as that of jurisprudence. Subsequently in the early days of Islam too law was neither inflexible nor so rigidly applied as one finds it in the latter days. At that time different and even contradictory laws relating to many problems could be tolerated on the basis of arguments. This is obvious from the differences of companions of the prophet after his death and for the practice of the early legists.

The Prophet, while laying down a law primarily considered the value and spirit of the action and not the form of the action itself. What was significant in this case was the obedience to divine commandments.

Companions of the Prophet

After the death of Prophet, the companions were spread out in different parts of the Muslim world. Most of them came to occupy the positions of intellectuals and religious leadership. They were approached by the people for decisions regarding various problems. Often they formed an opinion by looking to the 'Shariat' value, which led the Prophet to take decision. For example, once Ibn Masud was asked whether a woman would be entitled to dower if her husband died without fixing its amount and consummating the marriage. Ibn Masud at first replied that he had not heard any thing from the Prophet on the subject. But when he was requested to make a suggestion he opined that the woman would be entitled to the average dower which a woman of her social standing might expect. He further suggested that she could receive full share from the heritage of her husband and that there would be a period of waiting for her. Maqil-b-Sinen is reported to have stood up on the occasion and said that Prophet had given a similar decision. But Ibn Umar and Zayel-b-Thahil gave different decisions in a similar case. According to them such a woman would not receive any dower but instead could be entitled to her share in the heritage. The verdicts are followed in different countries differently. Same is the case with 'Hadith' too. Differences arose in Hadith due to several reasons like contradictory traditions reported from Prophet.

Different Schools of Law

Among the early schools of law, we repeatedy hear the names of Abu Hanifah, Abu Yusuf, al Shayabani, Malik and Al- Awzai in different regions. They won their fame for their independent 'Ijtihad' based on pure reasoning in the sphere of Islamic Law. They were influenced both by the practice and thought of their respective regions. So the long process of independent interpretation of law continued in different regions from the earliest time. While this process of crystallisation of legal opinion in different schools was still under way, Al-Shafii appeared on the scene. He studied the works of his predecessors, travelled to several towns in various regions and learnt Hadith from a number of specialists. Al Shafii says that when a tradition from the Prophet is established to be genuine, it must be accepted, but most cases were decided on the basis of personal opinion. There were no strict rules to bring about uniformity in their decisions, hence he formulated rules for 'Qiyas'.

The above analysis shows that the trend towards personal allegiance started roughly towards the middle of the second century of the Hijra. Apart from these groupings in different regions, people were generally engaged in independent thinking on law. Later on Al-Shafii developed his own legal theory and tried to bring about strict consistency in law. After him the regional character of the early schools began to be corroded and the influence of personal allegiance to one master and to his principle prevailed gradually.

Classical Legal Categories

We now see that according to Islam the ultimate source of authority is God alone. In the ideal of Islamic Law, everyone except God, including the Prophet and ruling authorities, is subordinate to Divine Law, which emanates from Divine Revelations. As Islam gives guidance in all walks of life, Fiqh, the law of Islam, as developed from the very beginning, comprehends with special law, religio-moral, social, economic and political aspects of human life. The Quranic rulings may be divided into two broad categories namely 'Halal' (permissible) and 'Haram' (forbidden). The classical legal categories owe their origin to these two terms frequently and by Quran. The Quran itself does not lay down the various degrees of permissibility and prohibition. These degrees came into existence later when 'Fiqh' developed as an independent science. The terminology used by early jurists is a little different from the five categories evolved later. These are Wajib, Haram, Makruh, (disapproved)

Mandub and Mudah (prohibited). This classification is based on moral assumptions and is primarily legal.

Sources of Law

The above categories are based on four foundations. According to the classical legal theory, they are : the Quran, the Sunnah, Ijma and Qiyas. Works on Islamic jurisprudence classical since the time of Al-Shafii and certain reports claiming to go back earlier, convince us that the present sequence of the sources of Islamic Law was in existence in the earliest days of Islam. Ijma, according to Al-Shafii, stands as an authority for those who have no legal knowledge, in case the scholars are agreed.

The primary source of Islamic Legislature is the Quran. The Sunnah explains and elaborates the Quran. While Sunnah undoubtedly constitutes also an independent source, it is closely linked with and is secondary to the Quran. Qiyas is the systematic form of *'raiy'* (राय) (considered individual opinion) and is based on the Quran and the Sunnah. Personal opinion results in Ijma when it receives the universal acceptance of the community. In a word the Quran, the Sunnah, Qiyas and Ijma are interlinked. The same spirit pervades these sources for which the final authority is the Quran.

Quran. We may now discuss briefly each of these sources of law. The Quran, as we said before, is the primary source of legislation. Several Quranic verses expressly indicate that it is the basis and the main source of law in Islam. It is, however, clear that Quran is neither a legal code in the modern sense, nor is it a compendium of ethics. The primary purpose of the Quran is to lay down a way of life which regulates the relationship of man with man and his relationship with God. The Quran gives directions for man's social life as well as for his communion with his creator. The laws of inheritance, rulings for marriage and divorce, provision for war and peace, punishments for theft, adultery and homicide, are all meant for regulating the ties of man with his fellow beings. Quran in addition abounds in moral teachings which go in making social laws later. However, the Quranic quasi-legislation is not couched in purely legal terms. There is an amalgam of law and ethics. A common reader begins to read the Quran with an idea that it is a versatile code and a comprehensive book of law. He does not find in detail the laws and bye-laws relating to the social life, culture and political problems. In his book *The Origin of Mohammedan Jurisprudence* Prof. Schacht holds that "apart from the most elementary rules, norms derived from the koran were introduced into Muhammedan Law almost invariably at a secondary stage". It is, therefore, said that Islamic Law underwent a long process of evolution. The interpretation of the Quran in the early period was not so complex and sophisticated as it developed in the later ages. The methodology of inference from the Quran grew more and more intricate and philosophical in the wake of the deep and minute study of the Quran by jurists in later ages. The corpus of Islamic Law is rich in examples, where with regard to a problem, some jurists argued on the basis of traditions or personal opinion, for these latter did not think the Quranic verse relevant to the point at issue. So the Quran, as we know, is not basically a code of law but a document of spiritual and moral guidance and the presentation of the details of legal rules does not fall under the basic objectives of the Divine Book but developed by later thinkers.

Sunnah. Another important source of Islamic Law is the Sunnah. Sunnah essentially means exemplary conduct of some persons. In the context of Islamic jurisprudence it refers to the model behaviour of the Prophet. The Islamic concept of Sunnah, therefore, originates with the advent of Prophet and since the Quran enjoins upon the Muslims to follow the conduct of the Prophet, which is distinguished as 'exemplary and great' it became ideal for Muslim community. It also describes the function of the Prophet namely announcing of the revelation before people, giving moral training to them and to teach them the Divine Book of wisdom. The Sunnah is, therefore, closely linked with the Quran and it is, therefore, rather difficult to maintain that these are two different soures and it is the Sunnah that gives the concrete shape of the Quranic teachings. The source of law is the ideal Sunnah or the model behaviour of the Prophet. Hadith is the index and vehicle of the Sunnah. According to Al-Shafii, the Sunnah coming direct form the Prophet in the form of Hadith through a reliabale chain of narraters is a source of law, irrespective of whether it was accepted by the people or not and even if it was an isolated tradition, he emphasised the value of the traditions from the Prophet in preference to the opinion of the companions or their practice.

Qiyas. The next source of Islamic law is 'Qiyas' (analogical deductions). It is in fact a systematic and developed form of *raiy* (राय) (considered opinion). We find that with a semi-technical use of the term 'Qiyas' in the alleged letter of Umar, the second Caliph, to Abu Musa. Umar is reported to have advised him to acquaint himself with the "parallels and precedents" (of legal cases) and then to "weigh up" the cases, deciding what in his judgement would be the most pleasing to lead and nearest to truth, from such beginnigs as this reported advice *'raiy'* appears to have developed later into legal and technical concept of Qiyas viz. to find out an essential common factor between two similar cases and to apply the rule of one to the other. Qiyas comes last in Al-Shafii's scheme of legal theory. He regards it as weaker than Ijma. He does not allow the use of Qiyas in the presence of a tradition *(khahar)*.

Ijma. The last source of Islamic Law according to the scheme, is 'Ijma'. 'Ijma' is a principle for guaranteeing the veracity of the new legal content that emerges as a result of exercising Qiyas and Ijtihad. It is in fact a check against the fallibility of Qiyas. The Ijma that allows no difference of opinion is generaly confined to obligatory duties *(faraid)*. This is known as Ijma of the community. Ijma is something static and formal having no room for disagreement. Therefore, only the Ijma of the community is valid according to Al-Shafii. Al-Shafii regards it as a source of law after the Quran and Sunnah of the Prophet and before Qiyas.

A mention of the theory of 'Naskh' (abrogation) appearing in Quran is essential. This theory contradicts the eternal validity of the Quran. From this, it follows that the abrogated Quranic injunctions were eternally operative prior to their abrogation but lost their eternity as a result of abrogation. Now despite their existence in the Quran, they are defunct and inoperative. Their mere existence in Quran is not the sign of eternity unless they carry a practical value. The concept of eternity of Quran presupposes that all its laws should remain effective in the Muslim Ummah for ever. Hence, in the face of this belief there can be no reasonable ground for the thesis that some of the Quranic verses are abrogated. The Quran was revealed peacemeal over a period of twenty three years and each revelation came down in the context of specific social conditions. The revelations that came earlier and were in certain circumstances amended or enlarged or modified later cannot be said to have been strictly abrogated. We can, therefore, generalise that the Quranic injunctions were revealed in a given situation and instead of abrogating the previous rulings by the subsequent ones, it seems proper to implement them in the conditions similar to those in which they were revealed rather than treating them as abrogated.

Sunnah—Its Earlier Concept and Development

Loosely speaking, the terms Sunnah and Hadith convey the same meaning namely the traditions of the Prophet. But Sunnah primarily means "Pathway", "Behaviour", "Practice", "Manners of acting" or "Conduct of life". Sunnah was not new to the Muslims. It was already in vogue in the pre-Islamic Arabia. The Arabs had used it for the past customs and exemplary conduct left by their ancestors i.e. for their customary or common law. Therefore, Sunnah, be it used in the sense of people's practice or an individual's behaviour, carries a normative element. But when this term is used in Islamic Law and doctrine, it refers to the normative practice set up by the prophet as a model, which so long as he was alive, was his unique privilege. In the succeeding generations, it stood for the usage of the early Muslims as representing the Sunnah of the Prophet.

Hadith—Concept and Development

Hadith is different from Sunnah as Hadith is the narration of the behaviour of the Prophet while Sunnah is the law deduced from this narration. In other words, Hadith is the "carrier" and "vehicle" of the Sunnah or Sunnah is contained in Hadith. During the life time of the Prophet, Sunnah implied the conformity of the acts of the companions to the acts of the Prophet. They regulated their lives according to the Quran as exemplified in and illustrated by the behaviour of the Prophet. The practice that originated from the lifetime of the Prophet continued in its pure form more or less until the time of the first four Caliphs. They managed to protect this continuous tradition and tried to close the avenues for the penetration of incongruent accretions. People around the companions would have asked them about the conduct of the Prophet on different problems. This narration of the behaviour of the Prophet by individual companions was known as Hadith. Now there were two channels before the people for knowing the real Sunnah of the Prophet namely (1) Practice so far it was pure and continous and (2) Hadith. The terms 'Sunnah' and 'Hadith', as already indicated, occur generally simultaneously in some writings. This, it is presumed, is to document the Sunnah by Hadith because the time was approaching when practice was no longer regarded as its own proof. Sunnah, however, carried in its content personal opinion of the jurists and the local colour of each region with the evolution of Islam in various regions as and when conquered by Muslims.

Early Modes of Ijtihad (Raiy, Qiyas and Istihsan)

The most fundemental source of law in the early phase was the Quran—as elaborated, exemplified and interpreted by the Sunnah. Thus, Quran—Sunnah constituted one source of law. But the law finished by the Quran-Sunnah source in the time of Prophet had to be supplemented and sometimes interpreted and elaborated to cover new problems in order to find answers for them. Islamic Law, therefore, developed with the emergence of new problems from time to time since the days of Prophet and was created and recreated, interpreted and re-interpreted in accordance with the varying circumstances, thinking, etc, and this process of rethinking and reinterpreting the law independently is know as Ijtihad. In the early days *'raiy'* (considered personal opinion) was the basic instrument of Ijtihad. It was a generic term which preceded the growth of law under more systematic principles of 'Qiyas' and 'Istehasan' but this term continued to be applied even to Qiyas by the right most wing.

Ijtihad

The term Ijtihad in the early period was used in a narrower and more specialised sense than it came to be in Al-Shafii and later on. It conveyed the meaning of fair discretionary judgement or experts' opinion. There is a report about 'Umar', the second Caliph that one day during the month of Ramadan, he announced the end of fast when the sun apparently set. After a while, he was informed that the sun was again seen in the sky. Upon this he remarked: "The matter is easy; we exercised Ijtihad (Qadijlahadna). This is an early example of the use of this term by the companions standing for discretionary judgement.

On going through the cases of Ijtihad of several companions specially of 'Umar', the second Caliph, we find that *'raiy'* was exercised even in the presence of the injunction in Quran or the Sunnah. The fact is that one companion singled out one verse or tradition for a situation while another pointed to quite a different verse. For example, it is a well known fact that Umar abolished a share of 'Zakah' being given to certain Muslims or non-Muslims for "conciliation of their heart" as required by the Quran. The Prophet used to give this share to chiefs of certain Arab tribes in order to attract them to embrace Islam or to prevent them from doing harm to the Muslims. But 'Umar' discarded the order which Abu Bakr had written in his Caliphate for donation of certain lands to some persons on this basis. He argued that the Prophet had given this share to strengthen Islam, but as the conditions had changed, this share ceased to be valid. Umar's action seems apparently contrary to Quran but in fact, he considered the obtaining situation and followed the spirit of the Quranic injunction. He thought that if Prophet had lived then he would have also decided so. Another example is :

Some slaves had stolen a she-camel, slaughtered and eaten it. When the matter was referred to 'Umar', he in the first instance ordered the cutting of the hands of the thieves but after a moment's reflection, he said addressing the slaves' master :

> "I think you must have starved these slaves out" He, thereafter, ordered the master of the slaves to pay double the price of she-camel and withdrew his order of cutting the hands of slaves "as thieves".

Raiy

The generic term *'raiy'*, the most widespread and natural mode of reasoning in the early period was, in the course of time subjected to a number of conditions and limits with a view to arresting its arbitrariness and to systematising the process of reasoning. This systematic form of individual reasoning in law came to be known as 'Qiyas'. 'Qiyas' has been derived from the Jewish exegetical term 'Hiqqish' meaning to hear together. However, though Qiyas is a systematic form of *'raiy'*, there is a big difference between the two. Raiy has a flexible and dynamic nature. It decides the cases in the light of the spirit, wisdom and justice of Islam. It is a well-considered and balanced opinion of a person, who aspires to reach a correct decision. 'Raiy' stands for the decision that would have been taken either by 'Revelation' if it were to come down on that occasion or by the Prophet if he had been there. Qiyas is a comparison between two parallels because of their resemblance. Qiyas indeed is an extension of a precedent. Its scope, therefore, is more limited than that of *'raiy'*. In *'raiy'*, we find the emphasis on actual situation, while in Qiyas the emphasis is on abstract analogy. Whatever the situation may be, Al Maqaffa cites an example of limited nature of Qiyas :

> "Suppose a man consults you on whether he should speak the truth or tell a lie. You could certainly suggest to him that he should speak the truth. Again he asks you whether on every occasion say when a person wants to kill another, he should speak the truth and give the pursuer the trail of the fugitive. Here Qiyas demands that he must speak the truth but *raiy* advises breaking of the law i.e. not to speak the truth but to do what is generally beneficial. An appraisal of the cases in which the companions exercised Ijtihad lead us to believe that their reasoning was characterised by *raiy* more than formal Qiyas."

Raiy in the early period, appeared in another form known an 'Istihsan'. It was a unique method of exercising personal opinion by setting aside the apparent and strict analogy in the interst of public benefit, equity and justice. 'Istihsan' is an 'unreasoned preference' to an established law in a certain situation or a decision based on absolute reasoning rather than on analogical reasoning. It depends indeed on one's legal acumen to distinguish where a rule is applicable and where it should be abandoned. Istihsan is not a whim and arbitrary opinion, but a way to take a correct decision according to situation. Umar's act of Ijtihad, e.g., stopping the amputation of the hands of thieves during the days of famine; declaring the *'talaq'* pronouncements as triple divorce; having the sale of slave mothers; prohibiting marriage with women of Ahl-al-Kitab in certain cases, and so on, in fact fall under Istihsan. Further, if an infidal enters Muslim territory under their protection and a Muslim steals his property or cuts his hand, the hand of the Muslim according to Abn Yusuf, will not be amputated.

Istihsan

He says that according to Qiyas, his hand should be cut but in this case he employs Istihsan to bring himself in agreement with those who hold this view. But this is a strange example of Ijtihad, which does not seem to be justified. The reason given for this departure is also not intelligible. The intention may be that he wanted to discourage the entry of foreigners to Muslim territory so that the Muslim society remains immune from their influence. Istihsan is not used in Iraq but its traces are there in Medinese. So, this is not universally applied. Also we donot find the term Istihsan in Al-Awzai's writings or cases decided by him 'preferring' public interest to the established rule. Rather his strict adherence to law is challenged by the Iraqis on the basis of Istihsan. For attacking a fort of non-Muslims by Muslims, if the non-Muslims stand on its walls and shield themselves by the children of Muslims. Abu Hanifa holds that the Muslims may attack them aiming at non-Muslims and not the children. Al- Awzai maintains that the Muslims should not throw arrows at them but in case any of non-Muslims comes out, he may be attacked. This is a case of Istihsan and not Qiyas.

Ijma in the Early Schools

Before we deal with main problem, let us briefly mention the classical theory of Ijma. Ijma has been defined in the classical Fiqh literature in different ways. One definition says, "Ijma is an agreement of the Islamic community on a religious front". Another definition states' "Ijma is a consensus of opinion of the persons competent for Ijma, when a religious issue arises, whether rational or legal". A third definition is "Ijma is a unanimous agreement of the jurists of the community of a particular age on a certain issue". The first two definitions have been criticised while the third has been accepted as the standard definition. Also Ijma is not subject to reason but is the privilege (Karâmah) of the community. Infallibility, therefore, inheres in the total community and not in the majority. But there is difference of opinion amongst jurists about total Ijma and the points on which it is used. Ijma, in actual Islamic history, seem to have been a natural process of solving problems through the gradual formation of majority opinion of the community. After the death of Prophet and close of Revelation, there arose the need for checking the fallibilty of 'Ijtihad'. The idea of Ijma, it seems, came into being as a socio-political necessity, approved of later on the basis of Quranic verses and traditions from the Prophet. The concept of Ijma was not available during the lifetime of Prophet as during that period words of Prophet were the final answer to any problem that cropped up in those days. Therefore, this concept arose to deal with new problems. It is, however, taken to be interpreted out of the provisions of Quran / Sunnah. To justify the idea of Ijma the jurists argue not only on the basis of traditions but also on the basis of the Quranic verses. But since the Quranic verses cannot be invented, we criticise them by saying that their interpretation and application are not correct.

Be what it may, Ijma plays a most crucial role in the development of Islamic Law. The existing body of Fiqh is the result of the agelong Ijtihad and Ijma process. This process is still operative and can add to the body of law. The major function of Ijma is to write the divergent opinions on a problem progressively and to ascertain the truth of a Qiyas. As a result of the difference of opinion on a host of problems in the various regions of legal activity, the need for a mainstay was acutely felt by the jurists themselves. The early concept of Ijma is quite distinct from the one developed in Al-Shafii's period. The classical theory of Ijma depicts it as something formal and static and not as living process of the Ijtihad-Ijma activity. That is why Ijma that took place in the past cannot be changed by another Ijma according to classical view. The early idea of Ijma was a forward-looking process using the Qiyas-Ijma complex as a living instrument for the revision and creation of fresh law for new needs.

Ijma of the companions represents the established practice during the time of the first four Caliphs. These Caliphs, especially Umar, the second Caliph, consulted the companions on fresh cases and announced their decisions in public meetings. For intance, Umar is reported to have consulted the companions on the problem of punishment of a thief. They reportedly agreed (Ijman) on cutting his hand if he commited theft for the first time, and his foot if he repeated it, and to put him in prison if he did so for the third time. Analysing the views of various schools of Iraq and Medina, we conclude that Ijma in various provinces meant only the average opinion of the lawyers of each province and not the universal Al Ijma of all regions. In each region, Ijma was crystallising progressively as a consolidated opinion averaging the individual opinions of jurists. Hence Ijma was anonymous in each region as no meeting was ever held to reach this agreement nor did there ever exist any such institution in Islam. Ijma in this phase was so much influenced by the regional character that even reference to Ijma of the companion by the early schools did not go beyond their particular regions.

8

APPLICATION OF MOHAMMEDAN LAW DURING MUSLIM RULE IN INDIA

Having studied the Islamic jurisprudence and the principles of Mohammedan Law, we have to see how these were made applicable in India by various Muslim rulers.

Before the birth of Prophet of Islam, Arabia was a country of idolators, who had no faith in resurrection and looked upon death as the end of life. They were divided into tribes, who lived in a nomadic state and roamed about from place to place. They had no organised Government amongst them. The only authority, which was respected was that of the tribal chief to whom they paid homage. Mohammed was born in 570 A.D. From his early life, Mohammed hated idolatory and regarded the worship of 360 idols in the Ka'aba as wholly useless. He asked the people to give up idol-worship and to recognise 'Allah' as the God worthy of adoration. He died in 632 A.D. He was succeeded by Khalifas. The first from Khalifas had no elaborate machinery of Government. Their problem was simple and they carried out their duties in a spirit of piety and benevolence. All authority, however, was centered in him. He was the head of all Departments in the state and had the control of the Bait-ul-Mal. He was the fountain of justice and was the chief authority in the state that appointed all officers. Below him were the Wazirs. The Wazirs were incharge of various Departments, the most important of which were Dewan-al-Khiraj (Taxes), Dewan- al-Jung (war), Dewan-al- Barid (Post), Dewan-al-Rastil (Secretariat), Dewan-al-Aata (gifts), Dewan-al Zaman (Accounts), and so on. Justice was administered by the Qazis and the Chief Qazi was called the Qazi-ul-Qazat. To assist them, there were the Adils. Criminal justice was administered by an officer called the Sahib-al-Mazalim. Also there were Muftis or juris consults, who expounded law and were subordinate to the Qazis. The police duties were performed by the Kotwal and the Muhtasib, the latter being responsible also for the morals of the community.

The earliest Muslims, who came to India, were traders, who reached the coast of Malabar attracted by the profits of trade. After the invasion of Mahmud of Ghazni, quite a stream of Muslim missionaries passed into India. But the king with army first invaded India to set up his kingdom was Subakatgin, who established his rule in Sind and subsequently conquered Multan and some other areas of Panjab. The first king to establish rule in Delhi was Mohammad Ghori, who after defeating Prithviraj Chauhan, became the first ruler of India. He left Qutab-ud-din as his vice and went back. Qutab-ud-din added further areas to his kingdom and became the ruler of practically the entire Northen India.

Mohammedan Law During the Slave Sultans

In the slave sultans, Balban cared for organising internal administration on a most efficient basis. It was half civil and half military. He was himself the fountain of all authority and enforced his commands with the greatest rigour. In administering justice, he never showed partiality even towards his own kith and kin and when any of his relations or associates committed an act of injustice, he never failed to grant redress to the aggrieved party. So great was the dread of the sultan's inexorable justice that no one dared to ill-treat his servants and slaves. A well established system of espionage is inseparable from depotism and Balban with a view to making the administration of justice more efficient, appointed spies in his fiefs, who reported to him all acts of injustice. These spies checked crime and protected innocent persons against the high-handedness of those in power, but their presence must have demoralised the community and led to the suppression of even the most legitimate and harmless amenities of social life.

Mohammedan Law During the Khiljis

Alauddin Khilji was opposed to the interference of the Ulema in matters of state and in this respect he departed from the tradition of the previous rulers in Delhi. The law was to depend upon the will of the monarch and had nothing to do with the law of the Prophet. This was the guiding maxim of the new monarch. He believed in the legal position of the sovereign power in the state in hands of the sultan. He upheld the royal prerogative of punishment and justified the mutilation of dishonest and corrupt officer though the Qazi declared it contrary to the canons of law. There sultan asked him, "That wealth which I acquired while I was a *malik* with so much bloodshed at Devagiri, does it belong to me or to the public treasury" ? The Qazi replied, "I am bound to speak the truth. The treasure obtained at Devagiri was obtained by the prowess of the army of Islam and whatever treasure is so acquired belongs to the public treasury. If your Majesty had gained it yourself alone in a manner allowed by law then it would belong to you". The Sultan flared up with wrath and asked the Qazi how such treasure could belong to the state. The Qazi meekly answered, "Your Majesty has put to me a question of law if I were not to say what I have read in the book and your Majesty, to test my opinion were to ask some other learned man, and his reply being in opposition of mine would show that I had given a false opinion to suit your Majesty's pleasure, what confidence would you have in me, and would you even afterwards consult me about the law".

The Qazi was confronted with a fresh question about the rights of the king and his children upon the public treasury. The Bet -ul-mal frightened by the sultan's stern demeanour, the Qazi screwed up courage with great difficulty to return a reply and said, "If your majesty will follow the example of the most enlightened Khalifas, and will act upon the highest principle then you will take for yourself and your establishment the same sum as you have allotted to each fighting man i.e. two hundred and thirty four *tankas*. If you would rather take a middle course and should think that you would be disgraced by putting yourself on a par with the army in general, then you may take for yourself and your establishment as much as you have assigned to your chief officers, such as Malik Kiran and others. If your Majesty follows the opinion of the politicians then you will draw from the treasury more than any other great man receives so that you may maintain a greater expenditure than any other and not suffer your dignity to be lowered. I have put before your Majesty three courses and all the crores of money and valuables which you take from the treasury and bestow upon women, you will have to answer for on the day of account".

The Sultan was filled with wrath and threatened the Qazi with severe punishment. When he again recounted his proceedings, the Qazi placed his forehead on the ground and cried with a loud voice, "My liege! whether you send me, your wretched servant, to prison, or whether you order me to be cut in two, all this is unlawful and finds no support in the sayings of the Prophet, or in the exposition of the learned". The exponent of the canon law knew that his fate was sealed but to his utter astonishment when he went to the court the next day, the sultan treated him kindly and handsomely rewarded him. With politeness which was agreeably surprising, he explained to the Qazi his doctrinc of kingship in these significant words, "To prevent rebellion in which thousands perish, I issue such orders as I conceive to be for the good of the state or/and the benefit of the people. Men are heedless, disrespectful and disobey my commands, I am then compelled to be severe to bring them into obedience. I do not know whether this is lawful or unlawful, whether I think to be for the good of the state or suitable for the emergency that I decree and as for what may happen to me on the approaching day of judgement that I know not".

The new doctrine of sovereignty was the outcome of the circumstances of the time. The people readily acquiesced in it and cared nothing for the claims of the Ulema. They tamely submitted to him because he gave them the much coveted gifts of peace and order. The support which he received from public opinion made him irresistible as long as he lived. He calmly sat down to find out the causes of political disorder and came to the conclusion that they were due to the four things :

1. Sultan's disregard of the affairs of the nation.
2. Wine drinking.
3. Friendship and frequent social intercourse of the *maliks*, army and grandees of the empire.
4. Superfluency of wealth which intoxicated men's minds and fostered treason and disaffection.

He, as a result, confiscated all gratuities, pensions and endowements to the state and all the villages that were held as *mulk* (in proprietary rights) or *inam* or *waqf* were incorporated in crown lands. He established an elaborate system of espionage. Spirituous liquor was strictly forbidden and the sultan himself set an example by giving up the habit of drinking and all glasses and jars broken. All festive gatherings and convivial parties were forbidden in private as well as in public houses, with the inevitable result that the amenities of social life disappeared and life became an intolerable burden. Hindus were treated with special severity. These reforms succeeded well enough. The increased strength and efficiency of the army guaranteed security against Mughal invasions and held in check the refractory Rajas and chieftains. All seditions were stamped out and men's habits were so disciplined that crime was considerably lessened. The cheapness of the neccessaries of life increased the happiness of the people and bound them more closely to the personal despotism of the emperor. He swept aside the dictates of religions and canons of law, if they interfererd with his policy. He had no regard for kindship and inflicted punishments without distinction. The fraudulent practices were sternly put down.

Mohammedan Law During the Tughlaqs

The administration of Ghiyas, contrary to Allauddin was based on the principles of justice and moderation. He took great care to prevent all abuses. The cultivators were treated well and officials were severely punished for their misconduct. The departments of justice and police worked efficiently and the greatest security prevailed in the remotest parts of the empire. But Muhammad Tughlaq adopted a policy which ran counter to the cherished prejudices of the orthodox school. He levied many taxes in addition to the four legal ones prescribed by the Quran and showered a greater regard for the religious susceptibilities of the Hindus than his predecessors had ever done. He deprived the Ulemas of the monopoly of the administration of justice. His love of justice was so great that he personally looked into the detail of the judicial administration and submissively accepted the decrees of the courts passed against himself. He made himself the supreme court of appeal and when his judgement differed from that of the Muftis, he overruled them and adhered to his own view. To curtail the influence of the orthodox party, he invested some of the distinguished officers of the state with judicial powers in spite of the fact that they were not Qazis, Muftis or professional canonists. He was very strict in administering justice. He laid his hands freely upon the members of the priestly class when they were found guilty of rebellion, upon sedition or embezzlement of public funds.

Neither birth nor rank nor piety availed, aught to afford protection to an offender from the punishment which his guilt merited and that is why Ibn Batuta, who had visited many lands and seen a great deal of men and affairs recorded the verdict when he was in his own country, no longer afraid of the Sultan's wrath that "Of all men, this king is the most humble and of all men, he most loves justice". He levied only four taxes allowed by the holy law namly the *khiraj, zakat, zeziya* and *khams*. The spoils of war and conquest won by the arms of the faithful were, to be shared by the army and the state in the proportion laid down in sacred law. He followed the Quran with the strictest fidelity. The *munsif* expounded the law and the Qazi delivered the judgement.

The legal system was reformed. Torture was abolished and leniency was shown in awarding punishment to the wrongdoers. The sultan was kindly disposed towards poor and the unemployed. The *kotwals* made lists of those who were in want and forwarded them to the Dewan where suitable occupations were provided for them.

Empire of Vijaynagar

The empire was a vast feudal organisation and the king was the apex of the whole system. He was assisted by a council composed of ministers, provincial governors, military commanders, men of the priestly class and poets. But the government was highly centralised and the king was a perfect autocrat. His authority was unlimited. He looked after the civil administration and directed the military affairs of the empire and acted as judge in cases that were submitted to him for decision. The principle officers of the state were the Prime Minister, the chief treasurer, the keeper of the royal jewels, the prefect of the police, who were assisted by a number of lesser officials. The Prime Minister was the king's chief adviser on all important questions. The prefect of the police was responsible for maintaning order in the city. The kings of Vijaynagar maintained a splendid court on which they spent huge sums of money. It was attended by nobles, learned priests, astrologers and musicians and on festive occasions, fireworks were displayed. There was a well regulated system of local Government. The empire was divided into more than 200 provinces, sub-divided into *kottams*, which were again subdivided into small groups of villages and towns. Each province was held by a viceroy, who either belonged to the royal family or was a powerful noble of the state. The province was merely a replica of the empire. The viceroy kept his own army, held his own court and practically acted as a despot within his jurisdiction. But he had to render account of his stewardship to the emperor. The system of local Government extended to villages. The village was, as it had been from time immemorial, the smallest unit of administration and managed their own affairs through its hereditory officers called the Ayagars. They decided petty disputes, collected revenues and enforced law and order. Justice was administered in a rough and ready fashion according of the discretion of the authorities. Petitions could be made to the king or to the Prime Minister. Justice in crime cases was dispensed according to the principles of Hindu Law and local usage. The criminal law was harsh and barbarous. Fines were levied and torture was frequently resorted to. Theft, adultery and treason were punished with death or mutilation. The members of the priestly order were exempt from capital punishment

Mohammedan Law During the Mughals

Babar. Babar had no time to devise new laws or establish institutions for the governance of the wide dominions which he had won by the power of sword. He accepted the system which he found in vogue in 'Hindustan' and parcelled out his empire into fiefs, which he entrusted to jagirdars, dependent upon himself. He was sovereign Indian ruler and fountain of Justice, A supreme commander, the supreme justice, the supreme owner of exchequer and a supreme administrator.

Sher Shah Suri. The Government of Sher Shah, though autocratic, was vigorous and enlightened. He was not content merely with the establishment of peace and order but reconstructed the machinery of administration. The whole empire was divided into 47 Divisions, each of which comprised a large number of *parganas*. There were 1,13,000 parganas but this might be the total number of villages and not parganas. Each pargana had a *shiqdar* and *amin*, a treasurer, a *munsif*, a Hindi writer and a Persian writer to write accounts. Besides these officers of the state, there were the *patwaris, chowdhuris* and the *muqaddams*, who acted as intermediaries between the people and the state. The *shiqdar* was a soldier, the amin, a civilian, whose main function was the assessment and collection of land revenues. The *shiqdar's* duty was to enforce the royal *firman* and to give military assistance to the *amin*, when he needed it. The *amin* was the principal civil officer and was responsible to the central government for his actions. The parganas were grouped into *sarkars*, each of which had a *shiqdar-i-shiqdaran* and a *munsif-i-munsifanan*, who looked after the work of the pargana officers throughout their division. Their duty was to watch the conduct of both the *amins* and the people to settle disputes regarding the boundaries of the parganas and to punish any acts of lawlessness on the part of the people.

Sher Shah dealt out even-handed justice to the high and low and no man could escape punishment by reason of his birth or rank. There were courts called the *Darul-adalat* in which the *Qazi* and the *Mir Adl* tried civil cases and administered justice. The Hindus settled their disputes relating to inheritance, succession and the like in their panchayats. But in criminal cases, they were amenable to the law of the state. The criminal law was severe; punishment was harsh and cruel and their object was not to reform the culprit but to set an example.

Even theft and robbery were treated as capital offences. The police organisation of Sher Shah, though primitive in many respects, was highly efficient. He tried to enforce the principle of local responsibility in the matter of preventing crimes, if a theft or robbery occured within the jurisdiction of an Amin or *shiqdar*, and the culprits were not traced, the *muqaddams* were arrested and compelled to make good the loss. When a murder occured and the murderer was not traced, the *muqaddams* were seized and asked to produce him. If they failed to produce him or give his whereabouts, they were themselves put to death. In any case, the responsibility of bringing to light an offence rested upon the *muqaddams* and regulations of the state operated harshly upon them. But the system resulted in the complete security of life and property. The travellers and way-farers slept without the least anxiety even in deserts and the zamindars themselves kept watch over them for fear of the king. Besides the regular police, there were the *muhtasibs* or cursors of public morals, whose duty was to prevent such crimes as drinking and adultery and to enforce the observance of religious laws. Spies are inevitable in a despotic state and Sher Shah employed diligent spies, who kept him informed of all that happened in his dominion.

Akbar. Akbar adopted a middle and reconciliatory path with the Hindus. But it shook the emperor's loyalty to orthodox Islam. He clearly saw the danger of allowing too much power to the Ulema. He could not allow them to be the sole arbiters of disputed questions and wished to write in his own person the power of the state and the functions of the supreme pontiff of the Muslim Church. He proposed to read the *khutba* from the pulpit in the Fatehpuri mosque which was composed by Faizi for the occasion. But more objectionable than the reading of this *khutba* was the emperor's assumption of the role of mujtahid at the suggestion of Shaikh Mubarak. As a result of this step, he was to become the supreme arbiter in all causes, whether acclesiastical or civil like Henery VIII of England. In 1579 the leading Ulema agreed to declare him the Imam-i-adil (*mujtahid*), the final interpreter of Muslim Law. Saikh Mubarak hastily drew up a document which he signed "With the utmost willingness". Its English translation is as under :

"Whereas Hindustan has now become the centre of security and peace, and the land of justice and beneficence, a large number of people, specially learned men and lawyers have immigrated and chosen this country for their home."

"Now we, the principle Ulema, who are not only well-versed in the several departments of law and in the principles of jurisprudence, and well-acquainted with the edicts, which are set not only on reason or testimony, but are also known for our piety and honest intentions, have duly considered the deep meaning first of the verse of the Quran. Surely, the man, who is dearest to God on the day of judgement is the Imam-I-adil, whosoever obeys the Amir, obeys thee and whosoever rebels against him rebels against thee. And of several of them proofs based on reasoning or testimony, and we have agreed that the rank of Sultan-I-Adil is higher in the eyes of God than the rank of a Mujtahid. Further, we declare that the king of the Islam, Amir of Faithful, shadow of God in the world Abul Fath Jalal-ud-din Muhammed Akbar Padshah Ghazi, (whose kingdom God perpetuates), is the most just, a most wise and the most God-feaing king. This document has been written with honest intentions for the glory of God and the propagation of the Islam and is signed by us, the principal Ulema and lawyers in the monthy Rajab in the year nine hundred and eighty seven (987)".

The Mughal system of administration was not original. The methods followed all over the Muslim world were those of Khalifas but the ideas of Muslims interfused with the customs and usages of this country. The Hindus continued to be employed in the Revenue Department and their customs and practices exercised a powerful influence on administrative arrangement. The Mughal administration was, therefore, a mixture of Indian and foreign elements and it was "Perso Arabic system in Indian setting". The head of the administration was the king himself. In theory he had unlimited powers but in practice he always deferred to the wishes of those, who were near him or who were affected by his decree. At a very early age, Akbar was a complete master of his kingdom and announced a policy which was based upon liberal and humanitarian principles. The disabilities imposed upon the unbelievers were removed and the administration treated the Hindus and Muslims alike in all matters. There was no exclusion from the offices of the state on religious grounds and the Hindus were granted complete liberty of worship. The principle of religious toleration guided the policy of Akbar. The emperor himself was the head of all administration. Below the king, the Wazir was the principal executive officer. He was, as it were, the alter ego of the emperor and was consulted in all matters. The chief Departments of Mughal Government were :

1. Finance under a Dewan.
2. The military, pay and Accounts office (Under Mir Bakshi).
3. The imperial house-hold (under Khan-I-Saman).

4. Judicial (under the Chief Qazi or Qazi-Ul-Quzrat).
5. Religious endowments and charitable institutions (under Sadr-I-Sudur).
6. Censorship of public morals (under Muhtasib).
7. Artillery (under Mir Atish or Darogah-I-Topkhana).
8. Intelligence and Posts (under Darogah-I-Dak chowkies).
9. Mint (under its own Darogah).

The king was the highest judicial officer of the realm corresponding to the Lord Chief Justice of England. The emperor, as the Khalifa of the age, was the supreme judge in all cases but generally he acted as the highest court of appeal. The Qazi was the chief judge in criminal cases which he decided according to Muslim Law. The *muhtasib*'s duties were to see that the people led their lives in accordance with the law of the Prophet to put down the practices condemned in the Shariat, and in general to prevent immorality.

The officer, who was responsible for maintaining peace in the cities, was the *kotwal*. His duties included keeping watch at night and patrolling the city, keep a register of houses and frequented roads; to employ spies ; to discover thieves; to examine weights and measures; to make a list of the property of those who had no heirs and of deceased and missing persons and not to allow a woman to be burnt against her will and to prevent circumcision below the age of 12. Kotwal was a familiar figure in big cities in Northern India and he still performs most of the duties entrusted to his Mughal prototype. It was the *kotwal*'s duty to prevent and detect crime ; to trace the whereabouts of offenders and to look after the daily life of the people in towns.

The emperor was the fountain of all justices. He was the highest court of appeal and the people had boundless confidence in his justice. He heard original suits of a certain kind as well as the appeal sent for disposal by the provincial Governments. On a fixed day all people, the high and low, were permitted to enter the court of justice and lay their complaints before him. Even when he was at tour, he held his court regularly and received complaints against his officials also. The Mir Aaz had to be present at the palace, all day and night. Below the emperor was the Sadr-i-Sudur, who decided important civil cases especially of a religious nature. The Qazi-ul-Qazat was the highest judicial officer in the realm, who was responsible for the efficient administration of justice. There were no law courts in those days with definite codes of law to guide the presenting officers.

The functionaries, who were mainly concerned with the disposal of cases were, (1) The Qazi, (2) The Mufti, (3) The Mir-adl. The Mufti expounded the law; the Qazi investigated the evidence and the Mir-adl deliverd the judgment. The Mir-adl was especially enjoined to look after the general interest of the state and to act as a counterpoise to the Qazi's influence. There were no professional lawyers, trained in law and conversant with social usages and regulations of the state and since the justice had to plead their cases in person, we may presume that justice was not always done to the simple villagers, who were helpless against a rapacious official or an influential opponent. The number of Mir-adls was not very large. They were generally associated with the Qazis, who were more conservative in their outlook and unresponsive to the larger consideration of public welfare. At one time, the emperor dismissed all reactionary Qazis, not to destroy the Muslim Law as is too readily assumed by his orthodox critics, but to induce a chastined mood in judges, who considered themselves infallible.

The Qazi's court had civil and criminal jurisdiction and tried cases of both Hindus and Muslims. But in deciding those cases in which the parties were Hindus, he was required to take into consideration the customs and usages of the Hindu community. The Qazi was expected to be just, honest and impartial and to hold trial in the presence of the parties at the seat of the court house and not in private place. He was ordered not to accept presents or to attend entertainments given by all and sundry and was asked to be proud of his poverty. But those injunctions were more honoured in the breach than in the observance. Most of the Qazis were haughty and corrupt and gave perverse verdicts. There was no written code of law, which the judge had to administer in Akbar's empire. The Quran was the ultimate authority to which all questions had to be referred. But the Quran could not be applied to all conceivable cases and therefore, its provisions had to be supplemented by the Hadis or sayings of the Prophet. The *fatwas* or decrees of the eminent judges or the Ulema constituted another source of law, but they were not binding upon the Qazi, who might or might not accept them. The criminal law was the same for all and in the matter of punishment, no discrimination was made on religious grounds. In civil cases in which the parties were Hindus, full regard to their customary and traditional law was paid and the Qazis were expected to acquaint themselves with Hindu usages. The courts had to follow the regulations laid down by the emperor in revenue cases. But the emperor was above the law. He could freely annul or reverse the decisions of his judges, who were always careful to avoid the imperial displeasure.

The punishment inflicted by the courts was often severe. Amputation of limbs was permitted but capital punishment could not be inflicted without the emperor's sanction : There was no regular jail system and long term prisoners were confined in forts. Those, who were guilty of particularly heinous offences, were thrown into dungeons and were treated with great rigour. Fines were not unknown and in certain cases exhorbitant demands were made to meet the ends of justice.

The king's regard for right and justice in the affairs of Government was remarkable. He took a very strong view of errors and misdemeanours committed by his officials in discharging their duties. He was sincerely anxious that guilty should be punished without malice indeed without undue leniency. All important cases were decided by the king himself and punishments were awarded after great deliberation. Moral offences were severely dealt with. Seducers and adulterers were either strangled or gibbeted. He had such a hatred on debauchery and adultery that neither influences nor entreaties, nor the great-ransom, which was offered, would induce him to pardon his chief trade commissioner, who had outraged the modesty of an unmarried girl. The wretch was remorselessly strangled. The chief executioners were provided with many barbarous instruments to inflict punishemnts upon malifactors, but no one was actually punished with them and they served to be intended rather to inspire terror than for actual use.

The administrative set up established by Sher Shah in the form of Subas, Sarkars and Parganas continued during Mughal period. The Governor/Subedar held his own court but he could not sit in the Jharokha or declare war or peace without the permission of the emperor. The emperor was the head of the judicial and military departments. He heard appeals from the decisions of the Qazis and Mir-adls. Below him were the Diwan, the Sadr, the Amil or revenue collector, the Fauzdars, etc. The courts in *subas* were pretty much the same as at the capital. The Qazi assisted by the Mufti and the Mir-adl administred justice to the people. The Subedar was the highest court of appeal in the province. When there was difference of opinion between the judicial officers, the decision of the Central Government was final. The *kotwal* was to brief the offenders to the court and trials were to be held promptly. No culprits could be detained in prison for more than one night without a trial. Appeals could be made to the emperor in important cases but the number could not have been very large.

Jahangir and Shahjehan. The administration of justice was carried on by the Qazis and Mir-adls but the emperor was not unmindful of his own duty in the matter. He was the highest judge in the empire and appeals in important cases were made to him. The emperor did not go to the Jharokha-i-Khas-or-Aam on Wednesday which was set-apart-for administering justice. On that day at the appointed hour the emperor came straight from the Jharokha-i-Darshan to the Hall of Audience, popularly known as the Ghusalkhana and disposed of the cases that were submitted to him by the Daroghas. The emperor sought the advice of the Ulema, who gave the view of the Shariyat and gave their verdict. The cases, which required local investigation, were sent to the Provincial Governors with instructions to find out the truth and to do justice and submit their report on such cases. Even in remote parts of the empire, wherever the eye of the emperor could reach, wrongs were righted and justice was done. There was no craze for litigation and there were fewer law suits and justice was expeditious. The punishments inflicted on the culprits were barbarous. Minor offences were punished with the mutilation of limbs, whereas for the more serious crimes, death and imprisonment for life were laid down as penalties.

Shivaji. Shivaji was an autocrat, but he was assisted by a council of eight ministers called the Ashta Pradhan. It was only an advisory body and had none of the characteristic of a modern cabinet. The eight Ministers were :

1. Peshwa (Prime Minister), who looked after the welfare of the state generally.
2. Amatya or the Finance Minister.
3. Mantri of the chronicler, who kept a diary of the king's daily doings and recorded everything that happened at the court.
4. Sumant or the Foreign Secretary.
5. Sachiva or the Home Secretary.
6. Pandit Rao and Dandadhakshya or the head of the ecclesiastical department, who looked after the grants to religious and learned men, decided theoligical disputes and questions relating to customs.
7. Senapati or Commander-in-Chief.
8. Nyayadhisha or the Chief Judge.

The administration of justice was of a punitive kind. There were no regular courts and no systematic procedure. In villages the elders held Panchayats to settle disputes submitted to them. Ordeal was common, and we read of men fearlessly grasping red-hot iron or

9

APPLICATION OF MOHAMMEDAN LAW IN INDIA : THE DIFFERENT SCHOOLS

Let us now study the principles of Mohammedan Law applied in India. The Prophet Mohammad, founder of Muslim religion was born at Mecca on 12th Rahi-al-awwal, corresponding to 22nd April 571 A.D. The Prophet was recognised as the supreme overlord and the supreme preceptor. Arabic was steeped in ignorance and barbarism, superstitions and vice. Female infanticide, drinking, lechery and other vices were rampant. However, the Prophet did not nominate a successor. But the successor was elected and called Caliphate. In course of time Ommayads of Damascus became temporal and spiritual head of Arabs with Damascus as the capital. Muavia was the first Caliph of the House of Ommeyya. It was during their period that the foundation of Islamic Law and jurisprudence was laid at Damascus but the real centres of learning continued at Macca, Medina and Kufa.

Schools of Islamic Law. The first broad division is between the schools of Sunni and Shia laws. There are four recognised schools of Sunni Law : 1. Hanafi school, 2. Maliki school, 3. Shafii school and 4. the School of Ahmad ibn Hambul.

Hanafi School. This is the most famous of the four schools of Hanafi Law. It was founded by Abu Hanifa and is also known as "Kufa School". The school was favoured by Abbasid Caliphs and its doctrines spread far and wide. Abu Hanifa earned the appellation "The Great Imam". The Imams left behind a number of books on jurisprudence based on Quran and called Shriyat. The books on the doctrine are *al-Hidaay* of Marghinavi. The *Fatwa-i-Alamgır* collected in Aurangzeb's time contain the doctrine of this school with other material.

The Malika School. This school was founded by Malik ibn Anas (713-795 A.D.), who was an inhabitant of Medina. He expounded the traditions. Malika's book *Kitab-al-Muwatta* systemised the law. Another important book containing Malika Doctrine is *al-Mukhtasan* of Khalil Ibn Ishak. By 854 A.D., the Maliki school law got firmly established.

The Shafii School. This school was founded by Mohammed-ibn-Idris-Al-Shafii (767-820 A.D.) He was a pupil of Malik-ibn-Anas but lived a part of his life at Baghdad and the rest at Cairo. Al-Shafii was foremost in jurisprudence and methodology of law. He was responsible for the doctrine of Qiyas but he ruled that an analogy may be based rightly on the Quran or Hadis or Ijmaa (infra). He established Ijmaa as a source of law and recognised only the Sunna (infra) of the Prophet. A large number of books have been written on Shafii school of which *Tuhfat-al-Muhtaj* of Hafai and *Nihajat-al-Muhtaj* of Ramli are standard authorities.

The Hambali School : Every modification of principles which took people away from the traditions of the Prophet caused a reaction among those who held to the traditions. This was practically so where '*Qiyas*' (Infra) was developed. The most exhaustive work on Hambali doctrine written by Muwaffak-al-Din. In India there is a sect known as Ghair Muqqallad, who do not strictly follow any school and who are akien to Wahabis.

The Shia School : Shia school owes its origin to Imam Jafaras-Sadik, the 6th Imam of the Imamias. This makes it earlier in point of time to most of the Sunni Schools discussed above. There are many differences in Shia and Sunni jurisprudence. Shias do not accept any tradition attributed to Prophet (Infra) unless it comes from the household of the Prophet. They also do not accept the validity of any decision not endorsed by an Imam. The Imamia Shias are divided into two main branches—'Akhbari' and 'Usuli'. The Akhbarias accept certain resolutions of former scholars but not the Usulis. The latter accept only those which are approved by their Imams. Ijma is valid only if the Imam could not be consulted. Conversely there is no room for equity, public policy or analogical deduction if the Imams were available. The Shias are found in Persia where they form the largest majority. Elsewhere they are in minority.

Degree of Obedience. Islam divides all actions into five kinds which figure differently in the sight of God and in respect of which his commands are different. This plays an important part in the lives of Muslims.

1. *First degree* : 'Farz'—whatever is commanded in Koran-Hadis or Ijmaa must be obeyed.
2. *Second degree* : Masnun, Mandub and Mustabah :

These are recommended actions.

3. *Third degree* : Jaiz or Mubah : These are permissible actions as to which religion is indifferent .
4. *Fourth degree* : Makruh : That which is reprobated as unworthy.
5. *Fifth degree* : Haram : That which is forbidden.

Sources of Islamic Laws

There are four sources of Islamic Law: 1. Koran, 2. Sunna or Tradition, 3. Ijmaa or consensus of opinion and 4. Qiyas or analogical deductions.

The Koran. Muslims believe in the divine origin of their Holy book which according to their belief was revealed to the Prophet by Gabriel. The Koran is Al-furgan i.e. one showing truth from falsehood and right from wrong. The Koran contains about 6000 verses but not more than 2000 verses deal with legal principles and if we leave out of account those which concern the state as such, there are about 80 verses, more or less, which deal with law of personal status. Most of them are concerned with inheritance, marriage, divorce and such like matters. The Koran does not even set them out as a code in one place. They are found in the position of the Koran revealed to the Prophet at Medina. The portion which was revealed at Mecca is singularly free of legal matters and contains the philosophy of life of religion and particularly Islam. The legal verses embody broad principles but do not explain or expound them. As the Koran is of divine origin, so are the religion and its times and the philosophy and the legal principles which the Koran inculcates. Since the Koran has no earthly source, it is obvious that none of this can be altered by any human agency or institution.

The Koran was compiled from memory after the Prophet's death from the version of Osman the third Caliph. During the Caliphate of Abu Bakr and Omar, the work of compilation of the Koran was begun under the supervision of Hazrat bin Sahit. The first version of Koran had no official standing beyond being a personal enterprise of Abu Bakr and Omar but a few years later this text acquired a great importance when the Caliph Osman set out to establish the economical text of the Koran.

Sunna or Tradition. The word 'Sunna' means 'the trodden path' and as this meaning shows, it denotes some kind of practice and precedents. At first this word was applied to custom and to the practice of early school of law, but later and finally it means the practice and precedents of the Prophet. The principles which were stated in the Koran found their aplication in the hands of the Prophet. This gave birth to Hadis (practice) of Prophet. As a source of law, Hadis is as binding as the principles of Koran. The term 'Sunna' is sometimes applied to the precedents created by authorities, other than the Prophet but this is a wrong use of the term and is better avoided. The two sources—the Koran and Sunna—may be said to form the fundamental root of Islamic Law.

Ijmaa. It was equally binding on the people to act on a principle (not contrary to Koran or Hadis), which had been established by agreement among highly qualified legal scholars of any generation. This was supported by the Hanafi Doctrine that the provisions of law must change with the changing times and of the Malikis that new facts require new decisions. The validity of Ijmaa, as containing a binding precedent, is based upon Hadis of the Prophet which says that God will not allow His people to agree on an error. Ijmaa has become a source of law. Ijmaa was a feature of all schools of Sunni Law and the rules deduced by Ijmaa are equally valid and binding in each school. As a matter of fact without Ijmaa, which is responsible for a vast body of principles, the rules of Islamic Law, as contained in the Koran would have been extremely sparce. Authority for Ijmaa is said to emanate from a verse in Koran, "The way is by counsel in their affairs."

Qiyas. This is the last source of Islamic Law. Compared with the other three sources, it is of much less significance. It consists in applying some text if the case can be demonstrated to be governed by the reason of the rule underlying it although the language may not apply. This is reasoning by analogy. There is a Hadis of the Prophet which is usually invoked in this connection. When Mouadh was appointed chief justice of Yemen, the Prophet questioned him to know how he would conduct himself and this is what was said :

Prophet-On what shalt thou base thy decision ?

Mouadh-On the Koran.

Prophet-If Koran does not give guidance to the purpose ?

Mouadh-Then upon the usage of the Prophet.

Prophet-If that also fails ?

Mouadh-Then I shall follow my own reason.

The Prophet fully approved of the replies of Mouadh, and praised God that his servant was on the right path. Qiyas does not involve the laying down of new principles but is a kind of permissible exegesis upon some text.

Fatwas. Though not a source of law, Fatwas as opinions of judges and Muftis in the light of facts are important. These have been instrumental in the development and enrichment of legal principles.

Introduction of Mohammedan Law into India

The Mohammedan Law is applied by courts in India to Mohammedans not in all, but in some matters only. The power of the courts to apply Mohammedan Law to Mohammedans is derived from and regulated partly by statutes of the Imperial Parliament and Article 225 of the Constitution of India but mostly by Indian legislation.

The rules of Mohammedan Law in India falls under three divisions viz :

1. Those, which have been expressly directed by the legislature to be applied to Mohammedans such as rules of succession and inheritance.
2. Those, which are applied to Mohammedans, as a matter of justice, equity and good conscience such as the rules of Mohammedan Law of Pre-emption.
3. Those, which are not applied at all, though the partis are Mohammedans such as the Mohammedan Criminal Law and the Mohammedan Law of Evidence.

Thus the only parts of Mohammedan Law that are applied in India by courts to Mohammedans are those mentioned in 1 and 2 above. In other respects, the Mohammedans in India are governed by the general law of India. Even justice, equity and good conscience rules may not be applied if they are in the opinion of the court opposed to justice, equity and good conscience but the rules referred to in 1 above are the rules that have been expressly directed by the legislation to be applied to Mohammedans and must be applied, though they may not in the opinion of the court, confirm with justice, equity and good conscience.

Shariat Act of 1937

From 7th Oct. 1937, in cases where the parties are Muslims, the Muslim personal law applies in a number of important matters. The Act operates throughout India. As per this Act, "Notwithstanding any custom or usage to the contrary, in all questions regarding intestate succession, special property of females, including personal property inherited or obtained under contract or gift or any other provision of personal law, marriage, dissolution of marriage, including talaq, ila, zihar, lian, kula and mubaraat, maintenance, dower, guardianship, gifts trust and trust properties and waqfs (other than charities and charitable institutions and charitable and religious endowments) the rule of decision in cases where the parties are Muslims shall be the Muslim Personal Law (Shariat).

Section 3 (1) of Shariat Act Provides :

"Any person, who satisfies the prescribed authority :

(a) that he is a Muslim ; and

(b) that he is competent to contract within the meaning of Section 11 of the Indian Contract Act ; and

(c) that he is resident of India.

May by declaration in the prescribed form and filed before the prescribed authority, declare that he desires to obtain the benefit of the provisions of this section, and thereafter the provisions of section-2 shall apply to the declarant and all his minor children and their descendants as if in addition to the matters enumerated therein, adoption wills and legacies were also specified."

Who is a Mohammedan. Any person, who professes the Mohammedan religion, that is acknowledges that there is but one God and that Mohamed is his Prophlet, is a Mohammedan. Such a person may be a Mohammedan by birth or he may be a Mohammedan by conversion. It is not necessary that he should observe any particular rites or ceremonies or be an orthodox believer in that religion as no court can list or guage the sincerity of religious belief. It is sufficient if he professes the Mohammedan religion in the sense that he accepts the unity of God and the Prophetic character of Mohammed.

Conversion to Mohammedan of a Hindu wife does not *ipso facto* dissolve her marriage with her husband. She cannot, therefore, during the husband's lifetime enter into a valid contract of marriage with any other person. Thus, if she after conversion to Mohammedanism, goes through a ceremony of marriage with a Mohammedan, she will be guilty of bigamy.

Mohammedan Sects. Mohammedans are divided into two sects namely Sunnis and the Shias. Sunnis are divided into four sub-sects viz. Hanafis, Malikis, Shafiis and the Hambalis. The Sunni Mohammedans of India belong principally to the Hanafi School.

The Shias are divided into three main sub-sects namely the Athna-Asharias, the Ismailyas and the Jaidyas. Most of the Shias belong to Athna-Asharias. The Mohammedan Law applicable to each sect of sub-sect is to prevail as to litigants of that sect or sub-sect. A Mohammedan, male or female, who has attained the age of puberty may renounce the doctrines of the sect or sub-sect to which he or she belongs, and adopt the tenets of the other sub-sect or any other sect and he or she will thenceforth be subject to the law of the new sect or sub-sect. A Sunni woman contracting marriage with a Shia does not thereby become subject to the Shia law and vice versa.

Succession and Administration. Unlike Hindu Law, the estate of a deceased Mohammedan, if he had died instestate, devolves on his heirs at the moment of his death. Under the Mohammedan Law, birth right is not recognised. The right of an heir apparent or presumptive comes into existence for the first time on the death of the ancestor, and he is not entitled until then to any interest in the property to which he would succeed as an heir if he survived the ancestor. There is no joint tenancy in Mohammedan Law and the heirs are only tenants in common. Therefore, an heir can claim partition in respect of one of the properties held in common without seeking partition of all the properties. Each heir is also liable for the debts of the deceased to the extent only of a share of the debt proportionate to his share of the estate. Now since the estate devolves on the heirs at the moment of the death of the deceased, the distribution is not liable to be suspended until payment of the debts.

In matters, not specifically mentioned elsewhere, the administration of the estate of the deceased Mohammedan is governed by the provisions of the following Acts to the extent to which they are applicable to the cases of Mohammedans, namely :

1. The Indian Succession Act 1925.
2. The Administrator-General's Act 1913; and
3. Bombay Regulation VIII of 1827.

Inheritance. There is no distinction in the Mohammedan Law of inheritance between movable and immovable property or between ancestral and self-acquired property. Further, there is no such thing as a joint Mohammedan family nor does the law recognise a tenancy in common in a Mohammedan family.

Birth-right not Recognised. The right of an heir-apparent or presumptive comes into existence for the first time on the death of the ancestor, and he is not entitled until then to any interest in the property to which he would succeed as an heir if he survived the ancestor.

There are three classes of heirs namely : (1) Sharers, (2) Residuaries and (3) Distant Kindered. Sharers are those, who are entitled to a prescribed share of the inheritance. Residuaries are those, who take no prescribed share, but succeed to the "residue" after the claims of the sharers are satisfied and Distant Kindered are all those relations by blood, who are neither sharers nor residuaries. The question as to which of the relations belonging to the class of sharers, residuaries or distant kindered are entitled to succeed to the inheritance, depends on the circumstances of each case.

Thus, if the surviving relations, be a father and a grandfather, the father alone will succeed to the whole inheritance to the entire exclusion of the grandfather, though both of them belong to the class of sharers and if the surviving relations be a son and a son's son, the son alone will inherit the estate, though both belong to residuaries. Similarly, if the surviving relations belong to the class of distant kindered, e.g., a daughter's son and a daughter's son's son, the former will succeed to the whole inheritance.

So, after payment of funeral expenses, debts, and legacies, the first step in the distribution of estate of the deceased Mohammedan is to ascertain which of the surviving relations belong to class of sharers and which are entitled to inheritance amongst them and then to proceed to residuaries and kindered in sequence.

Shia Law of Inheritance. The Shias divide heirs into two groups viz : (1) Heirs by consanguinity, i.e., blood relations and (2) Heirs by marriage that is husband and wife. Heirs by consanguinity are parents, children and other lineal descendants, grand parents, brothers and sisters and their descendants and paternal and maternal uncles and aunt and their descendants. Of these classes, the first excludes the second from inheritance and the second excludes the third, the nearer degree in each section excluding the more remote in that section. The husband or wife is never excluded from succession but inherits together with nearest heirs by consanguinity; the husband taking 1/4 or 1/2 and the wife taking 1/8 or 1/4 under different conditions.

Wills. Every Mohammedan of sound mind and not a minor may dispose of his property by 'Will'; the major being after attainment of 18 years of age. The 'Will' can be made either verbally or in writing. A Mohammedan 'Will', though in writing, does not require it to be signed, nor even if signed, does it require attestation; the reason being that a Mohammedan 'Will' does not require to be written at all. However, a Mohammedan cannot by 'Will' dispose of more than one third of the surplus of his estate after payment of funeral expenses and debts. Bequests in excess of 1/3rd cannot take effect, unless the heirs' consent thereto after the death of the testator. A bequest can be revoked, either expressly or by implication. In case of the person being on death bed, the gift of property can be made to the extent of 1/3rd after meeting the funeral expenses and debt.

Gifts. Every Mohammedan of sound mind and not a minor can dispose of property by gift but it can be limited to 1/3 rd after meeting the funeral expenses and debts, unless the more portion has the willingness of heirs. A gift in favour of minors and unborn children is void. As in the case of 'Will', gifts are not necessarily to be by writing. These can be orally declared too. For a valid gift, it is necessary that there is : (1) A declaration of gift by the donor; (2) An acceptance of the gift, express or implied by or an behalf of the donee; and (3) Delivery or possession of the subject of the gift by the donor to the donee. If these conditions are complied with, the gift is complete. Since writing of gift is not necessary, its registration too is not necessary.

Wakfs. Wakf means the permanent dedication by a person professing the Mohammedan faith of any property for any purpose recognised by the Mohammedan Law as religious pious or charitable. The term *wakf* literally means 'detention'. The legal meaning of *wakf* is the detention of a specific thing in the ownership of the *wakif* or appropriator and the devoting or appropriating of its profits or usufruct in charity on the poor or other good object.

The *wakf* may be in writing or the dedication may be oral. The subject of wakf may be 'any property'. A valid wakf may, therefore, be made not only of immovable property, but also of movable, such as shares in joint stock company, government promissory notes and even money but it must be belonging to the *wakif.* The following are valid objects of wakf :

1. Mosques and provision for insanes to conduct worship therein.
2. Colleges and provision for professors to teach in colleges.
3. Aqueducts, bridges and caravan *sarais.*
4. Distribution of alms to poor persons and assitance to the poor to enable them to perform pilgrimage to Mecca.
5. Celebrating birth of Ali Murtaza.
6. Keeping tazias in the month of Muharram.

7. Repair of imambaras.
8. Maintenance of Khankah.
9. Celebrating death anniversary of the settlor and members of his family.
10. Burning lamps in mosques.
11. Reading Koran in public places.
12. Performance of annual *fateha* of the settlor.
13. Construction of a '*ropat*' or free boarding house for pilgrims at Mecca.
14. Maintenance of poor relations and dependants.
15. Payment of money to *fakirs* and poors.
16. Grant to an Idgah.

Every Mohammedan of sound mind and not a minor may dedicate his property by way of *wakf*. The *wakf* may be made either verbally or in writing. It is not necessary that the term wakf be used in the grant if from the general nature of the grant itself, such a dedication can be inferred.

The *wakif* may provide for his maintenance out of the income of the wakf property. He may if he wishes, reserve even the whole income for himself for his life and the *wakif* may also provide for the payment of his debt out of the income of the *wakf* property.

Wakif property is not liable to attachment and sale in execution of the personal degree against the *mutawalli* nor can the rents and profits thereof be seized in execution.

Pre-Emption. The right of pre-emption or 'Shufaa' is a right, which the owner of an immovable property possessed to acquire by purchase another immovable property, which had been sold to another person. The following three classes of persons and no other, are entitled to claim pre-emption, namely :

1. A co-sharer in the property.
2. A participator in immunities and appendages, such as a right of way or a right to discharge water.
3. Owners of adjoining immovable property but not their tenants, nor persons in possession of such property without any lawful title. A wakif is not entitled to pre-empt as the wakf property does not vest in him.

The first class excludes the second and the second excludes the third but when there are two or more pre-emptors, belonging to the same class. they are entitled to equal share of the property in respect of which the right is claimed. The right in which pre-emption is claimed—whether it be co-ownership or participation in appendage—must exist not only at the time of the sale but at the date of the suit for pre-emption and it must continue upto the time, the decree is passed.

No person is entitled to the right of pre-emption unless :

1. He has declared his intention to assert the right immediately on receiving information of the sale.
2. He has with the least practicable delay affirmed the intention, referring expressly to the fact that the 'talab-i-marasibat' had already been made and has made a formal demand.

Marriage. Marriage (Nikah) is defined to be a contract which has for its object the procreation and the legalising of children. Every Mohammedan of a sound mind, who has attained puberty may enter into a contract of marriage. A girl of 15 years is said to have attained puberty. However, a marriage of a Mohammedan, who is of sound mind and has attained puberty is void if it is brought about without his/her consent.

Essentials of a Marriage. It is essential to the validity of a marriage that there should be a proposal made by or on behalf of one of the parties to the marriage and an acceptance of the proposal by or on behalf of the other in the presence and hearing of two male or one male and two female witnesses, who must be sane and adult Mohammedans. The proposal and acceptance must both be expressed at one meeting. A proposal made at one meeting and an acceptance made at another meeting do not constitute a valid marriage. Neither writing nor any religious ceremony is essential. A marriage may be valid, or irregular or void from the begining such as a marriage contracted without witnesses is irregular and not void.

A Mohammedan may have as many as four wives at the same time but not more. If he marries a fifth wife, when he has already four, the marriage, is not void but irregular. Conversely it is not lawful for a Mohammedan woman to have more than one husband at the same time. A marriage with a woman, who has her husband alive and who has not been divorced by him, is void. A marriage with a woman before completion of her *iddat* is irregular, not void (Iddat is the period during which it is incumbent upon a woman, whose marriage has been dissolved by divorce or death to remain in seclusion and to abstain from marrying another husband). The abstinence is imposed to ascertain whether she is pregnant by the former husband so as to avoid confusion of parentage.

The duration of the *iddat*, if the woman is subject to menstruation is three courses, if she is not so subject, it is three lunar months. If the woman is pregnant at the time, the period terminates upon delivery or four months and ten days, which ever is longer. When the marriage is dissolved by death, the duration of *iddat* is four months and ten days.

Valid and Void Marriage. A Sunni male may contract a valid marriage with a Shia female and vice versa ; the rights and obligations of the wife would be governed by the law to which she belonged at the time of her marriage.

A Mohammedan male may contract a valid marriage not only with a Mohammedan woman but also with a 'Kitabia' that is a Jewess or a Christian but not with an idolatress or a fire-worshipper. A marriage with an idolatresss or a fire worshipper is not void but merely irregular. Conversely a Mohammedan woman cannot contract a valid marriage except with a Mohammedan. She cannot contract a valid marriage even with a Kitabia that is a Christian or a Jew. A marriage, however, with a non-Muslim is irregular and not void.

A marriage which is not valid, may be either void or irregular.

A void marriage is one which is unlawful in itself; the prohibition against the marriage being perpetual and absolute. Thus, a marriage prohibited by reason of consanguinity, affinity or fosterage is void. An irregular marriage is one which is not unlawful in itself, but unlawful 'for something else' as when the prohibition is temporarty or relative, or when the irregularity arises from an accidental circumstance, such as the absence of witnesses, marriage with a fifth wife; marriage with a woman undergoing iddat, marriage with the spouse of different religion. The reason for being irregular and not void is that in such cases irregularity can be removed.

A valid marriage confers upon the wife the right to dower, maintenance and residence in her husband's house; imposes on her the obligation to be faithful and obedient to him, to admit him to sexual intercourse and to observe *iddat*. A void marriage is no marriage at all and so does not create any duties or liabilities. An irregular marriage may be terminated by either party, either before or after consummation by words "I have reliquished you"

Muta Marriage. Shia law recognises two kinds of marriages viz. Permanent and *Muta* or temporary. A Shia male Muslim may contract a *muta* marriage with woman of any religion but a Shia woman may not contract a *muta* marriage with a non-Muslim. A muta marriage does not create mutual rights of inheritance but the children conceived during that period are legitimate and capable of inheritance. The muta marriage, is for a specific term, and it ceases after the period is over.

Maintenance. The husband is bound to maintain his wife so long as she is faithful to him and obeys his reasonable orders but is not bound to maintain a wife, who refuses herself to him or is otherwise disobedient. After divorce, the wife is entitled to maintenance during the period of *iddat*. If the divorce has not been communicated to her until after the expiry of that period, she is entitled to maintenance until she is informed of the divorce. Where a wife, without lawful cause ceases to cohabit with her husband, the husband may sue the wife for restitution of conjugal rights.

Dower. Mehr or dower is a sum of money or other property which the wife is entitled to receive from the husband in consideration of the marriage. The husband may settle any amount he likes by way of dower upon his wife, though it may be beyond his means, and though nothing may be left to his heirs after payment of the amount. But she cannot in any case settle less than ten Dirhams. Where a claim is made under a contract of dower, the court should, unless it is otherwise provided by any legislative enactment, award the entire sum provided in the contract. The amount of dower can also be fixed before or after marriage and can be increased after marriage.A contract of dower made by father on behalf of his minor son is binding on the son.

Divorce. The contract of marriage under the Mohammedan Law may be dissolved in any one of the following ways :

1. By the husband at his will, without the intervention of the court.
2. By mutual consent of the husband and wife without the intervention of the court.
3. By a judicial decree at a suit by the husband or wife.

The wife cannot divorce herself from the husband without his consent, except under a contract whether made before or after marriage but she may in some cases obtain divorce by a judicial decree.

Any Mohammedan of sound mind, who has attained puberty, may divorce his wife, whenever he desires, without assigning any reason. The 'talak' may be effected : 1. Orally (by spoken words) or 2. By a written document, called a talaknama. No particular form is to be filled in for talak. The husband can only say 'thou art divorced;' 'I have divorced' or 'I divorce my wife'. The pronouncement of 'talak' amounts to dissolution of marriage. Talak, once given is irrevocable.

The Dissolution of Muslim Marriage Act was passed in 1939 with a view to consolidate and clarify the provision of Muslim Law relating to suits for dissolution of marriage by women married under Muslim Law and to remove doubts as to the effect of renunciation of Islam by a married Muslim woman or her marriage. The wife is entitled to obtain a decree for the dissolution of her marriage if the husband has neglected or has failed to provide for her maintenance for a period of two years; if the husband is insane; if husband treats her with cruelty or makes her life miserable or conducts himself as such even if such conduct does not amount to physical ill-treatment.

Parentage, Legitimacy and Acknowledgement

Parentage is the relation of parents to their children. Paternity is the legal relation between father and child. Maternity is the legal relation between mother and child. These legal relations give rise to certain rights and liabilities as regards inheritance, guardianship, and maintenance.

The maternity of a child is established in the woman, who gives birth to the child irrespective of the lawfulness or her connection with the begetter. Paternity of a child can only be established by marriage between its parents. The marriage may be valid or irregular but not void. Marriage may be established by direct proof. If there be no direct proof, it may be established by indirect proof that is by presumption drawn from certain facts. It may be presumed from prolonged cohabitation combined with other circumstances or from an acknowledgement of legitimacy in favour of a child. The fact that any person was born during the continuance of a valid marriage between his mother and any man or within two hundred and eighty days after its dissolution; the mother remaining unmarried, shall be conclusive proof that he is the legitimate son of that man.

Guardianship of Person and Property. Minor means a person, who has not completed the age of eighteen years as per Indian Majority Act. All applications for the appointment of guardian of the person or property or both of a minor are to be made under the Guardians and Wards Act 1890. Mother is entitled to the custody (*hizanat*) of her male child until he has completed the age of seven years and of her female child until she attained puberty. In default of the legal guardians, the duty of appointing a guardian for the protection and preservation of the minor's property falls on the judge as representing the state. A legal guardian of a minor has no right to dispose of immovable property except in certain stated circumstances where sale is necessary for maintenance of the minor; when there are legacies to be paid and there is no other source, etc.

Maintenance of Children and Grandchildren. A father is bound to maintain his sons until they have attained the age of puberty. He is also bound to maintain his daughters until they are married but he is not bound to maintain adult sons unless they are disabled. Children, in easy circumstances, are bound to maintain their poor parents, although the latter may be able to earn something for themselves. Similarly, a person is bound to maintain his paternal and maternal grandparents if they are poor but not otherwise to the same extent as he is bound to maintain his father.

10

ADMINISTRATION OF HINDU LAW DURING THE MUSLIM PERIOD

Most of the important commentaries and Nibandhas on Hindu Law were composed during the Mohammedan period. This indicates that Hindu Law did not die during Mohammedan rule in India. But during Mohammedan period, the natural and untrammelled growth of Hindu Law was simply arrested to some extent. The rulers were strangers to this country. They did not accept Hindu Law for themselves, nor did they abolish Hindu system of law altogether. Hindu Law was allowed to be reserved for the Hindus and the Mohammedan rulers did not interfere with this system in any appreciable way, so far as its civil aspect was concerned. The result was that in this way the Mohammedans followed their Mohammedan Law and the Hindus were allowed to stick to their own system of law. Thus arose the two separate systems of personal law which practically proceeded on parallel lines and which remained to be modified later only at the time of British administration. It was clearly understood that a successful subjugation of the conquered must depend on the respects shown to their sentiments in general and to their laws and manners in particular. This was with respect to civil law only. The case was different in respect of criminal law. Herein the law was administered mostly by the self same tribunals, which made no distinction between the Hindus and Mohammedans or their systems of law. As a matter of fact the ruler underlined criminal administration and inflicted just and deterrent sentences most impartially irrespective of any consideration of the status or personality of the accused person. Again, the fundamental concepts of crimes and their punishments were essentially similiar to a very large extent in the Hindu Law and the Mohammedan Law except, of course, the Muslim cannon law, which was specifically inapplicable to the non-Muslims. It appears from the

Fatwa-e-Alamgiri that the application, if at all, of the principles of Muslim Law to the non-Muslims would be governed by proclamations and the edicts of rulers from time to time. Thus, as eating or selling pig's meat was allowed by Hindu Religion, no Hindu could be prosecuted according to the Muslim Canonial Law for such an act of a Hindu. The Muslims or the followers of Islam alone could be tried and punished for such acts.

The distinction between the personal laws of Hindus and the Muslims, which began in India with the Mohammedan rule were also maintained by the British, but the tendency was to reduce the scope of the distinction to its minimum. During the Mohammedan rule, particulary speaking, only the criminal law was largely common to the Hindus and the Muslims with the exception of the application of oaths and ordeals. And the civil law was administered according to the personal systems. The British rulers, however, began to widen the scope of common or general law and, as far as possible it was uniform for the Hindus and Muslims. The Indian Penal Code, the Indian Contract Act, the Civil Procedure Code, The Criminal Procedure Code, The Transfer of Property Act, the Indian Evidence Act, the Indian Succession Act are some of the most important legislative enactments to show that the difference between the two personal systems of law, as they originally existed, was being obliterated. The most significant juristic expression "Justice, equity and good conscience" also was equally applicable to the Hindu and the Muslim systems of law.

Thus, though there were two parallel systems of personal laws in India during the Mohammedan period, still there was the minimum influence exerted by one upon the other. Of course here and there, somewhat similar concepts and institutions might come across, but any positive evidence of definite influence of one upon the other will be rather debateble. Thus, both the systems had a religious conception of law in the sense that they were ultimately supposed to have been based on revelation and that the law bound the kings, the judges and the subjects alike. The rule of law governed both the systems of law. According to the very message of Prophet Muhammed, God, the Omnipotent, "Being alone, had the attributes of sovereignity". The Prophet himself did not claim for him any better position than an ordinary man. Similarly, a Muslim ruler was regarded as a God's servant, responsible for the observance of His law by all alike. The Muslim criminal law did not make any distinction between the rulers and the subjects. The law of Shara applied equally to all without any discrimination or partiality on behalf of the officers of the king. So the monarch could sue and be sued. The Mughal emperors insisted on their confirming the death sentence, wherein actually they could find an opportunity to commute the capital sentences in suitable cases. Apart from these prerogatives, the rulers also had the right and also the duty to supervise the entire judicial administration of the country. The adjudication by the rulers themselves was often sought by the people for their quick and impartial decisions. So, both the systems of Hindu and Muslim Law were largely governed by the rule of law.

In the development of these two systems of law and their sources to which they owe their existence also, there were essential points of resemblance. The most important sources of Hindu Law are the Vedas (Revelation), the Smritis (traditions), the Nibandhas and the Commentaries (opinions and interpretations of jurists) and customs and equity (actual usages and their explanations by the courts). Exactly corresponding are the sources of Mohammedan Law which are the Quran (revelation) by Prophet Muhammed. The Sunna (traditions as the precepts and usages of the Prophet Muhammed), Ijma (the consensus of the jurists and lastly the Qiyas (analogical deductions based on customs and justice, equity and good conscience). The ultimate fates of both the systems of Hindu Law and Mohammedan Law were again more or less the same during the British adminstration in India.

Though politically there was a division between the believers and the non-believers, yet in the eye of law, all were equal. There was impartial and stern justice essentially based on Islamic Law—equally binding the king, the Qazis and the Magistrates. Justice and beneficence must be exercised alike for all subjects. The king is the shadow of God and gift of divine mercy is common to all the believers and the non-believers. The purely Islamic civil code governing the laws of inheritance, marriage and other analogous matters of the Muslims did not at all apply to the Hindus. The Hindus were allowed to be governed by their own law on these topics of civil law. The case was, however, different so far as the Islamic Penal Law was concerned. The conceptions of crime and the purpose and sometimes the methods of punishment being virtually identical, there could not be any very appreciable difference between the two systems of law from the standpoints of wider interests of the society and the state. Thus, the Muslim criminal law was applied more or less equally to both the Hindus and Muslims guaranteeing security of life and property.

The non-interference with Hindu Personal Law by Muslim rulers was not without reason. The Sultans, after ascending the throne of Delhi, had very little time or opportunity to devote attention for the administration of justice in the country. They chose, therefore, to leave the Hindu Personal Law alone—undisturbed and uninterrupted. It was deemed to be an imperative necessity from the standpoint of politics for the sake of expediency. The Muslim Law was, however, taken from Egypt or Turkey on the Abbaside models. The Muslims' administration of justice was of "Perso-Arabic" origin and the three important sources of Indo-Mohammedan Law, the Koran, Juristic opinion and precedents were all "Trans-India". So, the Muslim rulers did not interfere with the personal laws of the Hindus; on the contrary, they adopted many time-honoured principles and institution of the Hindus.

Administration of justice was regarded as a special responsibility of the Muslim rulers like the Hindu kings. The Prophet is reported to have said that a moment spent in the dispensation of justice was better than seventy years of devotion. A dominion can subsist in spite of misbelief but it cannot endure with the existence of injustice. The mode of administering justice during the Mohammedan period was simple, speedy and without any elaborate law or procedure. Jehangir and other Mughal rulers had tied a chain of gold to a box wherein the people could lodge their complaints. In case of unreasonable delay, even the judges and the Qazis had to compensate the parties. The Qazis were instructed to use their reason and discretion in deciding disputes without relying too rigidly on the letters of law. During Mohammedan period, litigation was never encouraged. Capital sentence required the sanction of the king for execution. The king did not want to vest much powers in the hands of Qazis and Magistrates for fear of corruption. Generally speaking, there was wonderful and essential justice. Even close friends, Amirs and Omarahs of kings could not escape punishment if and when found guilty. Once Mohd. Tughlaq asked Qazi the cases in which capital punishment could be inflicted. The Qazi told firstly in apostasy; secondly in shedding of innocent blood ; and thirdly ; an adultery. Tughlaq replied, "All this may be true but mankind has become much worse since those laws were made" and he flayed alive a man convicted of treason and exhibited his dead body in public while the executioner was ordered to proclaim, " Thus shall all traitors to their kings perish". There were 25 capital punishments in the reign of Akbar,

Jehangir and Shahjahan. During their period, the criminal code was severe and the punishment was deterrent.

No non-Muslim could be appointed a judge or a Qazi as in Hindu Law, a non-Brahmin could not be appointed a judge. Also generally a non-Muslim could not be a witness against a Muslim but in actual practice it was not rigidly followed. Iltutmish, for the first time, introduced the system of employing Pandits to expound Hindu Law for the Hindus on the Abbaside model. Village Panchayats could try cases of local character. The number of witnesses was not insisted upon though generally four witnesses were required to prove adultery and two witnesses for adjudging a man insolvent. The *wakils* were allowed to be engaged for speaking on behalf of the plaintiff or defendant.

As has already been noticed, the Sultans, after ascending the throne of Delhi had very little time and opportunity to devote attention for the administration of justice or its organisation. They chose, therefore, to have the Hindu personal law alone—undisturbed and uninterrupted. They introduced and maintained Islamic Law in the general administration of justice. The Islamic Law, however, was taken from Egypt or Turkey on the Abbaside model. The Mughal emperors also followed the Sultans in many respects. As a matter of fact there was hardly any regular and systematic machinery for the administration of justice during the rule of the Sultans, of course, occasionally cases were tried by the Sultans themselves or by some royal *farmans* issued to the provisional governors. Sher Shah, however, made some valuable contributions in the matter of administration, in general, and administration of justice, in particular. But after his death, the system did not survive long. Similarly, during the rule of Babar and Humayun, there was hardly any attention bestowed upon the administration of justice in the country except that these emperors chose to decide some cases in camps in the most summary way without any reference to any regular code or procedure. The reign of justice, however, became more and more regular, systematic and methodical during the reigns of Akbar, Jehangir, Shahjehan and Aurangzeb—all of whom were highly eminent in the sphere of administering justice and equity to all concerned without any discrimination of caste or creed and rank or position.

Akbar was not only a great ruler but was also a great administrator of justice and equity. According to him, justice was the divine element in the monarchy. He says, "If I were guilty of an unjust act, I would rise in judgement against myself, what shall I say then of my son, my kindered and others." He tried all capital cases and other highly important cases. The capital punishment was by crushing by elephants, impaling and hanging. Akbar was, however, in favour of reformatory punishment as far as possible. He used to insist upon clear finding by thorough investigation without merely relying upon ordinary routine evidence. He himself did not spare any pains to thoroughly investigate into an allegation from all possible angles of vision for arriving at a true finding and he would insist on his representative also to be equally circumspect in the matter of administering justice. Though Akbar had a very high standard of justice to be scrupulously followed by himself as well as his delegates, still he was not always above all human frailties. Sometimes, he would be unduly influenced by wrath and passion to inflict the most unexpected punishment, following the most irregular procedure. With the result, too heavy punishment was inflicted on too minor offence. Jehangir too had a great love for administration of justice. He scrupulously followed the practice of adjudging cases even when he was in pain or sorrow or was indisposed. He was responsible for having installed the golden chain of justice. The system underlined by the golden chain, was an exemplary one, as it was a very powerful instrument in putting an end to all sorts of injustice and oppression by the Govenment officers belonging to the different ranks and grades. In case the allegation of complainant could not be substantiated, the complainant was punished for having unnecessaily troubled the emperor in pulling the chain. Jehangir forbade the cutting of nose or ears and blinding as forms of punishment. He issued orders that no capital punishment be executed until the sunset. Shahjehan devoted the whole of Wednesday in administering justice without holding the public *darbar* on that day. From morning till noon, he would decide disputes. He had a very efficient system of judicial administration. His sense of justice was very stern and impartial. In Diwan-e-Khas at the Red Fort of Delhi, he had a Meezan-i-Adl (Balance of justice) painted on the wall. This would always inspire the sense of justice and impartiality while Shahjehan would go for holding court for deciding disputes. He was also helped by the Muftis, Qazis and the Ulema. Some nobles also usually attended his court. He used to inflict severe punishments, sometimes even thieves guilty of heinous offences were punished by hanging or tranportation to the other side of Indus. The most important contribution of Shahjehan was the establishment of a regular system of appeals and hierarchy of different grades of tribunals. From the courts of the first instance, appeals lay to the courts of the provincial governors or the Qazis of the *subhas*. From their decisions again appeals could be preferred to the court of the Chief Dewan or the Chief Qazi in matters of law. The emperor had both original and appellate jurisdiction. He would everyday spend sometime in administering justice. When he would go to the 'Jharokha Darshan', in the morning, he would sometimes let down a string, from the window so that people might tie down their complaints and petitions to it. He was very particular about prisoners, so that they might not be detained unduly and for unusually long periods. He inspected the fort of Gwalior twice allowing an interval of five years. With the result that after the second inspection there was no prisoner left in the fort.

Aurangzeb was one of the most ardent followers of Islam in administering justice with impartiality and equity according to strict principles of Mohammedan Law as enjoined by the Shara. He also tried himself to master the essential principles of Quranic Law from the writings of the different jurists traditions and commentaries. Like his predecessors, he too reserved one day for administration of justice without holding Darbar on that day. He used to adjudicate cases from morning till noon in the Diwan-e-Khas in the presence of Qazis, Ulemas and the Kotwal. No body was authorised to inflict capital punishment without the previous approval of the emperor sought and obtained. The judgements were executed and punishments inflicted on the very spot immediately after the announcement of the judgement. He spared no pains to investigate a case thoroughly and then came to a correct finding.

The Islamic Conception of Crime, Punishment and Evidence

As has already been observed, the Muslim rulers left Hindu Civil Law alone and administred the self-same criminal law for all the subjects—Hindus and Muslims—without any discrimination. The condition of Muslim penal law continued until it was modified by the British administration, who ultimately replaced it by the Indian Penal Code and the Criminal Procedure Code. The gradual changes and modifications that were introduced by the British are indicated in further chapters. The criminal law had occupied a greater importance in the administration of justice by the Mughal emperors, who used to exercise their discretion in almost all the judgements passed and the punishments inflicted by them. There was practically no code for their guidance. The *Fatwa-e-Jehangir*, of course contained some rules but they were also more administrative than strictly legal. The most important code of law ever promulgated by the Mughal emperors was the *Fatwa-i-Alamgiri*, which was compiled at the instance of emperor Aurangzeb. In this work, an attempt has been made to constitute a standard canon of law based on the essential principles of the Shara. It was undoubtedly the only written book of law worth mentioning. In 1672, Aurangzeb issued a *farman* to the Governor of Gujarat. This might be regarded as the Penal Code of Aurangzeb. It contains rules regarding the administration of criminal justice, specially with respect to the imprisonment of culprits. A minute examination of the rules of Farmans will reveal certain striking points of similarity and difference between Hindu and Muslim ideas of criminal law. In the first place there were, during Muslim rule, prisons, where offenders could be detained viz. prisons of Gwalior, Ranthambore and other places but no period, for which the offenders could be detained, was given. Mughal emperors were very anxious to see that the prisoners might not be detained unduly for long periods. They themselves examined the cases of prisoners individually and issued orders of their release unless they were found to have committed serious political offences.

There were prisons in ancient India too. But whereas in Hindu law there were different grades of fines, in Muslim Law, there was no question of fine as realisation of fines was illegal according to the Shariat. So, every offender was imprisoned, or dismissed or banished but never fined. There were common corporal punishments, including sentence of death in both laws.

Punishment in Muslim Law

The Muslims' conception of punishment was more reformative as it is indicated by the fact that offenders should be detained in prisons until they are repentant. In Hindu Law too there is provision of 'Prayschita'. In both laws the habitual offenders were liable to heavier punishments. In ancient Hindu Law, caste played an important part and the Brahmins were not liable to any corporal or capital punishment. But no such distinction is seen in Muslim criminal jurisprudence. The Islamic Law of crimes was crude and archaic; the law of punishment was horrible and inhuman and the law of evidence was artificial and technical. There was hardly any distinction, between public law and private law. The conception of crimes being offences against the state was not yet recognised. Offences like drunkenness and adultery were considered as offences against God and offences like murder and robbery were offences against men. Then, even murders and homicide were regarded as private grievances compoundable and pardonable by the relations of the deceased.

The punishment in Muslim law was broadly classified as Hadd, Kisa, Diya and Tazir. Hadd literally means boundary or limit. In this case, there were scheduled punishments for scheduled offences and the judges could not modify or alter them in any way. Such punishments wefe stoning or scourging for Zina for illicit intercourse; amputation of hands for theft and scourging for a false accusation of adultery against a woman. Kisa means retaliation. According to this principle, wilful killing and some kinds of grievous hurts and maiming entitled the injured person or his relations to inflict the same injury on the wrong-doer. Diya was the blood money or money compensation, which could be accepted in lieu of the retaliation. Tazir means the discretionary punishments. There were no specifications of this punishment either in quality or in quantity. Sometimes even new punishments or new modes of punishments could be devised by the judges and the kings.

Muslim Law of Evidence

The Muslim law of evidence was peculiarly artificial; hence conviction in many cases would become impossible or difficult. The evidence of an unbeliever could not lead to a capital punishment. In other cases, the testimony of one Muslim was regarded as equivalent to that of two Hindus. Again, the evidence of one man was equal to that of two women. The fixed number of witnesses was also insisted upon in Muslim Law. For conviction in a rape case, the evidence of four eye-witnesses was necessary. This would mean that such evidence would be next to impossible. For theft again, there must be two witnesses subject to the general rule that one man was equal to two women. In actual cases, there were many difficulties in adducing sufficient evidence for conviction. Direct evidence was always insisted upon and there might be innumerable circumstances giving rise to suspicion or doubt regarding the culpability of the offender. Thus Muslim law seems more adopted to offer redress to the party aggrieved than to inflict chastisement on the criminal and make an example to deter others. So, conviction could not be secured too readily. Therefore, Muslim law was not as atrocious as it appears to be in the first sight. The Mohammedan Law of crimes is mild for though some of the principles, it sanctions, be barbarous and cruel, yet not only is the infliction of them rarely rendered compulsory on the magistrate but the law seems to have been framed with more care to provide for the escape of the criminals than to find conviction on sufficient evidence and to secure the adequate punishment for offenders. On account of Tazir or discretionary form of punishment, there always remained the chance of sentence being either unduly severe or ridiculously lenient.

Defects of Muslim Law

The administration of justice during the Muslim rule as a whole had certain glaring defects. In the first place, the Muslim law being inseparably connected with the Muslim religion, could not be applicable to the Non-Muslims; in the second place, no precision even of the Quranic Law also could be expected, as the profession of law was in the hands of men, who derived their knowledge by inheritance or possessed it by intuition, without any previous study or application. In the third place, the courts would not maintain any register or proceedings at all ; the usual consequence being that even the self-same cause could be tried more than once according to the interests of the parties concerned, and lastly the heavy fees in the forms of *chauth* or one-fourth of the total amount decreed, was another very vital consideration for which most of the people usually resorted to arbitration as the mode of trial in civil suits. The confusion was worse confounded after the grant of Diwani in favour of the East India Company. Things also did not improve to any appreciable extent even after the establishment of the plan of supervision and control in 1769 as the supervisors and the members of controlling council were absolutely lacking in experience and knowledge of administration.

Constitution and Functions of Courts as they Existed Just After the Assumption of Diwani in 1765

The name of Islamic jurisprudence was 'Fiqh' based on the Quran, which was the ultimate source of Islamic religion and law. In theory, a non-Muslim had no right to full citizenship but there was some divergence between this theory and the practice. Hence the Hindus enjoined under the Mughal Government, a complete indulgence with regard to rites and ceremonies of their religion, as well as with respect to the various privileges and immunities—in matters of property and in all other temporal concerns—the Muslim law gave the rule of decision exempting where both parties were Hindus, in which case the point was referred to the judgement of the Pandits or Hindu lawyers. Under the early Arab conquerers—the Khalifa used to appoint the Qazi, either verbally or in writing, insisting on certain conditions of appointment and enumerating certain duties to be performed by him. According to Central Mughal judicial system too, the emperor, like the Khalifa, was the supreme judicial authority as he was the highest court of appeal and sometimes acted as the court of the first instance too. Besides the emperor, there was the Chief Qazi and the Diwan-i-Ala. There were also the Daroga-i-Adalat and the Chief Sadr. The administration of justice in the provinces, was a miniature of the central system, the Nazim being the vice-regent or the sovereign in the province. Like the Daroga-i-Adalat, at the center, the provincial Diwan also had his Daroga for civil causes. Every province thus had the following officers who were concerned with the administration of justice, law, and order. There was the Qazi, who was the judge of canon law—civil and criminal; there was the Muhtasib, who might be regarded as the censor of public morals and superintendent of weights and measures; there was the Sadr, who was in charge of religious and charitable endowments; there was also the Kotwal and the Bakshi, the former being the prefect and the superintendent of the city police and the municipal officer and the latter being the paymaster general. Moreover, there was a number of Wakya-Nawis (News Reporters), the Khufia-Navis (Spies) and the Harkaras (News agents). The provinces in their turn were divided into Sarkars which were subdivided into Parganas.

11

VILLAGE PANCHAYATS FOR ADMINISTRATION OF HINDU LAW DURING THE MOHAMMEDAN PERIOD

The Village Panchayats, as integral parts of the village republics, played a very important part in ancient and Medieval India and they are still playing a very important role in modern India also. In their judicial capacity, they decided local disputes. The importance of village Panchayats was emphasised by RR Diwakar, Governor of Bihar by saying, "I look upon the Panchayat as the basis of all democratic governments." It has also been said that neither Mauryan bureaucracy, nor Mohammedan invaders, neither the centralised administration of Akbar or Aurangzeb, nor the British Ryotwari or permanent settlement have obliterated the traditional rights of the village communities as described in the *Arthashastra*. The functioning of village Panchayats was hardly interfered with even though they gave very important decisions based on local customs in keeping with the law of the country. Today the Village Panchayat Acts have given very wide powers to the Panchayats. During Mohammedan period where the rulers were non-Hindus, the Hindus depended mainly on these Panchayats without seeking any redress from the alien rulers themselves, particularly in civil disputes. The Hindus really felt shy to approach the foreign rulers for adjudicating their own personal disputes which were to be decided with special reference to their personal laws and customs. The rulers too welcomed their idea and refused to interfere with the administraton of the local Panchayats or assemblies which to a great extent relieved the rulers of their judicial responsibilities.

It has already been seen that even from the early times of the Samitis there were many tribunals in the ancient India in the shape of assemblies of kinsmen, artisans, corporations and Parishads, which were more or less analogous to the village Panchayats in their jurisdiction and function. These different tribunals, according to Smritis, decided disputes amongst themselves. But there was one important point of difference between these tribunals and the Panchayats of subsequent period that the conception of Panchayats originated with that of the tribunals referred to above. During Samiti period, they were not exclusively private as appeals lay from their decisions to the king in the last resort. These tribunals were, therefore, linked up with the king, who could revise their decisions on appeal and unless set-aside in appeal, decisions of the tribunals were final and binding. These were relegated to the position of Panchayats during Muslim period as Muslim kings did not want to bind themselves with the tribunals having legal jurisdiction. The Panchayats were recognised by the Muslim rulers as well, who did not, however, associate themselves with them as intimately and as coherently as the Hindu kings. The scope of Panchayats was, however, widened to include even the non-Hindus within their jurisdiction. The present day Panchayats too do not imply an exclusively Hindu Institution.

The rudiments of the various kinds of popular assemblies can be traced even in the Rigvedic society. From the very earliest times, the constitution of Hindu Society was organised on the basis of the autonomous village, as its units. The different institutions based on these villages were not only recognised but also greatly emphasised during the subsequent Smriti epoch. The population comprised of tribes known as 'Janas' comprising of 'Janpadas' or a collection of villages, who were made of '*gosthis*' and these *janpadas* and gosthis had their own tribunals as discussed above. In Dharmasutras and Dharmashastras too we come across certain other terms such as Gana, Kula, Srenipuga, Vrata, etc., as discharging some judicial functions. The Gana and Vrata are found in Vedas too. The existence at that time of so many kinds of judicial tribunals indicates that perhaps the country hardly had any central judicial structure and all judicial disputes were settled by tribunals only and recognised and executed by the people accordingly. Brihaspati and Pitamaha also speak of courts beginning with Kula, etc. The hierarchy of the different courts has been explained by Pitamaha as under—"A suit should first of all be tried in the village

(Tribunal or Panchayat); then it should be tried in the town (in appeal); then in the provincial court and last of all the king should give the final decision as the highest appellate tribunal. There is no retrial of any case once decided by the king—rightly or wrongly. *Manu Smriti* also enjoins on the king that he should respect the laws of the Jati, Sreni and Kula."

Though he does not expressly mention that these bodies have got judicial powers, still it appears to be implied that such power of adjudication also was recognised on their behalf. If these courts were in reality required to be stabilised by the king, then no further injunction would have become necessary to say that the king must honour the courts of his own creation. It, therefore, concludes that these courts were adopted by Jati, Kula, etc, and adjudicated the cases as per local customs only which differed from Jati to Jati and Kula to Kula. So the Kula, Sreni, etc, were private arbitrations, but there could be appeal from these courts upto the highest tribunal of the king, indicates that they somewhat had recognition of the king if not established by the king. According to Brihaspati, these courts could not decide the cases of 'Sahasa', which necessarily had to be decided by the judges appointed by the king as per uniform canons of law in the country.

Having their precursors in the different popular tribunals of the ancient Hindu society, the village Panchayats played a much more important role during the Muslim rule in India. As it has been seen above, there were so many kinds of different popular courts in ancient India, there cannot be any room for doubt that they were not actually functioning in the ancient society. The ancient legal literature of the Hindus abounds in descriptions and illustrations of the different kinds of popular courts constitutionally interlinked with each other in the sense that appeals could lie to the king as the highest tribunal in the last resort. These courts existed right upto the end of the Hindu rule. But with the consolidation of Muslim rule in India, the character of these courts underwent a fundamental change. Their link with the king as the last resort was not to be found in Muslim rule. Hence these became only popular Panchayats unconnected with the Muslim royal courts. But in a sense so far as the Hindus and their personal laws were concerned, they became more important and they began to serve the legal purposes of the Hindus almost exclusively so far as the civil side atleast was concerned as the Hindus felt shy in approaching Muslim rulers or the royal courts presided over by Muslim officers and the rulers themselves felt relieved when they saw that the administration of civil justice was being carried on by the popular courts of Hindus themselves. Thus, the exclusive jurisdiction of the Panchayats over the Hindus became much more prominent and was serving a much more useful purpose.

There were many factors that contributed to the survival and even for strengthening of the Panchayat system during the Muslim rule. The royal courts and the kings could be hardly accessible to the ordinary litigants as the court officers and employees were in the habit of harassing those that would go to them for justice; there was also corruption rampant everywhere. These drawbacks were to some extent remedied by Mughal rulers but on the whole the village Panchayats proved more or less satisfactory and least expensive. Moreover, there were not many regular courts, which could be within the easy reach of the people. Similarly to go to the kings and the emperors at the capital was again not always very easy and convenient. Hence, the Indian villagers in Mughal empire had to settle their differences locally by appeal to the caste courts or the Panchayats or the arbitration of an impartial empire (Salis).

East India Company also found some local courts already functioning almost on the line of the village Panchayats. These courts were re-modelled from time to time by the Company, which also sometimes established altogether new courts of minor jurisdiction on the model of village tribunals or Panchayats. These courts were necessarily of minor jurisdiction following very simple and speedy procedure unattended by any rigid formality or technicality. These courts could decide civil cases upto the value of 50 Pagodas and could try criminal offences of minor nature. According to the scheme of 1672, the Central Court consisting of one judge was established at Bombay. Below this court was created another court of petty civil jurisdiction under the name of "Court of Conscience." This court was mainly intended for administering justice to the poor 'free of cost'.

The Charter of 1753, not only modified the jurisdiction of mayor's court, but also created a 'Court of Requests' at each of Presidency towns of Bombay, Madras and Calcutta. These courts were intended to dispose of petty cases speedily and cheaply.

During the rule of Maharaja Ranjit Singh also, the Panchayat system was widely prevalent. There were Panchayats in villages and small towns as well. They used to administer both civil and criminal law. As it is gathered from the light thrown upon the administration of Maharaja by the European scholars, the Panchayats consisted of two very honest, upright and experienced men of high character and integrity. Only such highly competent persons could be appointed as members of the Panchayats. Like the Indian Penal Code and Criminal Procedure Code of the present time, there was no law book binding on the Panchayats for substantive or adjective law. Cases of debts, marriage, thefts, forgery and disputes relating to property were settled according to the customs of the country. But the law of inheritance and partition was based on precedents and old decisions. The witnesses used to take oath by the Holy Grantha or the holy water of the Ganges. This procedure was more or less followed in the British Indian Courts also. Spies were engaged for tracing theft and stolen articles and if footprints of a thief were traceable in a particular village, the inhabitants thereof would be responsible for tracing the thief and getting him arrested through the Panchayat. Ordinary disputes like affrays, etc, were heard and decided by the head of the area concerned known as Talukdar, who could inflict fines and corporal punishment.

The Constitution of India has rightly provided for a 'Directive Principle of State Policy' by Article 10, which lays down : "The State shall take steps to organise village Panchayats and endow them with such powers and authority as may be necessary to enable them to function as units of self-Government."

The complicated legal machinery of the country, specially during the British administration, entailing too heavy expenditure and involving great delay, was causing great harassment to the village people, and was one of the greatest impediment in the programme of the village uplift. A less costly judicial system capable of speedy disposal of cases, was what was wanted for the amelioration of the economic conditions of the people. Hence every state had started Village Panchayats essentially with the purpose of ensuring the most efficient administration of the village. Reference may be made in this connection to the Punjab Gram Panchayats Act of 1953. It was passed for better administration in the rural areas of the Punjab by Panchayats. Provisions have been made for administration of justice—civil, criminal and revenue. Extra judicial powers and functions have been referred and enumerated. The provisions of the Code of Criminal Procedure 1898, The Code of Civil Procedure 1908 and the Indian Evidence Act 1872 do not apply to proceedings before Panchayats, save to the extent mentioned in the Act.

As has already been seen, the Muslim rulers including Sultans and the Mughal emperor underlined the administration of criminal justice and hence the royal and imperial courts, including the rulers themselves, used to administer Muslim Law of crimes to all including the Hindus and the Muslims. So far as the personal laws of the people were concerned , it is quite clear that the Hindu Personal Laws governing marriage, inheritance, adoption and other topics of law, more or less, connected with the religion of the Hindus, could not be and as a matter of fact they were never actually administered by the Muslim Courts. This was the general condition of the society prevailing upto the turn of the advent of the British Company. The personal system of the Hindu Law and the Muslim Law was actually in application is clearly indicated by the provision that had to be made in the judicial plan of Warren Hastings in 1772. According to this provision, the Diwani Adalats were directed to decide all cases of inheritance, marriage, caste and other religious usages and institutions according to the laws of Koran with regard to Mohammedans and laws of the Shastras with respect to the Hindus. The scheme of Warren Hastings also fully corroborates the prevalence of Hindu law among the Hindus, otherwise, perhaps, he could not have made provision for two systems of personal law. This inidcates a stern reality which could not be overlooked or ignored by the foreigners even.

Though the Muslim rulers did not administer Hindu personal law themselves or through their courts, there is hardly any doubt that the Hindu kings of ancient times and the Hindu rulers contemporary with the Muslim rulers, invariably applied the Hindu Law for the governance of their subjects. According to the Buddhist pilgrims Fahien and Hiuen Tsang, who visited India in 5th and 7th centuries A.D. respectively, fine was the usual form of punishment and amputation of limbs was prescribed for exceptionally serious and heinous crimes. These are the very punishments prescribed by the ancient Dharmasutras and Dharmashastras. Capital punishment was hardly in vogue though it was theoretically sanctioned. In the Marathi records and the inscriptions of Southern India, we find unmistakable indication that most of the administration of justice was effected by the caste-courts and village Panchayats which derived their inspiration from the ancient Smriti texts. Shivaji also had a council of eight ministers. The Nyayadhisha was the minister-in-charge of administration of justice. He was to be a Brahmin, well-versed in the Shastras. The whole administrative and judicial systems of the Maratha rulers in general, and Shivaji in particular, were essentially modelled upon the ancient *Arthashastra* and the Dharmashastras. Qualified judges were appointed in the towns also besides the capital. The Panchayats were the usual courts for administering civil and criminal justice. Murder was regarded as a crime as well as a sin; hence even when pardoned, a murderer had to expiate by performing penances according to the provisions of Shastras. In case of theft, if the property could not be recovered, the aggrieved party had to be compensated by the Police or the villagers, where the offence was committed. A village could be exempted from the liability only when it could show that the offender could be traced to some other village.

In Mysore also, it was found that the administration of justice among the Muslims was entrusted to the Qazis, who would apply Muslim Law for this purpose. But the Hindus among themselves were to be governed either by customs or by the rules of the Shastras. This was the general scheme of administration of justice during the whole of the Muslim period under the Muslim rulers. On the judicial system of Maharaja Ranjit Singh also, it will be clearly seen that the administration of justice under the Maharaja was essentially based on customs and the levels of the text books on Hindu Law. As, according to the Smritis, the king was enjoined to administer justice himself as well as through learned and otherwise qualified judges, so the Maharaja also used to decide cases sometimes personally and sometimes through the officers appointed for this purpose.

Though the Muslim power was consolidated in Northern and Central India by the close of the 12th century, still the Muslim penetration into the South began only towards the close of the 13th century. The Yadava Dynasty of Devagir came to an end in 1318 and Mohammad-Bin-Tughlaq ascended the throne of Delhi in 1325. The Sultanate of Delhi was overthrown by the founder of the Bahamani kingdom in 1347. Towards the close of the 15th century, the Bahamani kingdom was divided into five separate monarchies which were conquered by the emperor of Delhi towards the latter part of the 17th century. Shivaji succeeded in having established an independent kingdom in 1674 which existed in varying forms until 1818 A.D. The Muslim system of administration of justice was followed in the kingdom of emperors of Delhi and Hindu system followed in Maratha kingdom. According to the institutions of Mohammed-Bin- Tughlaq, the systems of judicial administration consisted of two parts viz the central and the local. The former consisted of the Sultan, the Naib and the Wazir and Qazi-u-

Quzat, the last named officer being the head of the Department of justice which was known as Dewani-i-Qaza. The latter consisted of graded units such as the Iqlim (Province), the Shiq (District), the Shadi and the village. For each of these units, different officers had to be appointed for the administration of justice. The Amir, who was an officer for the Shadi, was to be assisted by some Hindu officers, such as, the Mutsarif, the Chaudhary, the Patwari and the Muqaddam. The same system was more or less followed by the other Sultans also upto 1650. One of the most important innovations introduced by the Bahamani Sultans was the construction of Majlis—meant for each Pargana, Taluk and village.

Judicial System of Shivaji

But the most important modifications were introduced by Shivaji, who was followed by his successors, including the Peshwas even for some years after the close of 18th century. Shivaji made enthusiastic efforts to revive the Hindu traditions enshrined in the original Sanskrit texts regarding the administration of law and judicial institutions. At the beginning of his career, when Shivaji was a mere *jagirdar* under the Bijapur Government, he used to administer justice through Majlis, which was nothing but the combination of the royal officers and the Gotas. But after the coronation, when Shivaji became a king, he used to decide important suits with the help of the Dharmasabha, which was the development of the Majlis of a Pargana resembling its Hindu prototype, as described in the textbooks of Hindu Law. To perform the duty of the Hindu monarch according to the Hindu Shastra tradition, he included in his council two ministers, the Nyayadhisha and the Panditrao—trying suits through the Dharmasabha in the open courts including the Rajmudra. The judicial system of Shivaji was followed by his successors, but Shahu made certain modifications which might be conveniently characterised as 'Feudalisation of justice'. Shahu came to the throne in 1708 and his system was modified only by the Peshwas, who were the defacto rulers of the Marathas from 1750 to 1818. Shahu, his Rajmandal, consisting mainly of feudal lords and other officers of the state and the Sardars, constituted his Central Government. The jagirdars and the Sardars were responsible for the local administration of the territories under their jurisdiction according to the *mokas* and the jagir tenures. Being the highest judicial authority in the kingdom, cases were brought to him for his adjudication with the help of the Rajmandal, the Ministers and the Sardars. Sometimes the Dharmasabha or the judicial council also used to be called for adjudicating important disputes. The members of the Rajmandal and the Sardars also used to adjudicate cases with the help of the Majlis as well as the Panchayat and ultimately the former was replaced by the latter.

Some Sanskrit judgements or Jayapatras have been traced which give an independent and unmistakable evidence of the fact that the Hindu Law, as enshrined in the original text-books and commentaries, was invariably used in actual practice and also that in spite of various vicissitudes—both political and social—the tradition thereof was brought down to quite recent times to have been modified by the judicial system, as introduced during the British rule. The rules laid down in Hindu system were so detailed and practical and their development so natural that they must have been the result of actual experience in the daily administration of justice.

PART—IV

BRITISH PERIOD

12

BRITISH SYSTEM OF ADMINISTERING JUSTICE

As has already been seen, with the advent of the Muslims and the consolidation of the Muslim rule in India, the natural growth of Hindu Law was considerably arrested, in the sense that it practically ceased to be administered by Muslim royal courts. The criminal law was administered by the Muslim rulers through the different courts, presided over either by the rulers themselves or by the judges or the Qazis, appointed by them. The Muslim criminal law was equally applicable to the Hindus and Muslims alike without any distinction of caste or creed or rank or position. The civil law of the Hindus, as derived from the earliest sources, was mostly administered by their caste-courts or Panchayats, constituted by their own people. But the Muslim civil law, based as it was on the Koran or the 'Shara', was not entirely beyond the recognition of the Muslim Royal Courts. The distinction was essentially based on the question of religion. So, after the introduction of the Muslim criminal administration, the original Hindu system of crimes and punishments; the conception of sins and '*prayaschita*' came to be suppressed. Of course, the religious theories did not absolutely die out. The conception of crimes and sins to be expiated to some extent by '*prayaschita*' and other religious rites, were confined to their private sanctions which were never the subject matter of the Muslim rulers or their courts. The immediate effect of the Muslim rule was thus the necessary introduction of two parallel systems of law in India in place of the only original system of Hindu law.

A third system of law was yet to be introduced into India after the advent of the Britishers and the introduction of the British system of administering justice in India. The British system, more or less, equally affected the existing laws of the country namely the Hindu Law and the Muslim Law. The bias or prejudice that was to be seen explicitly or implicitly in the distinction between Hindu Law and Muslim Law during the Muslim period was for obvious reasons not to be noticed in the British period. During this period, Hindu Law and Muslim Law were affected almost in an identical way, so far as their subsequent development was concerned. The importance of the effect of British administration on the growth of Hindu Law can hardly be over-emphasised.

In the British period also, the administration of justice affected the Hindu Law as well as the Muslim Law almost in the same way as it was the general principles of the Britishers that in certain specific topics, Hindu Law was to govern the Hindus and Muslim Law was to govern the Muslims. Excluding these specific topics, the residue was affected uniformly in order to do away with the distinction between two parallel systems of law.

Originally the English law was to be applied by the governors and the Councils or their employees only in disputes concerning the servants or the workers of the Company. But in course of time, English Law was being applied to the Indians also, who happened to reside within the territorial jurisdiction of the company and sometimes to the Indians in general, irrespective of the question of residence or employment. Some courts were established by the Charters of the British Crown and they were known as Royal Courts, as contra-distinguished from the Company's courts. Although theoretically the Mughal rule in India lasted upto 1858, when the last Mughal emperor Bahadur Shah II was sent to Rangoon in exile after the mutiny. But by this time, the company had taken various measures to change the law of the land and introduced principles of English Law and the English system of judicial administration. Direct and material intervention began from 1772 shortly after the assumption of Diwani of Bengal, Bihar and Orissa by the East India Company in 1765.

The Charter of 1661 gave very wide powers to the Company. The most important provision of the Charter was that the Company was empowered to appoint Governors and Councils in their Indian settlement and that these Governors and Councils were further authorised to try all cases—both civil and criminal—concerning all persons belonging to the company or living under them according to the Laws of England.

The Charter of 1683 authorised the Company to establish admiralty courts in order to check illegal traffic and punish piracy, which became so common. This court was to try all cases —Mercantile and Maritime in nature—and all offences committed on the high seas or within the

Charter limits. In 1688, was started the Mayor's court at Madras on the strength of the Charter issued in 1687. The mayor and the elderman constituted the court and all of them being laymen, a man "Skilful in Law" was to be attached to each mayor's court as the 'Recorder'. This Mayor's court was different from Mayor's courts established in 1726.

The first judicial system in Bombay was ushered into existence in 1670. According to this system, two courts were started in two Divisions of Bombay. All the judges were honorary. There were some Indian judges too. Above these courts, there was the court of Deputy Governor and Council. This court had both original and appellate jurisdiction and could try civil and criminal cases. A new system was introduced in 1676 when a court consisting of a judge was established in Bombay. This court could try all civil and criminal cases. In 1718, a new court of judicature was established in Bombay. This court consisted of nine judges, including the Chief Justice, four of the puisne judges were to be Indians. Appeals from the decisions of this court lay to the Governor and the Council. This court continued to function until 1726, when Mayor's courts were established in the Presidencies of Madras, Bombay and Calcutta.

In Bengal, originally the Zamindars were entrusted with the collection of revenues and maintenance of law and order within their respective Zamindaris. There, the condition of administration of justice was extremely deplorable. The Zamindars, however, assumed without any definite authority, the power to administer justice, both civil and criminal, more for their own interest and exploitation than for the pure and honest administration of justice. Each Zamindar maintained a criminal court as well as a *kutchery* or *adalat* for the administration of civil law. On the criminal side, all cases, including capital offences, could be tried by the Zamindars. The Company also began to administer justice in Calcutta through a collector. The Collector's court tried cases among both the Indian and the English people. The serious criminal offences used to be tried by the Governor and the Council according to the Charter of 1661. Too many powers were given to the collectors, who continued to administer justice in a punitive and rudimentary manner until the establishment of the Mayor's court in Calcutta in 1727. This court derived authority from the Crown. Although the Mayors' courts had been established in 1726 in the Presidency towns, the actual working of these courts was far from satisfactory. The independence of the Corporation and Mayors' courts was very much disliked by the executive of the company. The laws and customs of India were not at all respected and hence the courts gave rise to some discontent amongst the Indian people. When the interferences of the courts were brought to the notice of the Governors-in-Council, they resolved that the courts were not authorised to deal with caste and religious questions of the Indians.

The Company assumed the Diwani of Bengal, Bihar and Orissa in 1765. This was an important landmark in the evolution of Indian legal history. The Company also undertook to administer civil and revenue law and the administration of criminal law remained with the Nawab. Warren Hastings, who was the Governor of Calcutta at the time, formulated a scheme in 1772 for the better administration of the revenue and law for Bengal, Bihar and Orissa. According to the Plan of 1772, in each District there was a court for deciding civil cases. It was known as Mafussil Adalat, which had jurisdiction in all civil cases, including property, inheritance, marriage, debts, accounts, contracts, and partnership, etc. Similarly, for each district, there was established a criminal court named Mafussil Nizamat or Faujdari Adalat. Besides District Courts, there were superior courts at Calcutta known as Sadar Diwani Adalat, and the Sadar Faujdari or Nizamat Adalat.

Establishment of the Supreme Court

The battle of Plassey in 1756 virtually transferred the political authority of Bengal to the Company. But the company, instead of taking the entire responsibility, placed the Nawab on the throne of Bengal. For a long time there was chaos and lawlessness in the province. The matter came to the notice of British Parliament, who, with a view to remedy the situation, passed Regulating Act of 1773. It made important amendments in the rules regarding the Constitution and administration of the Company. Some legislative powers were also given. But the most important innovation made was the establishment of a Supreme Court of judicature of Fort William. The most conspicuous provision made by the Regulating Act was regarding the establishment of Supreme Court in Calcutta by a Royal Charter. The Supreme Court was to consist of one Chief Justice and the puisne judges, who were to be appointed by the king from Barristers of not less than five years' standing and who were to hold office during the pleasure of His Majesty.

Powers of the Supreme Court. The powers of this court were very wide including civil, criminal, ecclesiastical, and admiralty jurisdictions. For the town of Calcutta, grand jury and petty jury consisting of Englishmen were to be used. It was also a Court of

Record. For treason and felony, this court could try even the Governor General or the members of his council. No law enacted by the Governor General and Council could be treated as valid and effective unless it was registered and published in the Supreme Court of judicature. The Supreme Court was to be a court of law as well as of equity and the judges of this court were to have the same jurisdiction and authority as the justices of the courts of King's Bench in England. The Mayors' courts and other courts were superseded. The only court that still continued working was the Court of Request. Appeals from Supreme Court could be taken to the King-in-Council. The system of advocates and attorneys was also introduced for the first time subject to control of Supreme Court. Nobody except the advocates or Attorneys, could appear and plead before the Supreme Court of Judicature. The judges could act independently and competently. The Supreme Court had full power and authority to hear and determine all complaints, whatsoever, against any of his Majesty's subjects for any crime, misdemeanour or oppression and also to entertain, hear and determine any suit or action whatsoever against any of His Majesty's subjects in Bengal, Bihar and Orissa.

Conflict Of Powers. There was, however, constant conflict between the Governor General and Council and the Supreme Court on account of different powers given to them. In the long history of conflict, three topics became most conspicuous—one of them was the claim of the Supreme Court to exercise jurisdiction over the English and Indian officers of the Company, employed in the collection of revenues and to punish them for corrupt and oppressive acts, done in the course of their official duty; the second topic was the right that was claimed by the Supreme Court to try the judicial officers of the Company in execution of their official functions and the third topic was the claim of the Supreme Court that any person in Bengal, Bihar and Orissa beyond Calcutta, who contended that he was not subject to the jurisdiction of Supreme Court must have to appear before it and plead accordingly. In 1781, the Parliament passed an Act of Settlement to remedy the defects that became manifest by that time. As a result of the Act of Settlement, provisions were made more favourable to the Governor General and Council and many important limitations were imposed on the rights of the Supreme Court. It was provided in the Act of Settlement that the Governor General and Council shall not be subject -- jointly or severally -- to the jurisdiction of the Supreme Court of Fort William in Calcutta for any act done in their official capacity. All matters arising out of inheritance and succession to land and goods and matters of contract and dealings between party and party, shall be determined in case of Mohammedans by the laws and usages of Mohammedans and in case of Gentoos (Hindus) by law and usage of Gentoos (Hindus). It was also provided that where any one of the parties shall be a Mohammedan or Gentoo (Hindu), the Supreme Court shall apply the laws and usages of the defendant. The Act of 1781 put the Hindu and Muslim inhabitants of Calcutta on the same footing as the Hindus and the Muslims of the Mafussil.

In 1797, the British Parliament passed an Act whereby the Crown was authorised to supersede the judicial system of 1753 and establish Recorders' Court in both Madras and Bombay. All the restrictions imposed on the Supreme Court of judicature at Calcutta by the Act of 1781 were also imposed on the Recorders' court at Bombay and Madras. In 1808, the Parliament passed an Act authorising the Crown to abolish the Recorders' Court at Madras and establish a Supreme Court of judicature instead.

Judicial Reforms : Warren Hastings and Cornwallis

Warren Hastings was to thoroughly reorganise the Adalat system in the Mafussil of Bengal, Bihar and Orissa which had become very corrupt. By the Scheme of 1780, in each of the Six Divisions of Calcutta, Murshidabad, Burdwan, Dacca, Patna and Purnea, a court of Diwani Adalat was established to try civil cases. These courts were to be presided over by Englishmen, who were to be known by designation of Superintendent of Diwani Adalat. They were the covenanted servants of the company. The most important feature of the 1780 Plan was the separation of the executive and judiciary. Sir Impey, the Chief Justice of Supreme Court at Fort Williams was appointed as the sole judge of the Sadar Diwani Adalat of Calcutta in 1780. This was also a part of the general scheme of Warren Hastings, who was making an earnest endeavour for the systematisation and improvement of the judicial system of the country.

The most glaring defect in Warren Hastings' scheme on account of the small number of courts was remedied by Impey, who provided for eighteen courts in place of only six and made separation between executive and judiciary by making express provision that the courts of Diwani Adalat were specifically debarred from taking cognizance of any revenue matter—directly or indirectly. Another important provision made by Impey was in respect of the duties of the judges and the law officers. "No judge of any Mafussil Diwani Adalat shall upon any pretence whatsoever, cause pending then before him, in order to make of any decree, by any officer or officers, or any person, whatsoever, other than in the cases specially mentioned in these regulations, nevertheless that it be competent to such judge to refer any question arising on the Mussalman, or Hindu Law to the Maulavies or Pandits of the court, respect being had to the law in which each is conversant."

The criminal aspect of the judicial administration did not improve to any considerable extent though Warren Hastings made some efforts for this purpose. Hastings appointed in 1772, the Court of Sadar Nizamat Adalat at Calcutta with a Muslim judge and some Muslim law officers and shifted the seat of Sadar Diwani Nizamat from Calcutta to Murshidabad to avoid interference of Supreme Court of Judicature.

Judicial reforms innovated by Lord Cornwallis constitute the most important contribution to the growth of Indian Legal History. Though he was the Governor General only for about seven years, still he could afford to introduce reforms in the judicial field in three most important instalments—firstly in 1787, secondly in 1790 and thirdly in 1793. First reform was to effect the economy when the number of District Courts was reduced from 36 to 23. An English covenanted officer of the company was appointed as the collector for each of the Districts. The collector was to be responsible for collection of revenues and trial of revenue cases; he was also to act as the judge of the Maffusil Diwani Adalat and over and above these duties, he was also to act as the Magistrate of the district. The Magistrates were asked also to try minor criminal offences according to the Scheme of 1787. Thus, three distinct jurisdictions were given to the collector, to writ, revenue, civil and criminal with different hierarchy of courts of appeal for each of these jurisdictions. It was found that the entire system of criminal administration was corrupt, inefficient and irregular. Murders, robberies and dacoities were rampant; the judges were ill paid and the scope of temptation was very wide. New scheme of Cornwallis for reform of the criminal administration was promulgated by the Governor General-in-Council on December 3, 1790.

The most important provision of this scheme was that the Nawab of Bengal was absolutely divested of his control over the administration of criminal law. The seat of Nizamat Adalat was taken from Murshidabad to Calcutta. The Sadar Nizamat Adalat was to consist of the Governor General and the members of his Council—assisted by the Chief Kazi of the province and two Muftis. The law to be applied was the Muslim Law as modified by the regulations. The Court was to sit atleast once a week. The record of the proceedings was to be kept regularly. Below this Sadar Nizamat were the courts of circuits that replaced the former Fauzdari courts, presided over by Muslim judges. The provinces of Bengal, Bihar and Orissa were divided into four divisions. Each of these divisions was further divided into sub-divisions. The court consisted of two covenanted civil servants of the company as judges to be assisted by the Kazi and the Muftis, who were to be nominated by the Governor General-in-Council. The magistrates were the lowest courts in criminal administration. They used to hand over the suspected culprits to be tried by the circuit courts. In minor cases, they could try themselves and punishments could extend upto fifteen *rattans* or imprisonment for fifteen days.

Though the new scheme of 1790 was to entail a heavy additional expenditure, Cornwallis was convinced that the money was worth spending. He said, "It is bad economy at any time to withhold the sums requisite for the support of the establishments necessary for the administration of justice." He also considered that with the new scheme in force, the murders, robberies and other criminal offences will not be more frequent than most, necessarily being expected from the vices and passions to which human nature is subject and which under the best regulated Government will always impel some individuals to commit the worst of crimes.

The last instalment of judicial reforms on the side of civil law was introduced by Cornwallis in 1793. The most important improvement of this scheme was the separation of executive from judiciary. The executive was not only separated from the judiciary, it was subjected to the jurisdiction of civil courts. Mainly for the economy of expenditure in administration, Cornwallis was compelled to recombine in 1787, the executive and judicial powers in the collector in defiance of separation that was effected in 1774. But by 1793 he became a champion of the cause of separation of the executive and the judiciary. Another very important provision made in 1793 was that the Government was equally subject to the jurisdiction of courts in the same manner as between the individuals. The proposal of Cornwallis was that "where Government was a party with its subjects regarding property, it should submit its right to be tried through the medium of its officers in the courts of justice."

According to the arrangement before 1793, there were no intermediate courts of appeal between the courts of Diwani Adalat and the Sadar Diwani Adalat at Calcutta. According to the 1793 scheme, four provincial courts of appeal were instituted at Patna, Calcutta, Dacca and Murshidabad. The Diwani Adalats in the District headquarters were very much overworked on account of a large number of cases—both big and small. However, the necessity was keenly felt for relieving the district courts by taking away the less important cases to be entrusted to some subordinate judiciary, which comprised the Commissions or the Munsiffs. Another court that was provided for by the regulation of 1793 was the court of Registrar, who was the covenanted servant of the Company. The Registrar was also appointed to relieve the Diwani Adalats by trying minor disputes. Cornwallis also directed his attention and vigilance to the other aspects of litigation namely court fee and the legal profession. Court fee varying from 2 to 5 per cent were imposed on the litigants in 1787 in order to put a check on litigation by indirect taxation.

With the introduction of "Rule of Law" legal profession also assumed very great importance. It was felt by Cornwallis that the legal profession should be put on a sound basis to be controlled and supervised by the courts on the strength of Sanads to be issued by the Sadar Diwani Adalat. Any pleader found guilty or promoting or encouraging litigation, of frauds, or gross misconduct, would be suspended. The lawyers were to charge moderate fees according to the schedule contained in the Regulations.

The judicial structure that was laid down by Cornwallis was altered and improved by his successors according to the exigencies of the situation. The first discouraging feature that had to be met by John Shore was an undisposed accumulation of judicial work. There were 30,000 suits pending and half of this accumulation was in last nine months. Wellesely planned to take out the judicial powers from the Governor General in Council to be vested in judges, who would be independent of and separated from the executive and the legislative organs of the Government. In 1801, the most important provision made was that the Sadar Diwani Adalat was to be presided over by these judges. Secondly, the chief judge was to be appointed by the Governor General-in-Council from among its members of the Council. Thirdly, the other two judges were to be appointed from among the covenanted servants of the company. Fourthly, the Chief Judge and the puisne judges were to constitute both the Sadar Nizamat Adalat as well as the Sadar Diwani Adalat.

In 1805, Cornwallis again became Governor General when the Doctrine of Separation of executive and judiciary was brought to its logical conclusion when he enacted that the Chief Judge of the Sadar Adalat, was no longer to be a member of the Council. This was, however, again reversed in 1807, when it was provided that the Chief Judge shall be a member of the Supreme Council. In 1821, Lord Hastings' magisterial powers were given to the collectors and they came to be designated Collector-Magistrate. These collectors and not the judges became principal officers in the District.

Bentinck's Judicial Reforms

Lord Bentinck was responsible for many wholesome judicial reforms in the rapidly changing conditions—both economic and political—of the administration of the company. The most conspicuous reform of Bentinck was the establishment of the court of Sadar Diwani Adalat and Sadar Nizamat Adalat at Allahabad, from Jan 1, 1832. This was necessary to serve Banaras and Oudh provinces conquered by the company. These provinces were originally under Calcutta. The establishment at Allahabad gave relief to the people, who were compelled to go to Calcutta. Bentinck further remodelled the courts as under :

The Munsiffs, the Sadar Ameens, Principal Sadar Ameens, the Zilla and city Adalats and the Sadar Diwani Adalats were established. The provincial courts of appeal were abolished. The criminal administration was also strengthened by the appointment of Indians as Magistrates.

Termination of Company Rule in India

The Indian High Courts Act of 1861, marks one of the most important stages of development in the judicial system of the country. This was passed in 1861 after termination of the Company rule from India and taking over of Indian territories by the English Crown. Upto 1861, there were two sets of courts functioning in India. One such set consisted of the Supreme Courts, which were "Crown Courts" and the other set comprised the courts, which were known as the "Company's Courts." Each High Court was to consist of one Chief Justice and not more than fifteen puisne judges; at least one-third of these judges including the Chief Justice were to be barristers of not less than five years' standing and not less than one third of the covenanted civil servants of the company and the remaining judges could be taken from amongst the barristers, who were not of less than five years' standing, Civil servants of at least ten years' standing having worked at least for three years as District Judges or of the small cause courts for at least five years and pleaders of Sadar Courts or the High Courts for at least ten years' standing. The judges were to hold office during His Majesty's pleasure. After the establishment of High Courts in Bengal, Bombay and Calcutta, the Supreme Court, the Sadar Diwani Adalats and the Sadar Nizamat Adalats were abolished. These High Courts had both original and appellate jurisdiction in all matters -- civil, criminal, admiralty, testamentary, intestate and matrimonial.

Appeals from the High Courts could go to Privy Council of England. Originally, the Indians could not take any great advantage of the Privy Council as the procedure to be followed there was quite unfamiliar to them and the distance and the means of communication also had their own difficulties. The first Indian appeal to the Privy Council was preferred from Bengal in 1799.

Position further changed with the demand for independence by the political parties in India. The British Parliament passed Government of India Act of 1935, which gave the limited right of governance to elected State Assemblies in provinces. According to the Act of 1935, which gave a federal structure to the governance in India, a Federal Court was established in India having exclusive original jurisdiction in cases between the federation and its constituent units, advisory jurisdiction and appellate jurisdiction of a limited character. Appeals from the judgements of the Federal Courts would lie to the Privy Council, when these judgements were given by the Federal Court in the exercise of the original jurisdiction or in any other case by leave of the Federal Court to His Majesty in Council.

In anticipation of the new Republican Constitution of India, which came in force from January 26, 1950, the Act of 1949 was passed by the Constituent Assembly of India, which provided for the abolition of jurisdiction of His Majesty-in-Council to entertain appeals or petitions from any judgement, decree or order of any Court of Tribunal in India in any matter, civil or criminal. The new Constitution of India ushered into existence the Supreme Court having original, appellate and advisory jurisdictions. This was now destined to be the highest Tribunal of the land and the jurisdiction of Privy Council for appeals ended.

13

DEVELOPMENT OF LEGAL HISTORY DURING THE BRITISH ADMINISTRATION

As it has already been seen that the Dharmasutras, the Dharmashastras and the *Arthashastra* of Kautilya, along with the different commentaries and Nibandhas reveal a state of Hindu society in which Hindu Law was highly developed, both in its civil as well as the criminal sides, including their substantive and adjective aspects. But this highly elaborate and perfectly developed Hindu system of law was almost entirely eclipsed by the Muslim legal system, when the Muslim rulers succeeded in establishing and consolidating an empire in India. So far as the royal courts were concerned, the Muslim Law became very prominent and the Hindu Law was reserved for its administration by the Hindu Panchayats only among themselves. In criminal law in particular, the Muslim Law happened to replace it altogether and Muslim Law was administered through Muslim Kazis and Muftis. The then prevailing Muslim system of law in general with its peculiar and archaic conception of criminal law in particular and the most artificial and useless law of evidence, gave rise to a very unhappy and chaotic state of things which required immediate improvement. Things became more favourable after the passing of the Charter Act of 1833, which made provision for the creation of an all India Legislature and appointment of a law member as well as the Law Commission. At that time, Lord Macaulay had said : "I believe that no country ever stood so much in need of a code of law as India and I believe also that there never was a country in which the want might so easily be supplied."

Appointment of the Law Commissions

The first Law Commission was appointed in 1834 with Lord Macaulay as the Chairman. As the criminal law was in the most chaotic condition, the Commission was specially instructed to draft an Indian Penal Code and it became Act in 1860. The first Law Commission made a very comprehensive proposal that an Act should be passed making the substantive law of England as the law of the land (Lex Loci) subject to certain conditions and restrictions. Though nothing very concrete came out of the proposal of the first Law Commission and though it was subject to vehement criticism, still it supplied the right thinking people with sufficient material regarding the codification of the Indian law. On its recommendation Caste Disabilities Removal Act of 1850 was passed. A Second Law Commission was appointed in England in 1853. This Commission amalgamated the Supreme Court and the Sadar Courts and framed uniform code of civil procedure and criminal procedure for all the Courts of India. Accordingly IPC was passed in 1860, C.P.C. in 1859 and Cr. P.C. in 1861. Limitation Act was passed in 1859.

The Third Law Commission was appointed in 1861 for the purpose of preparing a body of substantive civil law in India. It drafted Law of Succession, Law of Contract, Evidence and Negotiable Instrument. The most important of the above drafts from the standpoint of legal history was that which aimed at codifying the Law of Succession of all the persons in India except Hindus and Muslims. It was again amended in 1925 and 1928. Similarly very useful purpose was served by the Evidence Act of 1872 and the Indian Contract Act of the same year, alongwith, I.P.C., Cr. P.C. and C.P.C. already passed.

The Fourth Commission was appointed in 1879. This Commission drafted bills on Trusts, Easements, Alluvision and Deluvion; Master and Servant; Transfer of Immovable Property Act, and Negotiable Instrument Act.

Laws and Society in Modern India

One of the outstanding achievements of British rule in India was the formation of a unified nation-wide modern legal system. The word 'modern' is used here to refer to a cluster of features, which characterise, to a greater or lesser extent, the legal systems of the industrial societies of the past century. The salient features of a modern legal system include uniform territorial rules, based on universalistic norms, which apportion rights and obligations as incidents of specific transactions rather than of fixed statuses.

In pre-British India, there was innumerable overlapping of local jurisdictions and many groups enjoyed one or another degree of autonomy in administering law to themseleves. The existence of Dharmashastras, a refined and respected system of written law, did not serve to unify the system in the way the national law did in the West, as Hindu Law did not enjoy the political conditions for unification. But it was not only the fragmentation of jurisdictions and the extensive delegation to local authorities that obstructed the development of a modern legal system, the relative absence of written records, of professional pleaders and of appeals made even local unification difficult. The Mughals and other Muslim rulers had, in cities and administrative centers, royal courts, exercised a general criminal (and sometimes Commercial) jurisdiction and also decided civil and family matters among the Muslim population. These Courts operated according to Muslim Law—atleast in theory, for the application of Shariat was qualified by custom and royal decree, by corruption and lack of professionalism, and by arrangements allowing considerable discretion to the Courts of first instance. While a hierarchy of courts and a right of appeal existed, it seems that the activity of these higher courts fell short of any sustained and systematic supervision of lower courts. Hindus were generally allowed their own tribunals in civil matters. Where these matters came before royal courts, the Hindu Law was applied. The Government courts did not extend very deep into the countryside; there was no attempt to control the administration of law in the villages. Presumably the Hindu Tribunals proceeded on before Muslim rule, except that whatever ties had bound these tribunals to Governmental authority, were weakened. There was no appeal to the royal court.

While undertaking to administer the law in the Government's Courts, staffed with Government servants (rather than to exercise a merely supervisory control over administration of law by non-Governmental bodies), the British took the decisive step towards a modern legal system initiating a process that might be called the 'expropriation' of law. This expropriation, which made the power to find, declare and apply law a monopoly of Government, came about in slightly different way and at different times in different places. But the general movement was the same. Three distinctive stages can be discerned in the development of the modern Indian legal system. The first, the period of initial expropriation can conveniently be dated from Warren Hastings' organisation in 1772 of a system of courts for the hinterland of Bengal. This period was marked by the general expansion of Governments' judicial functions and the attrition of other tribunals, while the authoritative sources of law to be used in Governmental courts were isolated and legislation initiated. The second period, which began about 1860, was a period of extensive codification of law and of rationalisation of the system of courts while the sources of law became more fixed and legislation became the dominant mode of modifying the law. This period lasted until independence after which there was a further consolidation and rationalisation of the law and the development of a unified judicial system over the whole of India.

The law applied in the courts before 1860 was extremely varied. Parliamentary Charters and Acts, Indian legislation (after 1833), Company Regulations, English Common law and Ecclesiastical and Admiralty Law, Hindu Law, Muslim Law and many bodies of customary law were combined in the bewildering array. It was a fundamental and persisting British policy that in matters of family law, inheritance, caste and religion, Indians were not to be subjected to a single general territorial law. Hindus and Muslims were to be governed by their personal law, i.e., the law of their religious group. In other cases, the judges were instructed to decide according to justice, equity and good conscience. These were prior to 1860 when numerous attempts to reorganise and reform the Courts and to systematise and reform the law including some reforms which changed Hindu law were made. However, there was no major progress towards simplifying and systematising the law until the Crown took over the governing of India from the East India Company in 1858. The quarter of a century, following the take over by the Crown was the major period of codification of law and consolidation of court system. During this period, a series of codes, based more or less on English Law and applicable, with minor exceptions, throughout British India, were enacted. By 1882, there was virtually complete codification in all fields of commercial, criminal and procedural law. Only the personal laws of Hindus and Muslims were exempted.

What happened to indigenous law as a result of the formation of the modern legal system, is first its administration moved from informal tribunals into the Government's courts; second the applicability of indigenous law was curtailed ; and thirdly the indigenous law was transformed in the course of being administered by the Governments' Courts. The most striking impact of the provision of Governmental courts was the shift of dispute-settlement from local tribunals (and local notables) to the Government's courts. Nineteenth century (and later) observers speak of a flood of litigation, sometimes with the implication that these disputes would have been peaceably settled or indeed would not have arisen without the availability of official courts.

It was acknowledged early that Indians should be ruled by their own laws. Hastings' plan, which provided the model for the other Moffussil systems, set out to apply indigenous law. But in their search for authoritative bodies of law, the British made collections and translations of ancient texts and recent commentaries. However, Indian law proved to be elusive because of vast gaps and interspaces in the substantive law of India. In the written Shastras, large departments of law (as envisaged in modern concept of society) were scarcely represented and it was soon realised that Shastras were only a part of the law and that in many matters, Indians were regulated by less formal bodies of customary law. But even the customary law was not sufficient. For, when custom was recorded and the quasi legislative innovative role of the tribunals, that administered it, was restricted, it did not supply express rules in nearly sufficient number to settle the disputes occasioned by the increased activity of life and the multiplied wants which resulted from peace and plenty. The need to fill the left gap was ultimately to lead to statutory codification on the basis of English Law but in the meantime, the courts allowed to decide the cases on the basis of justice, equity and good conscience, filled the interstices of Shastra and custom with unamalgamated masses of foreign law. The customary law then was rigidified, restricted in scope and replaced by Dharmashastras. To ascertain the Hindu and Muslim Law, the Courts appointed law officers—Muslim Maulvis and Hindu Pandits—to select and interpret the relevant portions of laws of Hindus and Muslims for the English judges. At the same time, British set about collecting and translating authoritative books in the hope of making Hindu Law more accessible and certain and this led eventually to the elimination of law officers as intermediaries between the courts and the Hindu Law and the common law. Judges undertook to administer law directly from the existing corpus of material available due to general reorganisation of the legal system in 1860s. Earlier Shastras had changed and developed by successive commentaries and had maintained their flexibility by their complex and discretionary techniques of interpretation. British administration, not only dissipated these techniques but also narrowed the selection of authoritative texts. Courts were not to consult the whole of Shastric science but only those commentators accepted in the locality, a view which led to the elaboration of partially artificial schools of Hindu Law.

The modern legal system may be viewed as an important unifying element. Today, while India has no single nation-wide system of caste, kinship, religion or land-tenure, there is an all India legal system which handles local disputes in accordance with the uniform national standards. The legal system provides, not only a common textual tradition, but also a machinery for ensuring that this tradition is applied in all localities in accordance with nationally prescribed rules and procedure rather than dissolved into local interpretations. With this system goes what we might call an all India legal culture. Thus, the modern legal system provides both the personnel and the techniques for carrying on public business in a way that is nationally intelligible and free of dependence on particular religious or local authority. It, thus provides one requisite framework for organising Indian Society into a modern nation state.

The formation of an independent Indian nation provided a basis for further integration and consolidation of the modern legal system. With the coming of independence, enclaves previously outside the legal system, were integrated into it. A layer of constitutionalism was superimposed on the existing legal system and structure of Government. The Constitution established India as a secular federal republic with a Parliamentary system on the British style and a strong Central Government. The Constitution has established a unified judiciary covering the whole of India under a Supreme Court as a court of final appeal in all case. The Constitution includes a bill of Fundamental Rights, which are enforceable by the judiciary and to which all Governmental regulations and laws in every part of India must conform. Government is enjoined by these provisions to be indifferent to particularistic and ascriptive characteristics (e.g. race, religion, caste, place of birth and sex) in its dealings with citizens, whether as electors, employees, or subjects. A wide range of private conduct, involving the assertion of precedence of the imposition of disabilities—including venerable usages which had previously enjoyed religious and sometimes legal sanctions are outlawed.

The extention and consolidation of the modern features of the legal system can be observed in the treatment of two basic institutions of Hindu Society—the family and the caste. Although no unification of laws of Hindus and Muslims has yet been undertaken, the Parliament in 1955-56 passed a series of Acts known collectively as the Hindu Code, which affect a wholesale and drastic reform in Hindu law. Where earlier legislation introduced specific modifications into the framework of Shastric law, the code entirely supplants the Shastra as the source of

Hindu Law. Hindu Social arrangements are for the first time moved entirely within the ambit of legislative regulation; appeal to the shastric tradition is almost entirely dispersed with and the Shastra itself is no longer a living source of law. These rules are intermixed with rules from other sources and are administered in the common law style, isolated from Shastric techniques of interpretations and procedure. Still, local customary component of Hindu Law is a source of rules at a few isolated points, but it too has been abandoned as a living source of law. There is, however, one significant attempt to promote such indigenous law by developing certain judicial responsibilities to the local elective Village Panchayats.

India, thus has what we might call a dualistic or colonial style legal system—one in which the official law embodies norms and procedures congenial to the governing classes and remote from the attitudes and concerns of its clientele. Such systems are typical of areas in which a colonising power superimposes uniform law over a population governed by a diversity of local traditions. In a heterogenous society (differentiated horizontally by culture, or vertically by caste or class), the law expresses not primarily the aspirations and concerns of the society but those of the groups that formulate, promulgate and apply the law. There does, however, remain a gap between the official law and popular or local law, which is typical of most large political entities with intensive social differentiation.

Traditional Law

Traditional Law—Hindu, Muslim and Customary—has been almost entirely displaced from the modern Indian legal system. Today the Classical Dharmashastra component of Hindu Law is almost completely obliterated. It remains the original source of various rules of family law. But these rules are intermixed with rules from other sources and are administered in the common-law style, isolated from Shastric techniques of interpretation and procedure. In other fields of law, Dharmashastra is not employed as a source of precedent, analogy or inspiration except in case of Panchayats, which have existed in India for thousands of years and are a characteristic and distinctive institution of Indian civilisation. Literally, the term means the 'coming together of five persons', hence a counsel, meeting or court consisting of five or more members of a village or caste assembled to judge disputes or determine group policy. Although Indian civilisation contained refined and respected bodies of legal learning—the Dharamshastras (Hindu

Law) and later Muslim Law as well—and although there were royal courts in administrative centres, these did not produce a unified national legal system of the kind that developed in the West.

The Government's law did not penetrate deeply into the countryside. Throughout most of Indian history, there was no direct or systematic state control of the administration of law in the villages where most Indians live. In pre-British India, there were innumerable, overlapping local jurisdictions, and many groups enjoyed some degree of autonomy in administering law to themselves. Disputes in villages and even in cities would not be settled by royal courts, but by the tribunals of the locality, of the caste within which the dispute arose, or of guilds and associations of traders or artisans or disputes might be taken for settlement to the Panchayat of the localy dominant caste or to land owners, government officials or religious dignitaries. Some Panchayats purported to administer a faced body of law or custom, some might extemporise in some places and in some kinds of disputes, the process was formal and court like. Some Panchayats were standing bodies with regular procedures, but many of these tribunals were not formal bodies but were in the nature of extended discussions among interested persons in which informal pressure could be generated to support a solution arrived at by negotiation or arbitration. These Tribunals would decide disputes in accordance with the custom or usage of the locality, caste, trade or family. Development of village Government from 1920 to 1947 consisted primarily of the creation of Panchayat bodies, blending Municipal/administrative and judicial functions. Village Councils were elected bodies, in some, the franchise was limited by literary test. There were certain ex-officio members including the village headman, nominees of Government, certain classes of landlords and women, commercial groups and untouchables (after 1939). Judicial functions seem pre-eminent in the available accounts of the Panchayat institutions. These functions were sometimes performed by special village courts or by ordinary territorial Panchayats. Article 40 of the Constitution obligates the state to take steps to reorganise village Panchayats and endow them with such powers and functions as may be necessary to enable them to function as units of self-Government. The Constitutional directive to organise village Panchayats and to empower them to function as units of self-Government saw a steady fulfilment in the period 1949-59 which was followed by the introduction of PR (Panchayat Rajya) system in the period 1959-62 and thereafter, when Panchayats were given a wide variety of developmental and regulatory (local Governmental) functions. The number of Panchayats increased from 14,800 to 1,64,000 during first ten years of independence. The adoption of Balwant Rai Mehta Committee Report on democratic decentralisation (1958) led to the creation of three-tier system of PR. The three levels of reorganised local Government system are Gram Panchayat (Village), Panchayat Samiti (Block) and Zilla Parishad (District). Each, of the two higher levels, is indirectly elected from the tier below and also draws membership from legislators, cooperative officials and others. In 1965, there were 2,19,694 Gram Panchayats covering 99 per cent of villages and a population of more than 406 million besides 3485 Samitis and 246 Parishads. Micro level studies indicate significant and continuing changes arising out of the political diversion of PR. Although its scope and direction may vary, it has been universally acknowledged that political consciousness of the people has increased under Panchayati Raj. An average villager is more conscious of his rights today than before.

14

CONSTITUTIONAL DEVELOPMENT IN INDIA

Portuguese first came to India from Europe for trade purposes and having found it very paying, the other powers viz. French and English too came. A meeting was held in London on 22.9.1599 by some principle traders of England under the Chairmanship of Lord Mayor (Mayor of London). They requested the Queen of England to permit them to start trading with India and they were successful in getting a charter passed by the Government on 31.12.1600. This led to the formation of East India Company under the name and style "Governor and Company of Merchants Trading into the East Indies." The Company was managed by various committees and the joint sitting of the committees was called 'Court of Committees'. The members of these committees were elected by the shareholders. Later on this Company became a Joint Stock Company. The Company was given trading rights to trade via Cape of Good Hope for 15 years. During the period 1600 to 1765 A.D. there had been many ups and downs in the working of the Company, so much so, that during this period, the Company became ruler of India from a Trading Company.

The Charter of the Company was reviewed from time to time. The Charter of 1661 permitted each shareholder for 5000 pounds to be eligible for one vote. Each Governor-in-Council of the Company was allowed to decide the civil and criminal matters pertaining to the employees of the Company. The Company was also allowed to construct forts and keep some soldiers for their protection. The Charter of 1668 handed over Bombay port to the Company on a token amount of ten pounds per annum. This port was given in dowry by the King of Portugal in the marriage of princess Catherine of Bergenze and the Company was allowed to frame laws for the governance of the inhabitants of this port. The Charter of 1676 allowed the Company to cast their own coins. The Charter of 1683 permitted the Company to enter into battles and treaties with the countries of Asia, Africa and America. The Charter of 1693 confirmed some powers given to the Company after the previous charter. The shareholders could not purchase shares of the Company for more than 1000 pounds and the Capital of the Company was increased by 7,44,000 pounds.

During 1711, 1730 and 1744, several Acts were passed to increase the special powers of the Company. The Company was allowed to appropriate and distribute the booty and regularised the military force in India. In this way, each Charter strengthened the Company. The English got the powers not from the British Government alone but also from the Mughal rulers of India. In 1612, Thomas Eldworth obtained permission from Emperor Jehangir to establish a factory on the mouth of River Tapti, after they opened their trade centres in Burhanpur, Ahmedabad, Ajmer and Agra. Then Sir Thomas Roe obtained permission from Emperor Jehangir to establish factories in Mughal Kingdom. By 1672, English had not only established themselves in Madras but also got power of governance. Then they established their trade centres in Orissa and Bengal too. In 1698, English purchased the revenue rights of three villages—Sutanati, Calcutta and Gobindpur at the rate of Rs. 1200 per annum.

The manipulation by English and the revolution that came in governance of Bengal, made the Company's position stronger. Nawab Siraj-ud-daula formally confirmed the special powers given to the company through an agreement in 1756 and also permitted them to cast their coins and construct their forts. Then the Battle of Plassey took place in 1757 in which the Governor of Bengal (Siraj-ud-daula) was defeated by English by a treacherous act of Mir Jafar, who was enthroned as Governor of Bengal but English became the defacto rulers of Bengal. They then got lot of land and maintained their own army. In 1765, Mir Jafar was dethroned and in his place Mir Qasim was enthroned. He fought with English at Buxar in 1764 but was defeated. Then Mir Jafar was again made Governor of Bengal. Subsequently on his death in 1765, English became virtual rulers of Bengal. They could appoint anyone as Governor of Bengal and dethrone him any time when he did not act on English Company's terms.

From 1757 to 1772 there was a Dual Government in Bengal. The position of Nawab was only in name and British actually ruled. The Company's employees took advantage of the situation and collected lot of money. By now Company were the rulers of Bengal, Bihar and

Orissa and had revenue rights in these provinces. In Buxar, even the force of Mughal Prince Shah Alam was defeated. British after negotiations with the Mughal emperor handed over Allahabad to Mughal emperor on payment of 26 lakh rupees annually on subsidy and got a notification from emperor giving all revenue rights to the Company and also were now responsible for trying civil cases in their courts. Under the Dual Government, however, the Nawab and his men were still responsible for governing the provinces in name and all rights and revenue collection was with the English. The Governor thus became pennyless and corruption and lawlessness were the order of the day.

The Regulating Act

With the company having secured the governance of Bengal, Bihar and Orissa, the English became alert and urged for English Parliament's intervention in the matter. The House of Commons appointed a Committee in 1766 to look into the matter and give their recommendation. On the recommendation of the Committee, a Bill was presented in the House on 18-5-1773 called 'East India Company Regulating Bill' and after having been passed in 1773, it became 'Regulating Act'. The following system of administration was introduced:

Reasons for Passing

The reasons leading to the passage of this Act were :

1. After the Battles of Plassey and Buxar, company had become defacto ruler of Bengal, Bihar and Orissa. On the other hand, no employee of the Company could own any piece of land as per British Law. So, it was necessary to regularise the owning of these provinces by the Company for governance.
2. The Dual System of Governance had been introduced by Clive after the Battle of Plassey but it was only a stop-gap arrangement and none after two Governments—defacto (Company) and dejure (the Nawab)—being responsible to public for proper governance, there was lawlessness all around. It was, therefore, necessary to establish a Government by the company.
3. The Nawab and his employees had all become corrupt. The employees of the company too had become corrupt as they got huge amounts as gifts with every change of governor. They, therefore, changed governors frequently.
4. The company having obtained the revenue rights of Bengal, Bihar and Orissa, estimated their revenue to be around 16,50,000 pounds

annually and so they increased the dividend from 6 per cent to 10 per cent and then to 12 per cent. The rate of Company's shares in UK increased manifold. But the Company was, in course of time, unable to meet the rate of dividend decided and became a debtor Company leading to interference by the Parliament.

5. Due to defeat by the ruler of Mysore in 1769, the Company lost its prestige. Then there was a famine in Bengal in 1770 resulting in death of lakhs of people. The Parliament had to take action in the situation.

Due to the above circumstances, the Parliament passed two acts. According to first, the Company was given a loan of 14,00,000 pounds @ 40 per cent interest and the payment of £4,00,000 by the Company was deferred. The other was Regulating Act.

Board of Directors

1. The voting eligibility for election to Court of Proprietors was enhanced from equity holders of 500 pounds to 1000 pounds.
2. Even this eligibility should have been for a minimum of 12 months.
3. The duration of Directors was increased to four years.
4. The Directors had to present all correspondence with India in regard to Revenue matters before the Secretary of Exchequer.
5. All Governments in India had to obey the orders issued by the Directors and had to keep the UK Government informed about all matters involving interest of the Company.

Central Government of the Company in India

1. One Governor General and four Councillors were appointed at Fort William Presidency in West Bengal and the entire governance was in the hands of Governor General-in-Council. The administration of Bengal, Bihar, Orissa was also entrusted to him.
2. The first Governor General was to be Warren Hastings and General Clevering, Col Mousen, Richard Barvel, and Phillip Francis were to be members of the Council. The Governor General was to take a salary of 25,000 pounds every year and each member of the council was to get 10,000 pounds every year.
3. They could continue on their posts for five years but the king could remove them before the completion of five years on the recommendation of the Board of Directors.

4. All disputes within the council were decided on the basis of majority in the Governor General-in-Council.
5. The Madras and Bombay Presidencies could not start battle or enter into treaties with local authorities without the prior approval of the Governor General-in-Council except in cases of emergency or where such orders had been received from England.
6. The Presidency Governments had to obey the Supreme Government and keep them apprised of all matters of interest to the Supreme Government.
7. The Governors General-in-Council were empowered to make laws for the proper governance of the Fort William Settlement and the army.

Establishment of Supreme Court at Calcutta

1. A Supreme Court had been established in Fort William with one Chief Justice and three other judges, who had been barristers for atleast five years standing.
2. This Court had jurisdiction on all civil, criminal, admirality and eccelsiastical matters. This Court had to act as a Court of Record and Court of Oyer and Terminer and Gaol delivery for Fort William factory and other factories under it.
3. The Court had jurisdiction over all British Citizens living in Bengal, Bihar and Orissa and those others employed by the Company to serve the Company directly or indirectly.
4. The criminal jurisdiction did not cover the Governor General and the members of his Council except in matters of treachery or major crimes.
5. The Chief Justice and other judges could continue during the pleasure of the king. The salary of the Chief Justice was to be 8000 pounds and that of other judges 6000 pounds per annum.
6. The Governor General, members of his Council, and judges of the Supreme Court could not be prosecuted in Supreme Court or jailed.
7. The Governor General-in-Council and the judges of the Supreme Court were empowered and it was expected of them that they should act as Magistrates for the inhabitants of Fort William and other factories under it.
8. The Supreme Court had to get all matters considered by the Jury of the British Citizens of Calcutta and any appeal against their judgement lay to the King-in-Council.

Other Provisions

1. The Governor General, members of his Council or the judges of the Supr·me Court could not directly or indirectly accept any gifts, gratuity or monetary benefits. They could not also enter into any monetary transactions.
2. No employee of the force or other. under the king or the Company could accept any presents, gifts, gratuity or monetary benefits directly or indirectly.
3. The violators of above provisions could be punished to pay double the amount of such benefit and recalled to England.
4. No Collector, Supervisor or any other British Citizens posted in Bengal, Bihar or Orissa to collect revenues for the Company could except during the discharge of their duties enter into any trade, sale-purchased or any other negotiations about trade.
5. No British Citizen could lend money at an interest of over 12 percent.
6. The employees of the Company causing breach of trust could be fixed or convicted and put in jail or sent back to England.
7. Handsome salary was paid to Governor General, members of his Council, Chief Justice and judges so that they are not ternphid to accept bribery. It was 25000, 10000, 8000 and 6000 pounds per annum respectively.

Shortcomings of the Act

1. The Governor General was left at the mercy of the members of his Council as any decision could be taken against the orders of the Governor General by majority of members. The humiliation to the Governor General was at times so much that he had to think of resigning from his post.
2. The Governor General-in-Council was given overriding powers over the Presidencies of Bombay and Madras and they had to obtain prior approval of the Governor General-in-Council in all matters of starting battle or entering into any treaties with the local governments except in emergency. These Presidencies, however, to avoid obtaining prior approval of the Governor General, made each matter as emergency and started acting as per their volition.
3. There was no clear cut jurisdiction of the Governor General-in-Council or the Supreme Court and there was often overlapping. For example, the Supreme Court thought that they could issue

writ against any citizen under the Company and could summon them for evidence whereas the Governor General- in-Council opposed it. Similarly, there was dispute about jurisdiction in taking action against the revenue officers of the company for their defaults. Further, the Supreme Court thought that they could hear the cases against the other judges of the company for matters filed against them whereas the Governor-General-in-Council thought it was their jurisdiction.

4. It was not clear as to which law was to be followed by the Supreme Court—whether it was to be that of the defendent—or the English Law only.
5. With the increase in holding the equity for eligibility to vote for the election of members of court, the number of voters got reduced, and the Court of Directors became a body of the minority only.
6. The Parliament did not have adequate control over the Company. It was governed by the Governor General-in-Council only as made the Board of Directors weak.

Merits of the Act

However, in spite of the above shortcomings, the Regulating Act was an important milestone in the history of constitutional development in India as it was for the first time accepted that the Company was not a mere trading Company but a Governing Body as well.

1. The monopoly of the Company was reduced by appointment of first Governor General, members of the Council, Chief Justice and other judges of the Supreme Court by the king.
2. It was for the first time that a European Government established a Government of this choice outside Europe. No other European nation had so far established a Government abroad.
3. This Act lead to the centralisation of the governance of provinces.
4. It reduced corruption amongst the employees of the Company.
5. For the first time, the British Goverment took the responsibility of governing a country outside England.

Amending Act of 1781

After having seen the working of the Regulating Act for some years, it became necessary to carry out certain amendments to Act. The amendments made were :

1. The public servants of the Company were exempted from the jurisdiction of the Supreme Court in matters arising out of the

discharge of their duties. Similarly, the Governor General and members of the Council were put outside the jurisdiction of the Supreme Court in respect of the orders issued in public interest.

2. The jurisdiction of the Supreme Court was extended to all residents of the country but the law of defendant was made applicable instead of English Law.
3. It was made clear that the Supreme Court had to apply Muslim Law in respect of disputes over land, price of the commodities, succession, money transactions, etc., of Muslims and Hindu Law in respect of matters pertaining to Hindus and general usage in all matters.
4. The court was directed to respect the social and religious customs, usages, caste system of all Indians even if the same were against the Laws of England.
5. Against the decisions of the Country Courts, appeals could be filed before the Governor General-in-Council and their decision was final
6. The Governor General-in-Council was authorised to frame laws applicabale to all the Presidencies.

Pitts Indian Act 1784

This act primarily changed the structure of the Company in England and some changes were made in local Government as under :

1. A Board of Six Commissioners was constituted. It was known as the Board of Control and consisted of a Minister of State, the Chancellor of Exchequer, and four other members of the Privy Council and held office during the pleasure of the king.
2. The quorum comprised of any three members. In the absence of the Minister of State and the Chancellor of Exchequer, the seniormost Commissioner chaired the meetings.
3. The Commissioners were honorary and continued even if they were members of parliament.
4. They were, however, not allowed to appoint any one in the Company.
5. They had full powers to superintend, direct or control the working of the Company in relation to the revenues of the Company and its defence and non-defence jobs.
6. They had access to examine all documents of the Company and receive copies of action taken on all important matters, directives issued and messages received.

7. They were allowed to accept or reject the proposals put up before them or to accept with amendments and the directors were required to send such accepted or amended directives to their employees in India.
8. They could ask the Board to prepare proposals and issue directions on any matter in the interest of successful working of the Company. The Board could also prepare such proposals themselves and the Directors would then send those proposals to India in a way to indicate that those proposals had been sent by them.
9. The Board could send secret orders pertaining to secret matters on starting battle or entering into any agreement to the secret committee of the Board of Directors.
10. The Court of Proprietors was deprived its right of over-riding the decisions of the Court of Directors and ratified by the Board of Control.
11. The Parliament could grant an amount of 1600 pounds annually from the revenues of India to meet the expenses of its employees.
12. The secretary of State chaired the Board of Control and its decisions were taken by majority of votes. The Chairman had a casting vote.
13. The Governor General-in-Council was given the powers of superintending, controlling and directing the other Presidencies.
14. Only covenanted employees of the company could be appointed as members of the Governor General-in-Council. The members of the Council were reduced from four to three and the decisions of the Council were by majority, the Governor General having casting vote.
15. The Governor General-in-Council had been given full powers to decide all matters pertaining to war or peace with the Indian Governmants and about the use of the army.
16. The Act disapproved of the policy of intervention as followed by the servants of the Company in India.
17. The official offenders were not to be pardoned if they were found guilty of having committed any offence.
18. The Governor General and the members of his Council were appointed by the Committee of Directors with the approval of the Crown and the king could call them back or remove from the post.

Reason for This Act Being Considered as of Great Constitutional Importance in the History

1. It continued to be the base of constitution in India upto 1858. The job of Court of Proprietors was entrusted to the Board of Control, who supervised the political and military matters of the Company in India.
2. The centralised control of the Governor General-in-Council was established in all matters in India.
3. The position of the Governor General became strong.
4. It improved the structure of governance in India. The Governor General or Governors could carry out their proposals even if one member of the Council was in his favour.
5. It reduced the importance of the Court of Proprietors.
6. A special tribunal was established in England to try the defaults of the English in India.

Establishment of Dual system of Governance

As already indicated, the most important constitutional change through the 1784 Act was to establish a Dual system of governance of Company Affairs in India. This job was so far done by the Court of Directors, which was again under the control of the Court of Proprietors. All appointments of Governor General, the members of his Council, and other Governors and high officials were made by the Directors. This Act divided the Company's job of trade and political matters into two separate bodies. The trade was retained in the hands of the Board of Directors but the political jobs of the Company were given to the Board of Control. The Board of Control in course of time became very powerful.

Charter Act of 1793

The Charter of 1773 was issued for 20 years. Therefore, its renewal was taken up by the Parliament. Some industrialists and traders represented for having right of trading in India. The Charter of 1793 was issued with a little change for another twenty years. It provided that :

Provisions

1. The Governor General and Governors were given power to override their Councils.

2. The fact that the Governor General was up and above the Presidencies of Madras and Bombay was emphasised.
3. Governor General was given power to appoint a Vice President of the Executive Council from out of the members of the Council.
4. The Commander-in-Chief was not to be a member of the Council of Governor General.
5. No leave of absence out of India was allowed to the Governor General and Governors, the Commander-in- Chief and few other high officials.
6. Calcutta Supreme Court's jurisdiction extended to high seas.
7. Powers were given to appoint members of Civil Service as Justice of Peace; to appoint scavengers for the Presidency towns; to levy a sanitary rate and to prohibit sale of liquor without a license.
8. Payment of the members and the staff of the Board was made out of Indian revenues.
9. Two junior members of the Board of Control need not be Privy Councillors.

Charter of the Company was renewed for 20 years. It was repeated in this Charter that the proposal to win areas in India and extension of British territory in India was against the wish, image and policy of England but the necessities of circumstances and the wish of the persons in position acted quite contrary to this wish and the East India Company continued extending their territory after one battle or the other. The Charter of 1793 did not make any substantial change and was not constitutionally very important. It only invoked consolidation of the rules so far made with small changes. But the provision to make payment of expenses of the Board of Control from the Indian revenues was a wrong precedent. It continued till about 1919 Act. In fact, because of this precedent, English booked lot of expenses incurred in first and second world from Indian revenues under this provision.

Charter Act of 1813

After twenty years of the previous Charter, the question of its review came forth. Now the conditions were quite different, compared to what existed twenty years back and it was not found prudent to keep East India Company as a mere trading Company only due to :

1. Napolean had managed Continental Blockade in 1808 resulting in huge reduction in British exports. The traders, therefore, desired Indian trade to be opened to them.

2. The principle of Laissiz faire had gained importance and the traders had started criticising the autocracy of the East India Company.
3. The Christian missionary propagated inside and out of the Parliament for deputing their men to India for spreading Christianity.
4. Because of the policy of annexations of Wellesley, the British kingdom in India had become quite vast. Except Panjab, Sindh and Nepal, entire India was under British influence. This necessitated intervention by the Parliament.
5. The Company's financial position had become weak due to many battles. The Company was under debt for £ 2,10,00,000 and this had to be obtained by the Directors from Parliament. A Committee was appointed and as a result of the recommendations of the Committee, this Act was passed by the Parliament.

Provisions of the Act

1. The Company with the entire attained kingdom in India and its revenues were under the overall sovereignty of the emperors.
2. Trade with India, except trade in tea, was made open to all Britishers.
3. The British traders and Christian missionaries were allowed to settle in India.
4. The Governors and Governor General could, however, cancel the stay of any person whose conduct was not good and ask him to return to England.
5. The Justice of Peace could hear the cases of disputes between the British and local people.
6. The Company was required to maintain its Commercial and Provincial ascents separately.
7. The vacancies of Governor General, Governors, Commander-in-Chief, etc, could be filled by the Directors with the approval of the emperor.
8. The Company was expected to establish an office of a Bishop and other people under him.
9. An amount of one lakh per annum was set apart for the development of literature, encouragement to local educated people and starting technical education in British rajya in India.
10. The number of soldiers paid from Company's exchequer was fixed at 29,000. The Company could make conduct rules for

Indian troops.

11. The local Governments in India under the jurisdiction of Supreme Court were authorised to impose taxes on the local people and to punish them on non-payment of taxes.
12. The Control and powers of the Board of Control were made more extensive and specific.
13. The expenditure out of the revenues from India was regularised. First charge was expenditure on army; second for repayment of debt, and third on civilian employees and other employees. The remaining amount was distributed between the Company (to reduce the debt) and English Government in the ratio of 1:5.

Charter Act of 1833

This was the most important action between the Pits India Act and 1858 Act. This was to renew the Act of 1813 after its twenty years of validity. At this time there was liberalisation in the governance in England. The integration of trade and political sovereignty in India had destroyed the concept of governance in India. The Charter Act of 1833 had far reaching importance in the governance of India by the Company and the control over it from England.

Provisions

Its provisions were :

1. Shareholders of the Company were guaranteed a dividend of 10.5 per cent per annum out of the Indian revenues for next 40 years.
2. Restricted the patronage of Directors.
3. The President of the Board of Control became Minister for Indian Affairs.
4. Centralised the administration of the English Company in India. Governor General of Bengal became the Governor General of India and the other Governors were under the Governor General-in-Council.
5. Legislation was centralised by the Governor General-in-Council and not by Governors-in-Council.
6. Added a member to the Executive Council of the Governor General, and he was to be known as Law Minister.
7. Number of members of the Councils of the Governors of Bombay and Madras was reduced to two.
8. Bombay and Madras Governors were to keep their separate armies under the overall control of the Central Government.

9. Provided for the codification of laws in India for which a Law Commission was appointed.

In this way this Act can be called the Centralisation of Powers Act as it placed all military, civil governance, direction and legislation under the Governor General-in-Council. This Act reflected the good wishes the British leadership had for the Indian people. Hereafter the appointments to high posts were to be on the basis of ability judged through a competition and Indians could not be checked from holding any post in the Company simply because of the religion, race, caste or creed. This provision led to criticism but it reflected the feeling of betterment for Indian people. Further, so far the Hindu and Mohammedan Laws were applied by the courts but now uniform laws were required to be made and for this a Law Commission was appointed. This led to the formation of Civil Procedure Code, Criminal Procedure Code and Indian Penal Code and brought oneness in the judicial procedure and punishments in India. From jurisprudence point of view this Act was of utmost importance.

Charter Act of 1853

The Act of 1833 raised many hopes in Indian intellects to get appointment in high posts under the Company but those, who went to England for this purpose, returned in disgust and despair, so much so, that since 1833 when Indians were made eligible to hold high posts, not a single Indian was appointed during 20 years. Many petitions were sent to British Government for amending the rules to enable Indians to enter high posts. In this way, besides the Christian Missionaries and traders, who opposed the proceedings in Parliament considering 1833 Charter, now there was a third groups of Indians too. So, a Selection Committee was appointed to recommend amendments and on their recommendation the Charter Act of 1853 was passed.

Provisions

1. This Act renewed the Company's powers of governance in India without any time limit (unlike previous Charters valid for 20 years).
2. The number of Directors was reduced from 24 to 18 out of whom six were to be nominated by the crown.
3. The salary of the Board of Control along with its officers shall be changed to Indian revenues.
4. The Directors were now not entitled to make appointments of the

officers but these were filled through open competition, which was open to Indians as well.

5. A separate Governor was appointed for Bengal and the Governor General had only to oversee the working of all Governors.
6. In 1859, a Lt Governor was appointed for Panjab as a result of powers given to Board of Directors to create such vacancies in provinces other than Bombay and Madras.
7. The Fourth member of the Governor General's Council, who so far was a legal member, was made a regular member with voting right.
8. The legislative and executive powers of the council were separated. For legislative job, six more members had been appointed and all laws were made by this Council of 12 members.
9. The proceedings of the Legislative Councils were held like the British Parliament. This Council could also question the policies framed and executed by the Government.
10. After the expiry of Law Commission, commissions were appointed to examine their recommendations. This resulted in the formation of legal codes.

This Charter Act was very important from Constitutional angle. The Act having been passed without any periodic limit, gave an indication that the Company might not survive for long time now. Further, this Act made a separate Legislative Council, which practically became an Anglo-Indian House of Commons to whom the executive was answerable. This provision, however, lacked in the sense that this Council did not include any Indian as a member.

Government of India Act 1858

The mutiny of 1857, called by English as army revolt or mutiny or the first war of independence was actually an upheaval expressed against the British policy of annexations and exploitation of the country politically and economically. After the Mutiny had been suppressed, the British became anxious about retaining their power in India. They, therefore, took the governance of India directly under the Crown. Disraeley presented a bill in House of Commons on 26.3.1858 for transferring governance of India to under the Crown. This Act was called the "Act for the Better Government of India". Its provisions are :

Provisions

1. Most important provision of this Act was to transfer the governance of India from the Company to the Crown.
2. The revenues from India and Paramountcy of the Indian States and the tributes obtained from these states were all in the name of the emperor.
3. This Act finished the Board of Directors, Committee of Directors and Board of Control and their job was entrusted to a Minister of the emperor and the emperor was empowered to appoint a Secretary of State for Indian Affairs, whose salary was charged to India.
4. Council of Secretary of State consisted of 15 members, 7 elected by the Court of Directors and the rest to be appointed by Crown and the Secretary of State to preside over the meetings of the Indian Council.
5. Secretary of State for India was declared to be a corporate body which could sue and be sued in England and in India.
6. Indian revenues were not to be re-employed for military operating outside India except with the consent of Parliament.
7. It divided the patronage between the Government of India and the Secretary of State in Council. All appointments and promotions continued to be made in India. Appointments to Civil Service to be made by open competition as per rules made by the Secretary of State in Council.

After the governance of India was passed over to the Crown of England, and the mutiny had been subdued. The Queen of England visited India in 1858 and held a Darbar of Allahabad on 1st November 1858. There, she declared the assumption of the Government of India by the Crown and inter-alia declared :

1. No extension of present territorial possesions and shall respect the rights, dignity and honour of the native princes as their own.
2. All subjects of whatever race or creed be freely and impartially admitted to the offices in Indian service.
3. It assured the Indian princes that their territories shall not be annexed by the British Government and they shall be given the right of adoption.
4. Servants in India shall not interfere in the religious affairs of Indians.

After this, for full thirty one years, there was peace as Indians had been discouraged by the suppression of the mutiny and subsequent killings made by the British to develop an awe in their minds. The British Government too did not consider it necessary to give a further instalment of reforms to the people of India.

The Act of 1892

Ultimately Act of 1892 was adopted on pressure from Indian National Congress established in 1885.

Provisions

1. The Act enlarged the functions of Legislative Councils. They were authorised to discuss annual financial statements.
2. The members of the Council were given the right of addressing questions to the Government on matters of public interest.
3. The number of additional members in the Council was increased.
4. It allowed election to be held in India under the rules.

Although the Act of 1892 fell far short of the demands made by the Indian National Congress, it was a great advance upon the existing state of things. By conceding the principle of election and giving the Legislative Councils some control over the executive, it paved the way for future progress on those lines which were destined to place in the hands of Indians a large measure of control over the administration of the country.

Minto-Morley Reforms Act of 1909

The revolution for attaining independence had been attaining momentum, particularly after the British proposal of Partition of Bengal, against which the entire country stood as one piece to fight against British. Then with a view to create a division between Hindus and Muslims and subdue the demand for independence, Minto and Morley held a meeting with the representatives of Muslims at Simla and presented a Bill in British Parliament containing further reforms in the Direction of self-rule in 1909.

Provisions

The essence of these reforms of 1909 lay in conceding what at once was evacuated of all meanings. Thus, the elective principle of Democracy was adopted. Yet at the same time the anti-democratic, communal representation was added. The official majority was done away with but the elected representatives remained in a minority. The membership was considerably enlarged but an emphatic disclaimer was issued simultaneously that the new Councils in no way meant the introduction of Parliamentary system. The Council of India and even the Viceory's Executive Council were open to some very few selected Indians but the liberal aspect of admitting Indians to the arena of Government could in no way disguise the fact that real power remained safely in British hands. This Act did not satisfy the people and particularly the nationalist movements. Indian National Congress represented for more liberalisation but it had no effect on British. There were also other reasons for non-satisfaction such as :

Reasons for Dissatisfaction

1. Spread of Plague in the country for which the Government did not take proper care. Lakhs of people were killed due to this ailment.
2. Famine in 1899 due to drought in which again lakhs of people were killed. When there was famine in one part of the country, the English had been exporting foodgrains from India to England to feed their people.
3. Lord Curzon had taken several repressive measures such as Partition of Bengal in 1905 bringing Indian universities under Government control; posting of non-Indians only on high civil posts.
4. Division between Hindus and Muslims.
5. Japan's victory over Russia : In 1896 Abysinia's victory over Italy and Japan's victory over Russia, led to the fall in the image of European superiority over Asians and Indians too projected their claim for independence.
6. Disrespect to Indians in Canada, South Africa and Fizi had its effect on Indians involved in revolutionary movement.
7. In the beginning of twentieth century, the economic condition of the country had deteriorated. The revenue on land had been doubled; the irrigation cess had been increased several times; the essential things for living had become very costly; Indian industries had closed down and India was at the mercy of English industries, who had started supplying their products at high rates; unemployment had increased in the country.
8. The media and speeches of the leaders had inspired the people to boycott English materials and owned Indian made good.

9. Militant nationalism had come up and the youth had followed the path of revolution. They had started indulging in robbing Government treasuries; killing Europeans in isolation and to work for snatching independence from Britishers rather than requesting them for the same, which had no effect.
10. The mild group in Congress had been working with patience in the direction of securing independence but with the campaign of the militant nationalist becoming more popular, the mild groups had also started becoming tougher.
11. To stop the revolution, English had armed Muslims against Hindus so that they could fight within themselves and English continue to rule.
12. In 1905 Liberal Government had taken over and they were sympathetic towards Indian cause.

The Government of India Act of 1919

Provisions

All these resulted in the enactment of 1919. Its provisions were :

1. The Secretary of State for India was paid out of Indian revenues. Now it was decided to be paid from British revenues.
2. It set up bicameral legislature at the Centre in place of one house. The names of the two houses were Central Legislative Assembly and the Council of States.
3. The life of Central Legislative Assembly was three years and Council of State five years.
4. It provided for direct election for both houses of Central Legislature.
5. In the case of Council of State, the voters were assessed either to income tax on an annual income of not less than Rs. 10,000 to Rs. 20,000 or to land revenue of Rs. 750 to Rs. 5000. For Central Assembly, the qualification were either payment of municipal tax amounting to not less than Rs. 15 to Rs. 20 per annum or occupation of ownership of a house of the rental value of Rs. 180 or assessment to income tax on an annual income of not less than Rs. 50 to Rs. 150.
6. The Governor General was given the power to summon, prorogue and dissolve the chambers and right to address the members of the two houses.

7. Central Legislative could make laws for whole of British India.
8. Central Budget was passed by Central Legislature. There were some non-votable items too.
9. The members of Executive Council of Governor General were nominated members.
10. It provided for two lists of subjects—Central list and Provincial list.
11. Size of Provincial Legislature was enlarged.
12. It introduced Dyarchy in the provinces. Under this system, subjects to be dealt with by the Provincial Government were "transferred" and "Reserved". The Reserved subjects were administered by Governor with the help of Executive Council and the transferred were dealt with by Governor with the help of Ministers.

The Government of India Act of 1919 was a step forward in technique of responsible Government but not in practice as the Governor General remained the real authority as he could rule by ordinances. India, after First World War, began to take part in international affairs and his representative appeared at the League of Nations and at many other international conferences. At this time due to delay in operation, disturbances in Panjab came up leading to imposition of martial law and culminating in Jalianwalla Bagh Massacre in 1919. These were followed by communal riots in 1923. Muslim League which had been virtually moribund since 1916, was revised in 1917. One of the Provisions of 1919 Act was that its results should be examined after ten years. In 1927, the Conservative Government in England appointed a Commission of investigation consisting entirely of British Members of Parliament under the Chairmanship of John Simon. The Commission visited India in 1928 but was boycotted by Nationalist leaders. Its report was issued in 1930. The Congress in their session at Lahore in December 1929 declared that its aim was complete independence and decided to boycott the forthcoming conference in London and began Civil Disobedience movement from 6-4-1930 with Gandhi's famous march to Dandi against Government's self monopoly policy of mass strikes; boycott of English goods and violence. In repression, many were killed, many injured and 60,000 were imprisoned. Government abandoned its repressive measures and released political prisoners and Congress called off civil Disobedience movement and joined Round Table Conference. But no action was subsequently taken. Gandhi was again arrested in 1922 and Congress was declared an illegal organisation.

More than 1,20,000 people were again arrested and there was wholesale violence.

Government of India Act, 1935

Then came the Government of India Act of 1935, which was to come into force in 1937, with following main provisions :

Provisions

1. It provided for an All India Federation. The Act provided for three lists—Federal List, Provincial List and Concurrent List.
2. It provided for diarchy at the center, abolishing diarchy from provinces. Certain federal subjects were reserved in the hands of Governor General to be administered with the assistance of not more than three councellors appointed by him. These subjects were Defence, External Affairs, Ecclesiastical Affairs and Administration of Tribal Areas. In the administration of other subjects, the Governor General was to be aided and advised by a Council of Ministers, whose number was not to exceed ten. They could administer all departments except those in reserved subjects.
3. Federal Legislature comprised of Federal Assembly and the Council of States. Assembly was to have a life of five years and Council of States was a permanent body of which one-third members were to retire after every three years.
4. The Indian Legislature was debarred from making any law affecting sovereign or royal family on succession to throne, or suzerainty or Crown or any part of India, or Army Act, Air Force Act, Law of Prize Courts, amendment to Act of 1935. There were many non-votable items of expenditure also.
5. Establishment of a Federal Court with jurisdiction over states and provinces, consisting of Chief Justice and two puisne judges.
6. It abolished the Indian Council of Secretary of State.
7. The Governor, through the Governor General and the Governor General himself, were made strictly responsible to the Secretary of State.
8. The Legislature could not legislate on a large number of subjects. Also the Governor General or the Governors could override their ministers and legislators in certain circumstances.
9. The constitution of 1935 was rigid and only British Government had authority to amend the constitution.

10. The most important characteristic of the Act of 1935 was the provision of provincial autonomy.
11. It provided for the establishment of a Federal Court. This Court came into existence from 1 Oct 1937 and comprised of a Chief Justice and six other judges, who were to be appointed by the emperor. The number of judges could be increased on the recommodation of the Governor General. The qualification for appointment of the judges were :
    - (i) Should have been chief justice of any provincial court for the last five years.
    - (ii) Barrister of England or Ireland for at least ten years.
    - (iii) Member of Faculty of Advocates of Scotland for at least ten years.
    - (iv) A Lawyer of ten years standing in one of the Federal Courts.

Jurisdiction of the Federal Court

The Federal Court had original and appellate jurisdiction. In original jurisdiction, it decided the cases pertaining to disputes arising out of the interpretation of the Constitution between Centre and State/States; between a state and the princely territory or between two or more states. It also disposed of cases pertaining to interpretation of the Constitution.

In appellate jurisdiction it heard cases of appeals against the judgements of the high courts; where the high court certified the case to be fit for appeal to Federal Court and where some important point of law was involved as a result of orders passed by the Governor General-in-Council.

The Constitutional bench of Federal Court could also hear cases when the amount involved was more than Rs. 50,000 or an amount of over Rs. 1500 payable as for any Act or immovable property of this much amount is involved. Appeals could also be heard about cases arising out of the merger of any unit in Federation.

Advisory Jurisdiction. In addition to the original and appellate jurisdiction, the Federal Court also acted as an advisory court in cases referred to it by the Governor General for its advice on a matter of law. Such advice was given in open Court.

As Highest Court of Justice. The Federal Court had been assigned the category of highest court of justice in the country. In this capacity it made laws and procedure to be followed by various courts.

Additional Jobs. The Governor General could entrust any other job to any judge of the Federal Court.

In spite of being the highest court in the country, the Federal Court was not the highest as appeals could be filed against its judgement to the judicial committee of the Privy Council in certain specified matters such as interpretation of constitution or orders issued by the Governor General-in-Council or matters arising out of the interpretation of any agreement entered into with any native state. Cases could also be referred to Privy Council after approval by the Emperor.

Court of Record. The Federal Court also acted as the Court of Record. Its judgements and proceedings, were kept in record and could be projected in lower courts as precedents.

The Act of 1935 came into force in 1937, when elections were held for all provinces. After this election, Congress formed ministers in seven out of eleven provinces. In some provinces, Muslim League wanted to form coalition ministeries with Congress but Congress refused. Congress administrations were reasonably successful and the prestige of the organisation had grown to such an extent that its membership reached five million in 1939. Second world War broke out in 1939. Congress refused to Co-operate with the Government and all Congress ministries resigned in November 1939 but with German armies having been victorious in Europe, Congress offered to Co-operate with the British Government if a provisional national Government was formed at the centre. This was refused in 1940 but an offer was made to set up the national government after the war. A body to prepare a new constitution to enlarge Viceroy's Executive Council with more Indian members and create a War Advisory Council of representatives from British India and princely states had been formed. Congress rejected the offer and a new Civil Disobedience Compaign was begun. After the fall of Rangoon to Japanese in March 1942, and the possibility of an immediate attack on India, British Cabinet Minister Sir Staford Crips came to India with what was virtually the same offer as that of August 1940. In the meantime the Muslim League Ministries had not resigned at the outbreak of war and had become totally estranged from Congress. On 8th August, 1942, Congress called for a widespread return to mass civil disobedience. Government declared Congress illegal and arrested its leaders resulting in riots and sabotage throughout India. Over 60,000 people were arrested; 18000 detained without trial; 940 killed ;1630 injured in clashes with police and troops. After 1944, Labour

Government again came to power in Britain and decided to hold fresh elections in India. These were held in 1946 in which Congress won overwhelmingly.

On 19 February, 1946, British Prime Minister sent a mission to India with new proposals within the British empire. These were accepted by Muslim League but rejected by Congress. On 20 February, 1947 British Government announced its intention of leaving India by June 1948 and appointed Lord Mountbatten as Viceroy to carryout transfer of power. Muslim League started violence, arson and murders and Congress reluctantly accepted the fact that if independence was to be achieved, India must be divided. On 3 June, 1947, Viceroy broadcast a declaration of British Government policy for partition of India. Congress and Muslim League accepted the plan and the Indian Independence Act was passed through Parliament on 1 Feb, 1947. The date set for transfer was 15 August, 1947. On that day, India was declared a dominion within the British Commonwealth and Mountbatten was to be its first Governor General. In Karachi, Jinnah was chosen the first Governor General of Pakistan and thus British Indian empire came to an end.

Indian Independence Act, 1947

Provisions

1. The Act provided for the partition of India and the establishment of two dominions of India and Pakistan from 15 August, 1947.
2. The legislatures of the two dominions were given full powers to make laws having extra territorial jurisdiction.
3. The British Government was to have no control over the affairs of the dominions, provinces or any part of the dominions after 15 August, 1947.
4. Until a new constitution was framed for each dominion, the Act made the existing constituent assemblies the dominion legislatures for the time being. The assemblies were to exercise all the powers which were formerly exercised by the central legislature, in addition to its power regarding the framing of a new constitution.
5. Pending framing of new constitution, each dominion and all provinces were to be governed as per the Act of 1935.
6. The Governor General could modify or adopt Government of India Act 1935 till 31 March 1948 after which Constituent Assembly could modify or adopt the Act of 1935.
7. The right of the king to veto laws or to reserve laws for his

pleasure was given up.

8. It provided for the termination of suzerainty of the Crown over the Indian States, the existing arrangements between the Government of India and Indian States to continue pending detailed negotiations between the Indian States and the new dominions.
9. Agreement with the tribes of N.W.F.P. of India were to be negotiated by the successor dominions. The office of the Secretary of state for India was to be abolished and his work was to be taken over by the Secretary of State for Commonwealth Affairs.
10. The title of 'Emperor of India' was to be dropped from the royal style along with the titles of the king of England.
11. The Act terminated British authority over India ; set up two independent dominions, each with full authority to make any constitution, it pleased. Both the dominions were given full powers and rights to leave the British Commonwealth of Nations, if they so desired.

As indicated above, a Constituent Assembly was set up in India to draft a constitution for the country. After detailed deliberation, the Constitution of India was enacted by the Constituent Assembly, which came in force from 26 January, 1950.

New Constitution of India

Provisions

1. It established a Soveregin, Democratic, Republic. It declares that sovereignity vests in the people of the country. It also refers to justice, liberty, equality and fraternity.
2. There will be one Central Government and Governments of States and Union Territories.
3. It prescribes the conditions of Indian citizenship; there shall be single citizenship.
4. It provides for a large number of fundamental rights, guaranted to each citizen like right of equality before law; prohibition of discrimination on grounds of religion race, caste, sex or place of birth; equality of opportunity in matters of public employment; right to freedom of speech and expression; right to assemble peacefully; right to form union and associations; right to move freely throughout the country; right to reside and settle in any part of India; right to secure, hold and dispose of property; right to practise any profession, trade or business; right to life and

personal liberty; right to practice and propagate any religion; and right to constitutional remedies.

5. It also contains Directive Principles of State Policy.
6. It provides for a President of Indian Republic.
7. It provides for a Vice President and ex-officio chairman of Council of States.
8. It provides for Parliament consisting of two Houses viz. Lok Sabha and Rajya Sabha.
9. It provides for a Council of Ministers to assist President.
10. It provides for the Supreme Court of India consisting of Chief Justice and other judges.
11. It provides for Union Public Service Commission and State Public Service Commissions.
12. It provides for a controller and Auditor General.
13. It provides for distribution of powers between Union and the States with Union List, State List and Concurrent List.
14. It provides for freedom of trade, commerce and intercourse throughout the territory of India.
15. It provides that Hindi in Devanagari script shall be the official language of the union and English to continue for 15 years.
16. It provides for the procedure for amendment of constitution.

Index